Girl
in the
Grave

and other true crime stories

CARLTON STOWERS

Stephen F. Austin

Nacog

LIBRARY OF CONGRESS CATALOGING-IN-PUBLICATION DATA
Stowers, Carlton
    Girl in the Grave: And Other True Crime Stories / Carlton Stowers
    ISBN: 978-1-62288-053-9

1. Crime—United States—Nonfiction. 2. Crime—Texas.

Designed by Renee L. Williams

Manufactured in the United States of America

Stephen F. Austin State University Press
P.O. Box 13007 SFA Station
Nacogdoches, TX 75962
sfasu.edu/sfapress
sfapress@sfasu.edu

Distributed by Texas A&M University Consortium
www.tamupress.com

For Janet Manus and Howard Swindle, in memory

...and to the kind editors of the publications that first gave these stories a home: *Abilene Reporter, Dallas Morning News, D Magazine, Dallas Observer, Houston Chronicle, In Cold Blog, Paris Match, Polo, San Antonio Current, Teen People* and the *Irish Independent.*

Contents

Introduction

Some years ago, I read a quote from famed Texas author Larry McMurtry in which he described himself as a "Minor Regional Novelist," even posing in a T-shirt with the title proudly stenciled across its front. This, of course, was in his younger days, long before he'd won a Pulitzer Prize, written an Academy Award-winning screenplay, and regularly occupied best seller lists. Yet, despite delayed prosperity and fame, little seems to have changed as the one-time literary prodigy from Archer City has matured.

Talent and riches aside, the thing I most admire about the man is his stubborn insistence that the best subject matter is still found in his own backyard—that he still holds firmly to a belief that he need not travel East, West, or Abroad to seek out universal truths.

That awareness, frankly, is the only kinship Mr. McMurtry and I enjoy. Before you read on, consider yourself duly warned that my own success is light years from that of *Lonesome Dove*, that I've never paraded along red carpets, and that I no longer even bother to check the *New York Times* list for my name.

Yet as I've pursued a career as a journalist and author of non-fiction books, I, too, have been reluctant to stray too far from my own backyard. I am, by determined dedication, a regional writer, a literary homebody. Send me on an assignment beyond the Texas borders and my confidence and interest decline with equal speed. Only when writing about my native state, speaking its language, describing its landscape, sharing its mores and history, do I feel I'm giving my readers a fair shake for their investment in time and cover price.

Maybe I should get a T-shirt.

And before you question the wisdom of such self-imposed tethering, consider that the well I've regularly visited for lo these many years is deep; the boundaries to which I've limited myself are indeed far-reaching. (In this collection, it should be noted, you'll find that there are two exceptions to my Regional Rule. My only defense is that I found the stories fascinating— and they were written for a Texas-based publication.

Once, while residing in the picturesque Texas Hill Country, attempting to jump-start a freelance career by hacking out endless articles for newspaper Sunday supplements and magazines you've never heard of, I received an urgent call from an editor in Chicago, desperately in need of some story being played out in Texarkana, on the state's far northeastern border. Time, he insisted, was of the essence. Could I drive there quickly and get the story to him in 48 hours? "Physically impossible," I replied. He seemed more than a little nonplussed and no doubt viewed me as something of a smart-ass when I pointed out he was actually closer to Texarkana than I was.

What he had no grasp of is the fact Texas is one big place: urban and rural, deserts and dense forests, sweeping plains and sandy beaches; inhabited by the filthy rich and the dirt poor, famous and infamous, saints and sinners. We don't find it unusual that we've got our hustlers and con men living next door to the hard-working, God-fearing Joneses or that one man's nutty religious zealot is another's Heaven-bound role model. It's all here: the good, the bad, and the downright ugly. So far, we can still brag that the latter remains in the minority (though, not having yet read today's paper, I cannot swear that statistic still holds). Our football teams have won Super Bowls, we've sent men off to the White House to lead the Western World, and we have damn good chili and chicken fried steak and an ample supply of locally brewed beer. Plus, country music icon Willie Nelson is ours, born and bred, not to mention Mr. McMurtry, who is, for my money, the best wordsmith the state has ever produced. What more to ask for?

As a writer, I can think of nothing.

Usually within a quick drive or short plane ride, I've sat down with an incredible variety of people in equally fascinating places, gathering information that has allowed me to introduce readers to someone or something of interest.

Still, the battle to earn a living in a confined space goes on. New York publishers, many still convinced that fiddlin' contests and horse operas are the only thing playing down here in the Lone Star State, remain a hard sell. If I had a buck for every book proposal or story suggestion I've had turned down because some tweedy, pipe-smoking Easterner viewed it as "too regional," I'd be loaning McMurtry money.

For example, back in the mid-'80s, following a lengthy career in newspaper journalism, I decided time had come to devote more effort to book-length projects. I knew only that I wanted to tell non-fiction stories that offered the widest range of human emotion possible. I hadn't a clue what that meant or where it might lead me—until an old high school and college buddy dropped by for a visit. Ned Butler was then a prosecutor in the McLennan County District Attorney's office, preparing for the trial of a Waco man accused of the murder of three teenagers. As he sat on my patio that summer evening, telling the nightmarish story, it was not the details of the murders that particularly interested me. Rather, I was far more engrossed by his remarks about the shortened lives of the victims; how their devastated parents had dealt with the evil forces and unanswered questions that had invaded their once-normal lives; the effect on law enforcement officers duty-bound to involve themselves in such an evil and troubling tale, investigating, and seeking resolution and justice.

The story had all the dramatic and emotional elements I was looking for. And New York editors could not have cared less. Almost without exception, their rejections included the polite but tired litany, "too regional." Finally, having grown weary of the refrain, I fired off a response to the latest nay-sayer, summoning the same smart-mouth wit I'd used on the Chicago editor years earlier: "I wonder," I wrote, "just how many people in New York had heard of Holcomb, Kansas before Truman Capote traveled there to gather material for his legendary and award-winning crime book, *In Cold Blood!*"

Of course, I got no reply. But eventually I did get a contract with Taylor Publishing, a small Texas company based in Dallas that offered encouragement, a measure of enthusiasm, and even a small amount of advance money to help get me through what would be a two-year project. I snapped it up and went to work. And in 1985, the hardback edition of *Careless Whispers* was published. It is appropriate, I suppose, that it was initially distributed primarily to Texas book stores. But the sales were good, most reviews warm, and, lo and behold, it was honored by the New York-based Mystery Writers of America as the year's Best Fact Crime Book (the same award that had been presented several years earlier to the urbane Capote and his *In Cold Blood*).

Suddenly, one of the same Big City publishing houses that had viewed the book as "too regional" was making a substantial offer to publish it in paperback. West Coast movie-makers were calling. Foreign rights were being purchased. As this is written, *Careless Whispers* is celebrating its 25th year in print here in the U.S. and has been published such faraway places as Germany and Japan. If you are prone to insomnia, you can still catch the rerun of the TV movie it spawned.

In darker moments, I like to refer to it as my Revenge of the Regional Writer. In kinder times, I see it only as a simple reminder that a good story, fact or fiction, can leap beyond all geographic boundaries.

You'll not likely find the description in any literary texts, but, simply put, I am a match-maker. I seek out people and places, situations and circumstances that interest me to a degree that I feel duty bound to share them with others. Whether it is internationally famous Houston attorney Richard "Racehorse" Haynes spinning colorful tales of headline-making cases, or convicted rapist Donald Good telling his heartbreaking story of how DNA testing done two decades after the fact proved him innocent of the crime, their unique stories are prime grist for a writer's mill. I'm delighted to serve as the middle man.

And while, admittedly, I've sometimes tended the mortgage and made car payments by accepting travel fare to faraway places, there to interview celebrities ranging from self-important movie stars to stuffy politicians and business world wheeler-dealers, rarely do I recall them as moments of any great achievement and will mention them no further than to say it helps pay the bills, even if one is occasionally forced to type with one hand while holding his nose with the other. It's what you do if you aren't Stephen King or haven't experienced the good fortune of Aunt Suzy passing along that small fortune she'd secretly rat-holed through all those scrimp-and-save years down at the Old Folks Home.

Truth is, however, financial reward seldom enters the picture when one stumbles onto a magical subject that begs to be written; the one nobody else has discovered or has somehow failed to see its merit. If I have a valid talent to claim, it is in the recognition of (and appreciation for) stories that lend themselves to broader readership than one might first expect.

They are out there, along the backroads, off the interstate, in the big city back alleys, and I have long been their happy hunter.

For the better part of the last two decades, when my agent and/or editor would ask what I planned for my next book project, they already had the answer in mind. It did me absolutely no good to suggest some sweeping historical tome or a visit to the Hundred Best Barbecue Joints in Texas. Their response to such ideas was predictable: Why not write another true crime book?

Which I did at 18-month to two-year intervals, always careful to pick nearby settings. In the small town of Midlothian, I wrote of a young undercover police officer who, while posing as a high school student in an effort to ferret out teenaged drug dealers, was shot and killed by the 16-year-old son of a Dallas police officer. The crime and all of the tragic irony in *Innocence Lost*, however, played second chair to the story of the devastation it rained down on a once-quiet and peaceful community. When, after five years of futile investigation, the Richardson police finally determined that a wealthy socialite had orchestrated the hired murder of her husband's girlfriend, I chose to write *Open Secrets* and chased a serpentine and bizarre case from Texas to France and back. After I spent considerable time in Alvin, a little town south of Houston, *To The Last Breath* resulted, telling the story of three remarkable women—a private investigator/grandmother, a police detective, and an assistant district attorney—who combined efforts to prove that a ne'er-do-well father was, in fact, responsible for the death of his two-year-old daughter.

Along the way, I detoured briefly to help an FBI agent tell his war stories, coauthored the recollections of a Texas prison chaplain whose job it was to keep condemned prisoners company in their final hours, and was the ghostwriter for a Texas private eye with an uncanny ability to solve the unsolvable. When it occurred to me that so many people had openly and candidly confided how their once-private lives had been upset by unspeakable crime, I realized I could do no less. After long consideration and numerous starts and stops, I finished writing *Sins of the Son*, an autobiographical reflection on the troubled relationship between my long imprisoned first-born and me.

Even the magazine editors who called had begun to increasingly request crime stories. People wanted one on an East Texas funeral home attendant and church choir member who, after killing his aging and contrary female benefactor, neatly hid her body away in a freezer. Others wanted profiles of forensic specialists and jury selection experts, or haunting tales like the one played out in tiny Bangs, Texas, where a family, remodeling the attic of their rural home, discovered in a crawl space the mummified remains of three infants.

Not to say there weren't lighter moments. My favorite came from an editor at *Texas Parks & Wildlife* magazine eager for a story on the midnight bulldozing of a bird sanctuary that had defied several city ordinances and enraged naturalists. "We'd like for you to write it," the editor suggested, "like one of your true crime stories." I didn't know whether to be flattered or amused.

In time, I began to feel that I had spent about all the time walking the dark side of human nature that I wanted and began thinking it might be time to reinvent myself professionally. More and more, I considered focusing my writing on people who were still alive, well, and relatively carefree.

Breaking away, however, did not come easy.

One evening, a long distance call came from a young Wichita Falls woman named Catie Reid, asking in a pleasant voice if I was the person who had written *Careless Whispers*. No sooner had I acknowledged authorship than she began to spin a remarkable tale: Her older sister and one of the Waco victims whom I'd written about years earlier had, for a time, been best friends. And, she went on to say, her sister had also become a homicide victim just months after the Waco murders made headlines.

Small world, this Texas.

There had, in fact, been a series of killings in Wichita Falls, beginning in the winter of 1984. Three unsolved cases—the murders of Catie's sister and two other young women—had languished for fifteen years before a bricklayer-turned-district attorney's office investigator had determined that one man had committed the crimes. An arrest, I was told, had finally been made. The long and tragic saga now had a beginning, a middle, and, at long last, an end, she gently explained, and she felt the complex tragedy should be told in book form.

It didn't take me long to agree. The story presented a new challenge, that of weaving several stories into one, providing the reader some insight into how families, none known to the other, had negotiated through a decade and a half of not knowing who had taken the lives of their children.

Once again the research process put me into the company of a remarkable cast of characters and in a vast and stark part of Texas about which I'd never before written.

No one I encountered was more interesting than the 30-year-old woman who had first alerted me to the story. Catie, just thirteen at the time of her sister's death, had for years been the family rock, never faltering in her belief that justice would one day be served. In the acknowledgments of *Scream at the Sky*, completed two years after our first telephone conversation, I wrote that if I'd had a daughter I would have hoped her to be just like Catie Reid.

When the book was published, I followed my traditional routine of sending copies out to those whose lives I'd been allowed to chronicle so they might have the opportunity to read it before it appeared in stores. It is always an anxious time, filled with sleep-robbing concerns that those who had so willingly confided in me might somehow feel betrayed, however unintentionally.

Catie Reid, as I'd expected, was the first to respond. "I just finished your book," she told me late one evening, "and I'm so very proud of it."

It was far and away the best review I'd ever received.

◆ Carlton Stowers

(A version of this essay was first published in *Notes From Texas: On Writing in the Lone Star State*, edited by W.C. Jameson.)

The Girl In the Grave

The manila file folder containing information on the case had become dog-eared, the writing across its top edge badly faded after almost six years. It was thin compared to most files kept by police on a homicide investigation: a few dozen pages of offense reports, an itemized list of evidence gathered, copies of statements taken from two suspects who had ultimately pled guilty to the crime, fingerprint cards, and the cold, clinical details of death provided by the medical examiner.

Technically, Case Number 86-HOM001 had been closed since the summer of 1986, quickly solved through the cooperative efforts of police from Dallas and the neighboring community of Midlothian.

But for Sandy Baxter, senior dispatcher for the Midlothian Police Department, the resolution was far from satisfactory. A major piece of the tragic, puzzling story was still missing. It was for that reason that the file remained on her desk instead of being stored away, forgotten, in the department's filing cabinets.

While the murder was solved, the identity of the victim remained a disquieting mystery.

Less than a mile from the police station, in the tree-shaded, neatly manicured Midlothian Cemetery, only one unidentified body was buried; at the foot of the grave site sat a simple marker donated by a local funeral home. It read:

> Unidentified Caucasian
> Female
> Date of Death
> July 2,1986
> Age 16 to 20 Years

Statistically, she was just one of the 169 unidentified victims recorded in Texas since 1975 by the National Clearing House for Missing Persons and Unidentified Bodies. The Dallas County Medical Examiner's Office says it alone averages 12-15 "unknowns" annually.

To 42-year-old Baxter, a gentle, soft-spoken mother of four, being another figure in a sad collection of statistics was no fitting epitaph. Nor was it a proper ending to the investigation.

In today's violent age, when reports of senseless murders crowd the morning headlines and the evening news, law enforcement officers have less time than ever to dwell on yesterday's human indignities. Baxter understands. And that's why, on the day of the Ellis County-funded burial of the unidentified victim, she privately vowed to do all she could to learn the identity of the girl in the grave.

"I felt that somewhere," she says, "someone had to be grieving over the disappearance of their daughter. They had a right to know what had happened to her. And the girl deserved something more than an unmarked grave. Someone owed her the courtesy of finding out who she was."

Baxter wouldn't be satisfied until some measure of dignity was afforded the girl's death.

In all likelihood, Baxter felt, the young victim was probably a runaway. "That," she says, "made it hit close to home. When I was growing up, I had a sister who would run away from home, sometimes being gone for months at a time. I remember the agony everyone in the family went through each time she would disappear, not knowing if she was dead or alive for long periods of time."

Midlothian police chief Roy Vaughn, who was not in office when the murder occurred, admires Baxter's dedication. "Because of Sandy," he says, "everyone in the department worked on this case at one time or another, trying to find something that might provide a lead to the girl's identity. Frankly, we didn't have much to go on, but because of her, nobody was willing to give up."

Clues were scarce. According to the autopsy report, the girl was approximately 5'5" and weighed less than 100 pounds. She had slightly wavy black hair and wore salmon pink polish on her fingernails and toenails. In her pierced left ear were three tiny earrings: one red, white, and blue in the shape of a diamond; one blue and black and pear-shaped; another of yellow metal with a tiny red stone. She had also been wearing a small chain necklace with a gold pendant in the shape of a unicorn.

Though the coroner fingerprinted the young woman, computer searches locally and nationally failed to produce a match. The medical examiner found no evidence of dental work, ruling out yet another time-honored method of identification. Aside from the 21 stab wounds inflicted on the body at the time of the murder, there were no distinguishing marks—no surgical scars or tattoos. While the report listed her as Caucasian, the possibility of the girl being Hispanic or even Indian was not ruled out.

Said Midlothian PD lieutenant Billy Fowler, who helped Baxter with the case before his death of cancer in 1992, "The only real lead we had was the fact she wore the three earrings in one ear. Back in '86 it wasn't common for young women to have their ears pierced for multiple earrings."

* * *

There were times in recent years when Baxter felt she might be close to an answer. Entering the description of the murder victim into the National Crime Information Center (NCIC) system that collects data on missing persons throughout the United States, she encountered several promising leads. But after extensive follow-ups, nothing positive resulted. For a time, there was a missing girl from Florida who seemed a possibility, but she ultimately returned home safely. A young woman matching the general description of the victim had disappeared from a halfway house in Memphis, Tennessee, just a month before the Midlothian murder, but after several days of phone calls and teletype communications, she was found alive and well. Baxter made inquiries to agencies as far away as Hawaii and Montana without success.

Still, she continued to search the NCIC database at regular intervals, hoping that a needle-in-a-haystack match might one day occur. And in those times when she was free from her regular workload, she would pull out the case file, rereading the few pieces of information it contained, searching for some previously overlooked clue.

In time, it was all but committed to memory; still, it was never easy for her. The file tells a graphic and nightmarish horror tale that caused Baxter more sleepless nights than she cares to remember.

* * *

On the Monday night of June 2, 1986, 19-year-old Chris Wahnee and his 20-year-old cousin, Randy King, were driving along Ferguson Road in a red Camaro borrowed from a friend. They had been drinking all evening.

As they neared the intersection of Ferguson and Highland, they saw a young woman walking along the sidewalk and stopped to ask her if she'd like a ride. The girl got into the backseat, but after a short distance became uneasy and asked to be let out of the car. Ignoring her, Wahnee laughed and sped eastward down Ferguson Road.

It was when she leaned forward and began to choke Wahnee, insisting that he stop the car, that he started cursing his passenger, U-turned in the direction of the freeway, and headed south.

The Camaro had just passed the Dallas County line on Highway 67 when Wahnee turned onto a blacktop road and wound his way into the isolated farmlands of Ellis County. Stopping near a field bordered by a barbed wire fence, he walked around to the passenger side of the car and ordered the girl to get out. He also asked Randy King for his knife.

Pulling the struggling young woman to the rear of the car, Wahnee plunged the knife into her stomach. The insanity had begun.

He began removing her clothes, and then, with King's help, carried her limp body through the barrow ditch and lifted her over the fence. In the darkened field, Wahnee raped his victim and stabbed her repeatedly. Later, he would explain that he killed her "because she was making a lot of noises."

The only words Wahnee remembered hearing from his dying victim were, "I'm sorry."

Returning to the car where King waited, Wahnee pitched a purse and a small necklace he'd taken from the girl's body onto the dashboard. King picked up the small chain that held a tiny gold unicorn figure and slipped it around his neck. As they sped back toward Dallas, they tossed the purse from the car.

* * *

At 7:30 on Thursday evening, June 5th, investigator J. E. Gallagher answered the phone in the homicide division of the Dallas Police Department and listened for several minutes as a young man spoke in a hurried, frightened voice. Gallagher briefly stopped his note-taking to snap his fingers in the direction of partner P. E. Jones, signaling for him to pick up and listen on the extension.

What the detectives heard was a bizarre story of brutal murder. Two friends, the caller told Gallagher, had picked him up several days earlier and driven him to an isolated area south of Dallas, boasting of killing a woman and leaving her body in a field. They were drinking wine as they told the story, the caller said.

The more wine they drank, the more details they provided: "While we were riding around, they said they had picked her up somewhere along Ferguson Road and took her out in the country and stabbed her. After a while, we started driving through Oak Cliff, and I asked where we were going. They said they were going to show me where the body was," the caller said.

Convinced the call was legitimate, Detective Gallagher suggested a meeting to discuss the matter further. After a brief hesitation, the young man agreed but said he didn't want them coming to his home. He would meet them at the entrance to Eastfield College at 8:30 p.m.

"The kid was scared to death," Jones recalls. "It had taken him a while just to get up the nerve to contact us. He was convinced that if the guys who did the murder found out he was talking to us his life would also be in danger."

At the Eastfield meeting, the teenager's story grew in detail: The three young men had driven out Highway 67, past Duncanville and Cedar Hill, and into Ellis County, before turning off on a country road that led to the pasture where the body had been left. "They tried to get me to get out of the car and go out into the field with them to look at her," the informant said, "but I told them I wouldn't do it. So they got out and walked about a hundred yards out into the field and just stood there in the weeds, looking down for a couple of minutes. Then they pulled the girl's clothes out of a tree and walked back toward the car, laughing as they got in. I was sitting in the back seat, and they threw the clothes on me and laughed some more.

"They said her body had flies all over it...and that her eyes were gone."

Gallagher and Jones asked if he could direct them to the location. "Yes," he said. "While they were out in the field, I dropped a wine bottle out of the car window to mark the place."

Realizing that it would be dark before they reached the murder site, the two detectives, their frightened informant in tow, stopped by the police station to pick up flashlights before driving south.

A grizzly scene awaited them.

Walking into the field shortly after 10 p.m., the detectives found the nude body of the young woman lying in knee-deep weeds. As they focused the flashlights on the body, it was obvious that the victim had been stabbed repeatedly in the chest and stomach. Predators and days of 90-degree temperatures and intermittent rains had added to the horror of their discovery.

Even for the experienced homicide investigators, it was a scene that would be forever burned into their memories. "I wish it wasn't the case," says Jones, "but I can still close my eyes and see it all, just like it was yesterday. Some investigations just stay with you more than others."

At the time, however, emotion was set aside. The first order of business, the detectives agreed, was to determine whose jurisdiction the case would fall to since the body had been discovered outside Dallas County. Gallagher left Jones to protect the crime scene while he drove back to a nearby service station. Not wanting to discuss the matter on his police radio, he telephoned headquarters.

"But, even before he could get back," recalls Jones, "I saw a caravan of car lights approaching at high speed—the Midlothian Police Department, the Ellis County Sheriff, and one of the Dallas television stations. The media had apparently picked it up on its police scanner when our office notified the Midlothian PD."

Knowing that a mob scene would soon evolve, Jones' thoughts flashed to the frightened informant who had remained in his car. Concerned with protecting his identity from reporters, Jones ran through the field to the car and told the youngster to hide in a nearby drainage culvert.

"Don't come out until I come get you," the officer ordered.

* * *

In his three years on the Midlothian police force, Officer Roy Lake had never investigated a homicide. "Back then," he says, "we just didn't have murders in Midlothian. It hadn't taken on big city ways. It was just a quiet little country town where the police's job was to make sure nobody's business got burglarized and settle an occasional domestic dispute."

On that June evening, however, Lake felt the rush of adrenaline as he hurriedly drove toward the crime scene, alerted that, since the body had been found inside the town's city limits, it was his case to work.

Seeing that the Dallas officers had already secured the area, Lake immediately made arrangements for a photographer then contacted the local funeral home with instructions to be ready to transport the body to the Dallas County Medical Examiner's office once the on-scene investigation was completed.

Only after members of the media and a handful of local curiosity seekers left did Detective Jones tell Lake about the informant hiding in the drainage culvert. "We didn't want to take him to the station for fear some of the reporters might have gone there," Lake recalls, "so we went to DeeTee's Restaurant. It was closed, but I had a key given me by the owner, and we went in, put on some coffee, and took the young man's statement."

His friends, the frightened youngster said, were American Indians named Chris Wahnee and Randy King. He provided Lake and the Dallas officers with their descriptions and addresses as well as additional details of his conversation with them. "Chris said he was the one who killed the girl. He told me he stabbed her nine times," the informant said. "He showed me the butterfly knife he had used. It still had dried blood on it."

Neither Wahnee nor King had given any indication that they had known the victim.

As the teenager spoke, Lake remembers, his mind kept flashing back to the girl's tortured body. "Anyone who tells you he gets used to seeing something like that is lying," he says. "I found it impossible to believe that someone could be that savage, could have such little disregard for human life. I kept thinking, 'This is one helluva way to get introduced to homicide investigating.'"

* * *

The mind-numbing brutality of the crime aside, it was, by all measures, a relatively simple case to solve. "Open and shut, really," Lake admits. "All I had to do was get the arrest warrants from the local Justice of the Peace. The Dallas officers took it from there, making the arrests and gathering the evidence. They called me when they had Wahnee and King in custody, and by the time I got to Dallas, they were already in the process of taking their confessions."

From the time the informant called the Dallas police until Wahnee and King signed their respective confessions, less than eight hours had elapsed.

All that remained was to determine the identity of the victim.

"Though it was officially Midlothian's case once we turned Wahnee and King over to them," Jones says, "we did quite a bit of leg work in an attempt to find out who the girl was. The medical examiner had given us a fairly good description to work from, and we knocked on some doors and visited the grocery stores, service stations, and a couple of teenage hangouts in the area where the men said they had abducted the girl. But we drew a total blank at every turn.

"After a while, other things came up that required more immediate attention. Unfortunately, crime didn't stop with that little girl's murder, and we had to move on."

Lake, too, was hitting nothing but dead ends. He spent days walking the barrow ditches along the road where the crime occurred, looking for the woman's purse, which the killers said they had thrown from the car. He entered the description of the victim into the NCIC computer system with no success. "There were a couple of times that I got a 'hit,' a name of a missing person whose physical description generally matched what we were looking for, but nothing ever worked out.

"It became a very frustrating situation, knowing that we had resolved the legal aspects of the case but couldn't take care of the moral issue. That bothered me a great deal."

No longer in law enforcement, Lake says he just recently found himself thinking back on the case. "When you have loose ends," he says, "you always look back and wonder if maybe there was something more you could have done, something you overlooked. I came real close to getting into my truck and driving back out there to look for that purse again."

* * *

The body of the victim remained at the Southwestern Institute of Forensic Sciences in Dallas for almost three months. But as hope of identifying the girl dimmed, it was decided that burial arrangements should be made. Lake contacted Ellis County officials who agreed to an expenditure of $650, then phoned a Midlothian funeral home and requested that it make plans to travel to Dallas to get the body.

On a late October afternoon, the unidentified girl was buried with only Lake, fellow Midlothian officer Don Blanton, and two representatives from the funeral home present to hear the scripture and brief prayer offered by a local minister. "The whole thing didn't take more than 15 minutes," Lake recalls. "I think we all felt we should do something more or say something. But what? I remember leaving the cemetery with a really lousy feeling that hung on for days."

Long before the burial, Wahnee and King had entered a plea bargain with the Ellis County District Attorney's office. Wahnee was sentenced to 55 years in prison; King was given fifteen. "I thought we had a solid capital murder case, a death penalty case," reflects Lake, "but the D.A. said it would be difficult to try since we didn't know who the victim was. It made no sense to me."

"I made the decision not to try the cases," says Ellis County District Attorney Mary Lou Shipley, "after considering a number of factors. We had very little physical evidence aside from the statements given by Wahnee and King. That, combined with the fact there was no family of the victim to put on the stand, no way to humanize her for a jury, would have made it very difficult. In my judgement it didn't appear to be a case where a jury was likely to come back with a death penalty verdict."

While Wahnee remains in prison, his sentence recently extended an additional fifteen years following his assault of a fellow inmate; King was released on parole in 1991.

* * *

Meanwhile, Sandy Baxter continued her frustrating quest, making small progresses that kept her going. Along the way, she waged battles with tangles of red tape and faulty information. For months, she had unsuccessfully sought to find the earrings the girl had been wearing. First, she was told they had been stored in the property room of the Dallas police. Dallas records, however, indicated that all evidence in the case had been turned over to the Midlothian Police Department. No records there, either.

Then one day as she was talking with the funeral home director who had arranged the victim's funeral, he made an off-hand remark that sent her hopes soaring. "When my father and I went to Dallas to get the young woman's body," he recalled, "there was a small envelope attached to the body bag. We didn't even pay any attention to it until we got back to the funeral home."

The envelope, he said, had contained the girl's earrings. "I told my dad about them and asked if we should bury them along with the body. He said no, to file them away because someday someone might come looking for them."

Then, just weeks later, the girl's necklace, worn by King at the time of his arrest, was located by Detective Gallagher in the Dallas Police Department's property room.

Sandy Baxter's most significant discovery, however, came when she found a memo written in September of 1986, indicating that the medical examiner's office had agreed to do a reconstruction of the victim's face from which a composite drawing could be made.

"Everyone," she says, "seemed to have forgotten about it. I couldn't find anyone who had ever actually seen any photograph or drawing. Finally, though, the M.E.'s office gave me the name of a man who most likely would have done the work if, in fact, it was actually done."

The man, she was informed, was no longer in Dallas and no record of the reconstruction could be found. After numerous phone calls, Baxter located the artist in Chicago where he was teaching at the University of Illinois. He remembered the case, had a vague recollection of doing a drawing of the victim, but wasn't sure he had a copy in his files. He promised to do some checking.

What resulted was another dead end. If there was, in fact, any reconstruction or composite drawing, no one could locate them.

Baxter's inquiry, however, did spark a renewal of interest in the medical examiner's office. Autopsy photographs of the unidentified girl were sent to a detective with the Dallas Police Department with a request that he attempt a drawing.

A self-taught artist, the detective, assigned to the Physical Evidence Section, had begun doing the drawings of unidentified homicide victims and suspects as little more than a hobby just months earlier. Despite the decomposition of the victim's face, the detective diligently set out to create a drawing of what he felt the dead girl had looked like.

In September of 1991, Baxter received an envelope from the Dallas County M.E.'s office. For the frustrated dispatcher, the drawing provided renewed motivation. Pulling it from the envelope, Baxter felt a sudden mixture of sadness and elation at getting her first glimpse of the girl's face.

It was something new to go on; another tool that might help her move forward in her seemingly endless search.

* * *

Then, late in the summer of '91, Sandy received a phone call that caused her to set aside her nationwide search and focus on the possibility that the victim might well have resided in the very neighborhood where her abduction had taken place.

A freelance journalist working on an article about Baxter's lengthy quest had learned that Randy King had been recently paroled. The writer contacted King's parole officer, seeking an interview with King in hopes that he might shed some light on the victim's identity. Though King refused a face-to-face interview, he did finally agree to answer questions passed along by his parole officer. During the course of the unorthodox interview—the writer asking the parole officer his questions on the phone; she then posing them to King, who was sitting in her office; him answering; her relaying his answers back to the writer—King continued to insist that he did not know the girl's name. He did, however, ultimately make an off-hand comment that had not appeared in any statement previously given to the police. "When I asked Chris why he [Wahnee] killed her," King remarked, "he said something about her having gone to Gaston Junior High [in Dallas] with his [Wahnee's] sister and that he was afraid she might have been able to identify him."

The reporter passed the information along to Baxter, who immediately went to work. In short order, she learned that Wahnee's sister had been a junior high student, and Baxter secured computerized enrollment records from the school. From a list of almost 1,000 names, she launched into a time-consuming process of elimination. Making endless phone calls, checking driver's license records, I.D. card records, even criminal histories, she was able to determine that all but four of the girls on her list were still alive.

Two months of work had finally drawn her closer to the name she sought.

* * *

With the death of Lieutenant Billy Fowler, Sandy Baxter had lost more than a longtime friend. An officer with a quarter century of investigative experience, he had long championed her cause, quietly working on any leads she came up with and constantly lending advice and encouragement. With no investigative training, Baxter worried that she might not find another officer she could interest in the aging case.

Her concerns were short-lived. Sergeant Donnie Reeves, 41, had joined the Midlothian force in 1987 and, since he was assigned to work the late night shift, knew little about Baxter's obsession until he happened by her desk one morning as he was going off duty and saw her pouring over her worn file. As soon as she had explained what she was attempting to do, he volunteered his help.

Soon, his daytime sleep was routinely cut short as he logged off-duty time following up on any leads Baxter developed.

It was Reeves who suggested her next step be to seek out the enrollment records of Gaston Junior High students who had graduated to nearby Bryan Adams High School, warning that the task would be demanding.

His words were prophetic. The new computer printout she secured from the high school included the names of 2,000 female students. In time, however, she managed to narrow the list to 300 before a school official suggested that the student medical records kept back at Gaston Junior High included far more information than did the high school enrollment cards. Thus, Baxter and new helpmate Reeves returned to Gaston and spent two hours in the school's musty, airless basement, searching for the long-stored medical records of students who attended the school during the '85-'86 and '86-'87 school years.

When she finally located the box, Baxter shook her head in disbelief at the number of files. "Where do we start?" she asked. Reeves suggested she concentrate on the names of the 300 students she'd not eliminated from the high school list.

Working nights at her kitchen table, Baxter slowly whittled away at the mountainous task. Ultimately, there were 27 girls she could not account for. Their names went onto what she and Reeves labeled their "priority list."

"When I would finally locate anyone on the list and verify they were still alive," Baxter says, "I would ask them if they remembered any girl who had just suddenly dropped from sight during the time of the abduction and murder.

"Late one evening, I reached a girl on the phone, and when I began questioning her, she mentioned that she remembered the article that had run in the Dallas Morning News and told me that the composite drawing which accompanied the story resembled a girl who had once been her older sister's best friend.

The friend's name, she remembered, was Kimberley Hustead, and she had not seen her or heard anything of her since 1986. Yes, she said, Kimberley had attended Gaston Junior High, but only for a couple of months.

Though the name hadn't appeared on any of the school records which Baxter had searched through, school officials were finally able to locate an old address for the girl. Baxter added it to her list.

By the fall of 1992, eighteen girls had not been accounted for. With nothing more than a batch of six-year-old addresses, Baxter decided to draft a letter to mail to each of the women on her list, along with a copy of the composite drawing.

She mailed the letters on October 16. On the 20th, the Midlothian P.D.

received a phone call and forwarded it to Baxter's home. The woman caller said, "I understand you're trying to reach my daughter."

During the course of the conversation, Baxter learned that the woman had moved from Dallas to a small town in Arkansas in late 1985. Her children—16-year-old daughter Kimberley and an 18-year-old son—had accompanied her but soon grew weary of life there and moved back to Dallas to live with their stepfather.

Asked to describe her daughter, whom the woman admitted she'd lost touch with after Kimberley's move back to Dallas, the caller offered a physical description that closely resembled the girl Baxter had so long been hoping to identify.

"I felt strongly that this might be what we were looking for," Baxter remembers, "and I just froze. I couldn't think of the right questions to ask. I was shaking. Finally, I asked her if I could call her back in ten minutes, explaining that I had to go to the office and get my file. I immediately phoned Donnie at home and asked him to call her."

Reeves immediately telephoned the woman and, after only a few minutes of conversation, told her that he and Baxter would be on their way to her house.

"When we got there," Reeves says, "I explained to her what we were trying to do and asked her to look at the composite drawing." The divorced mother stared at the drawing for some time, saying nothing. Then she slowly handed it back to the officer and shook her head. "I don't think so," she finally said. "That's not my daughter."

She did, however, provide him with photographs of Kimberley and the address of Kimberley's brother. She also suggested they might want to talk with a girl who had once been Kimberley's best friend.

Walking from the house that evening, Sandy Baxter was distraught. She had been so certain the woman would acknowledge that the girl in the drawing was her daughter. Reeves placed an arm around her shoulders. "Did you see her reaction when she looked at the drawing?" he asked. "Believe me, Sandy, she knows that's her daughter.

"You've found her. Your girl's name is Kimberley Hustead." The mother's refusal to identify the drawing, he was certain, was nothing more than her way of denying that her daughter was dead.

Returning to the Midlothian police station, they telephoned the police department in the city where the brother lived, explaining they were faxing the drawing along with a request that an officer take it to the residence of Kimberley's brother to see if he might identify it. The officer Baxter spoke with assured her it would be done as soon as possible but was quick to point out that their department was in the process of moving into a new building. It might be a couple of days, he told her.

Not satisfied to sit and wait, Baxter and Reeves located the girlfriend the mother had mentioned and drove to Dallas the following day to interview her, taking with them the drawing as well as the autopsy photographs and the earrings that were taken from the victim's body. Seeing that the woman was pregnant, Reeves was initially hesitant to have her view the disturbing autopsy pictures.

However, when the woman said that she was reasonably sure that the drawing was of Kimberley Hustead, she asked to be shown the photographs. As she looked at each of the pictures she nodded her head. "That's Kimberley," she said.

Reaching into a nearby drawer, she took out several photographs of her friend and handed them to Baxter. The pictures, Sandy noticed, had been lying atop a folded copy of the newspaper article that had appeared earlier.

Then, as Reeves emptied the small pieces of jewelry from an envelope, the girl gasped. As she pointed to the pear-shaped earring, all color vanished from her face. "I gave that to her," she said. She volunteered to sign an affidavit stating that she was certain the girl in the autopsy photographs and the drawing was Kimberley.

By that afternoon, little doubt remained. After Baxter and Reeves located Kimberley's former boyfriend, he too made a positive identification and signed an affidavit stating that the victim was the girl he had dated for over a year. "There's no doubt in my mind," he said. In fact, he filled in some of the blanks about the evening on which she had been abducted and murdered.

It had already gotten dark, he recalled, and he, Kimberley, and her brother were in the car with her stepfather, driving along Ferguson Road. There was an argument—he couldn't recall what about—and Kimberley had demanded that her stepfather stop and let her out of the car. As she got out, she said she was going to walk over to a friend's house.

It was the last time he had seen her.

Why, Reeves wanted to know, had he not been concerned when he didn't see her again after that evening? "We were breaking up at the time," the young man explained.

* * *

Now, finally, it had come to the matter of making it official. At the Southwestern Institute of Forensic Sciences, a medical examiner had already used a technical process of matching overlays of the pictures that the mother and girlfriend had provided to the autopsy photographs and concluded they were, in fact, the same girl.

It was within the legal authority of the medical examiner's office to identify a body on the basis of the evidence that had been gathered, the Midlothian investigators were told. An affidavit from a family member, however, would be preferable.

Baxter, her nerves frayed and patience depleted, had waited too long and worked too hard for there to be any doubt.

Five days had passed since the request had been made to the out-of-state police, and still no effort had been made to locate Kimberley's brother. On a Wednesday night, Reeves phoned Baxter following a brief meeting with police chief Roy Vaughn. "Get us plane reservations," Reeves told her. "First flight out in the morning."

* * *

Sitting in his apartment, the brother went through the same routine as had his mother. "Yes," he finally said, "that's my sister. There's no doubt."

Reeves asked that he, too, write and sign an affidavit stating he had positively identified the girl. Only after the young man finished writing his brief statement did Reeves speak. "All through this," he said, "we've promised that if we identified the girl, we would tell her family everything we know about the case. Are there any questions you would like to ask?"

The brother stared sadly at the officer for several seconds, then slowly shook his head. "No," he finally replied.

On the flight back to Dallas, Sandy Baxter sat in silence, pondering the events of the past few days. It was over, yet the feeling of elation she had so often imagined was missing. The answer she had sought for six years had only yielded more questions: Why had no one even bothered to file a missing person's report when a 16-year-old child disappeared? How could a girlfriend who had seen the newspaper article and thought the story was most likely about Kimberley have simply put it away in a drawer, never bothering to contact anyone? How could a boyfriend not find it unusual that his girlfriend had just suddenly vanished? Why, damn it, had no one cared?

As the question spun through her mind, quiet tears began sliding down her cheeks. Reeves, as if reading her thoughts, reached over and gently squeezed her hand.

"*You* cared," he whispered.

* * *

As news of Baxter's accomplishment spread through the tiny community of Midlothian, donations for a headstone to be placed on the grave of Kimberley Hustead began arriving at the police department and funeral home.

A week after her visit from Reeves and Baxter, Kimberley's mother summoned the courage to travel to Midlothian and visit the grave site of the girl she had initially hoped was not her daughter. "I just didn't want to accept the idea that she was dead," she explained. "I wanted to think that she had just gotten angry about something and run away." Yet her reason for never having filed a missing person report, she said, was her fear that something tragic had happened to her daughter. "I just couldn't bear the idea of one day having to look at autopsy pictures."

Even looking at the drawing shown her by Reeves, she said, "was the hardest thing I've ever had to do."

While in Midlothian, she stopped in at the police department and was given her daughter's property—the tiny earrings and the unicorn necklace. "I remember the necklace," she said. "A lady who she did babysitting for had ordered it from the Avon catalog and gave it to her; Kimberley loved unicorns."

Her son returned home during the Thanksgiving holidays to join his mother in a quiet family service at the Midlothian Cemetery.

"I'll never be able to properly thank Sandy Baxter for what she did," the mother says. "It must have been the hand of God that drew her attention to Kimberley."

Baxter's attention has now returned to her duties as a police dispatcher. The case file of the long ago murder no longer sits on the corner of her desk. On a hot Texas summer day in 1993, advised that the new headstone bearing Kimberley's name was in place, Sandy finally visited the grave of the lonely little girl who had been so much a part of her life in recent years.

She brought with her a gift—a white porcelain unicorn—and placed it near the granite marker, admiring it and the words chiseled into it:

Kimberley Hustead
July 14, 1969
June 2, 1986
"In Loving Memory"

♦ *Dallas Life Magazine, Dallas Morning News*, September 1991

Haunted House

This is a story without beginning or end, only a middle where there is horror and confusion, unspeakable tragedy, and a dark, haunting evil that cries out for understanding. Stephen King should be telling it. It takes place in the quiet shadows of rural church spires, in an isolated and bucolic part of the Texas heartland populated by God-fearing, hard-working people. Good country folks.

And at least one faceless monster.

On the final Thursday in October of 2003, Stephen and Deena Roberts stood in the vacant upstairs of the large A-frame home they'd moved into three years earlier, contemplating a major remodeling project. Their two elementary school-aged children were fast reaching a time in their lives when they would be demanding more privacy, and the understanding parents, both in their 30s, had decided to oblige them by converting the unused upstairs space into two small bedrooms.

Comfortable in the downstairs portion of the house that sits off Brown County Road 153, a half dozen miles southeast of the whistle-stop community of Bangs, all but hidden by the large, gnarled live oaks that dominate their thirty-acre plot, the Robertses had paid what they referred to as "the attic" little mind since purchasing the house in late June of 2000. Until there came the need for additional room.

And now the husband and wife, an auto repair shop owner and a day care worker, were surveying it, assessing the structural changes to be made and the electrical wiring to be done. In the far corner of the room, just past the bright patterns made along the wooden floor by slender rays of sunlight that peeked through a small window, was a closet built out from the wall. When Deena Roberts opened it, she noticed a small door in back that obviously led to a crawl space behind it.

It was there—for how long, no one knows—that lay a horror which would change their lives, driving them to seek counseling, place a "No Trespassing" sign on their gate, and refuse all interview requests from the media. A planned holiday vacation was abruptly canceled. They are, friends say, now seriously considering moving from their once happy home.

Opening the door and peering into the dull grayness of the crawl space, Deena saw a single plastic trash bag just within arm's reach. She initially assumed it most likely contained some old clothes left behind by the previous residents. Only when she retrieved the bag and began to examine its contents did she turn to her husband, unable to speak.

Inside the trash bag was a paper sack. Inside the paper sack, a small sheet. And wrapped in the sheet was something neither of the Robertses was willing at first to believe. At first they thought—hoped—that perhaps it might be the remains of a small animal. It was, in truth, only wishful thinking. The reality was too horrifying to comprehend. What they had found was a tiny mummified human corpse.

Badly shaken, they hurried downstairs and placed a call to the Brown County Sheriff's Department in nearby Brownwood. Stephen Roberts was finally able to voice their worst fear to the dispatcher who took his call.

"He told us," recalls Chief Deputy Mike McCoy, "that he thought they had found the remains of a dead baby."

* * *

Over the course of two and a half decades of law enforcement work, McCoy has responded to more scenes of violence than he can recall—the blood and tangled metal of traffic accidents, murder victims' bodies unceremoniously dumped in barrow ditches and hidden in shallow graves, the aftermath of drunken domestic arguments turned deadly—but nothing like what he saw that afternoon after driving through the gate leading to the Roberts home.

During the twenty minutes it had taken to make the trip, he'd passed fields where goats, cattle, and horses leisurely grazed; he sped by brimming stock ponds, manicured grain fields, and well-kept farmhouses. It was not unlike racing through a two-lane Andrew Wyath painting—until he reached his destination.

The homeowners had already carried the large plastic bag from the house and placed it in the front yard. Next to it was the paper sack and sheet in which the tiny body lay. McCoy needed only a quick glance to determine that ·the darkened, leathery form was, in fact, human. Fellow Brown County deputy Scott Martin, who arrived just minutes later, agreed.

Nearby, Deena Roberts silently stood near her husband, her body trembling.

For the veteran deputies, myriad questions quickly arose. Had they, in fact, arrived at the scene of a long past homicide, or had the baby died of natural causes and just been cruelly hidden away? Who was this tiny person who had likely lived no more than a few days or weeks? Was it possible the people who had called them to the scene could somehow be responsible for the ghastly sight? Had there been other residents of the house sometime in the past? Would a check of old police and hospital records yield information on a missing infant from years ago?

Agreeing they would need help finding answers, McCoy immediately contacted Texas Ranger Nick Hanna, just recently assigned to the Brownwood office, asking that he join them at the Roberts home. Sworn in as a Ranger only two months earlier, Hanna was soon driving toward what he would later call "a puzzle in which none of the pieces seem to fit."

The three lawmen quickly agreed that the body should be immediately transported to the Travis County Medical Examiner's Office in Austin. And, rather than search the larger bag it had come from, the decision was made that it should not be disturbed in case it might provide badly needed evidence. It, too, would be sent to Austin. The Davis Morris Funeral Home in Brownwood was summoned to deliver the body and the bag; Scott, his right arm still in a sling as a result of shoulder surgery, was assigned to follow and witness the examination.

In Austin, neither he nor Dr. Elizabeth Peacock, Deputy Chief Medical Examiner of Travis County, had any reason to expect that the already bizarre case might take on an even more terrifying twist.

* * *

Inside the brightly-lit examining room, everything delivered by the funeral home was placed onto a gurney. Gently pulling back the sheet and looking down at the tiny mummified form, Dr. Peacock quickly determined that the science she practices was unlikely to provide satisfactory answers. The absence of internal organs, decomposed by the passage of time, eliminated the possibility of their yielding the traditional clues an autopsy might reveal. There was nothing on the small body to indicate a cause of death; no crushed skull or bullet wound. She could not, in fact, even determine the gender of the corpse, only that it was a newborn and had been dead for a minimum of six months, the length of time necessary for a body to completely mummify.

"While I was standing there, observing," says Scott, "I saw one of the technicians look into a plastic sack still inside the larger bag and lift the corner of what appeared to be a towel. He quickly turned to Dr. Peacock and called her attention to a small bone that was barely visible."

The M.E. immediately instructed her assistant to search no further. Instead, they would first X-ray the bag in an effort to determine its contents. The stark black and white film ultimately revealed skeletons of two additional small bodies, also newborns, Dr. Peacock surmised.

Scott phoned McCoy, who was anxiously awaiting a report in Brownwood. "We've got two more," the investigator said.

Three tiny bodies. Triplets? Unlikely since one appeared to be a bit larger than the others. Dead for how long? Hidden away by whom? What manner of unspeakable evil had been played out in the house on County Road 153?

* * *

The investigation—and the local talk—began almost instantly. In the small community of Bangs, where word of the grim discovery quickly spread, the reaction was what one might anticipate: things like this just don't happen here. Down at the Shell station, owner Mike Stephens called it "disgusting." At the Allsup's Grocery, one of the stories being circulated was that the bodies were not actually infants, as reported, but rather older children who had been severely malnourished. The nightmare was even the topic of discussion in chemistry class at the local high school. Not unexpectedly, a few of the more imaginative residents voiced concern that some manner of Satanic baby sacrifice ritual might have been carried out. And there was coffee shop speculation about an illegal abortion clinic hidden away somewhere in the countryside.

Wire service reports of the discovery had soon spread the story nationwide. Then came the queries from network television shows like *20/20, 48 Hours,* and even *Oprah.* All were disappointed to learn that, beyond the fact the bodies had been found, there was little story to be told. No beginning, no end. No place to direct blame. Not even identities to assign the victims.

Dallas true crime writer Patricia Springer, whose recent *Blood Stains* chronicles a 1993 Brown County child murder committed by Ricky McGuinn, says the case may well even interest non-fiction writers eventually—but only if and when the case is solved. "More likely," she says, "it is going to be one of those horror stories that grows into local folklore over the years."

"The whole thing makes my stomach turn," says veteran *Abilene Reporter-News* journalist Celinda Emison, mother of two teenage boys, who was assigned to the story. "I've covered murders, an execution, seen awful crime scene pictures, but nothing as upsetting as this. As a reporter, I find the mystery aspect of it quite interesting, but the fact there are children—babies—involved makes it all so sad, so tragic. And, wherever the story finally goes, the ending can only be ugly."

"It's the strangest thing I've ever heard," says Bangs police chief Bill Copeland, hired to his position only 60 days before the discovery. And, he candidly admits, he is relieved that the bodies were not found in jurisdiction. "If there's anything I can do to help," he says, "I'll certainly do so. But I've got to say I'm glad this isn't my case."

Those to whom it did belong—the Brown County Sheriff's Department and Texas Ranger Hanna—had never before worked a "cold case." "Our first priority," says Hanna, "has been to try and determine the identity of the children then establish a time line that would provide us a history of the residence where the bodies were found." From the get-go, they have approached the case as a multiple homicide investigation.

A search of old law enforcement records revealed no reports of missing children. Hospital records were non-productive. At the Brown County courthouse, however, investigators located a building permit that had been issued to a local electrical engineer named James Bowling in 1987. He'd built the country house and lived there with his wife, Doris, daughters Traci Ann and Constance, and son, Eddie. Shortly after the elder Bowlings died—James in 1999, his wife in 2000—the siblings put the house up for sale and moved away.

The tree-shaded A-frame, according to Brown County Appraisal District records, was in probate when the Roberts purchased it in July of 2000. From February until the new owners moved in, the house had been vacant.

"At this point," says McCoy, "we've got to treat everyone who ever lived in the house as a suspect." There is, however, little optimism in his voice to suggest a quick resolution of the mystery. "Everyone we've spoken with is being very cooperative."

The distraught Robertses quickly agreed to give DNA samples to prove they are not related to the infants. The two Bowling daughters, now living in small towns in the Texas Panhandle, expressed disbelief when investigators told them about the discovery and also volunteered to provide DNA samples to be compared to those the medical examiner hopes will eventually be extracted from the bodies. The women, now in their 40s, have been very cooperative, McCoy and Martin say. "One is a physical therapist," Deputy Martin notes, "and the other is a housewife with five children."

Only the Bowling son, a hairdresser reportedly living in the Corpus Christi area, has yet to be located and interviewed. "We aren't even sure he knows about what's happened," McCoy says. "Neither of his sisters had read or heard anything about it before we interviewed them." The last time either of the women had spoken with their brother, they told investigators,. was "at least a year ago."

It is a case, the officers agree, that defies even the most twisted logic.

McCoy all but dismisses the Robertses as suspects. "If they'd had anything to do with this," he reasons, "why, after such a long period of time, suddenly report what they found to the authorities? That makes no sense at all."

And what of the three surviving Bowling family members—each separated in age by six years and "not particularly close to each other"—who sold the house and moved away following their parents' deaths? "If you are trying to sell a house, it doesn't make much sense to leave three dead bodies hidden inside."

As Ranger Hanna says, it's a puzzle with no fitting pieces.

What, then, of the five-month time period in 2000 during which the house was vacant? Is it possible a trespasser—perhaps someone familiar with the house, even a stranger—might have used it as a place to hide the crime? "We're certainly not dismissing that possibility," McCoy says.

Sitting behind his desk recently, he admitted frustration. "You feel like there are things you should be doing," he says, "but what? We've gone through the house with a fine-tooth comb twice. We've dug through records and conducted interviews. Now, we're at a point where we're at the mercy of the scientists."

Specifically, the investigation depends on the findings of Denton's Dr. Harrell Gill-King, director of the University of North Texas' Laboratory of Forensic Anthropology, one of only two licensed forensic anthropologists in Texas. "This investigation," admits Deputy Martin, "now hinges on what Dr. Gill-King can determine and pass along to us."

* * *

Early in November of 2003, Dr. Gill-King drove to Austin and picked up the tender cargo he would take back to his laboratory for study. Good-natured and quick to laugh, he has spent the last two decades examining skeletal remains, testifying in grizzly and celebrated court trials, and teaching his strange craft to the next generation of forensic scientists. In the aftermath of the 9/11 disaster in New York, he was among those called in to help identify the remains of victims.

And while he says that it is his policy not to discuss any case on which he's still working, he does explain that he will conduct what is called a necropsy, rather than an autopsy. In layman's language, his examination will be conducted with a variety of high-tech X-rays, measurements, and photography. His goal: to determine when the infants died, their gender, if they are related, and, if possible, how they met their deaths.

The latter, experts say, is unlikely. Still, DNA material can be extracted from bones, ultimately providing authorities with comparisons to make with each of the bodies and any suspects developed in the course of the investigation. "When we get some DNA evidence to work with," says Ranger Hanna, "then I believe we'll be able to move the case forward."

Dr. Gill-King has told investigators that it might be as long as six to eight weeks before his testing of the bodies is completed.

Scientists at the Texas Department of Public Safety laboratory in Austin recently began examining the bags and wrappings in which the infants' bodies were found, searching for fingerprints and trace evidence like hair and fibers left behind by the person or persons who hid the bodies.

Martin, however, agrees that chances of ever determining the cause of death of the babies is "slim to none"—unless someone eventually steps forward to confess. "Right now," he says, "we're more focused on learning who the victims are and who they might be connected to."

And so, everyone waits on Dr. Gill-King. And only after the anthropologist has extracted DNA from the remains will samples be officially requested of those on the investigators' "persons of interest" list.

For McCoy, things are moving too slowly. As he waits, he scours databases for similar cases, solved or unsolved, that might somehow be linked to his investigation. And while he's found nothing that appears to tie in to the rural tragedy, he's learned that the mysterious event that now commands his every waking thought is not as unique as he assumed.

"Just the other day," he says, "I was reading about a case of a woman who gave birth to triplets in New York back in the '80s, then apparently murdered all three. For years, she moved here and there, always taking their bodies with her in a box. Finally, she evidently left the box in a storage building out in Arizona." Eventually, she'd stopped making rental payments and the contents of her storage space were removed and her crime discovered. "She was living somewhere in Pennsylvania when they finally arrested her last year."

As a footnote to the chilling story, McCoy points out that the accused murderer grew up in Hondo, Texas.

Additionally, he says he's received calls and emails from fellow law enforcement officials who have worked similar cases over the years.

Dallas forensic pathologist, Dr. Linda Norton, a highly regarded expert on infant deaths, says such cases are not unusual. "And," she says, "neither is the killing and discarding of new-born infants. If the truth were known, there are probably far more instances than we'd ever want to imagine. A baby is so easy to hide. Put it in a dumpster and most likely it winds up in a landfill, never to be seen again. Bury it and in no time the body decomposes to a point where there is virtually nothing left. It sounds horrible, but when you talk about the things supposedly civilized people do, it too often becomes stranger than any fiction you'll ever read."

Only last week, a headline in the local papers reported a just-born child discarded in a strip mall trash bin in Hurst, Texas. Sad, horrifying, but hardly front page material these days.

After reviewing the facts of the case, Dr. Norton agrees with investigators that their most likely suspects are those who have resided in the house. "Or," she adds, "someone connected to someone who lived there.

"I'll bet you this: The person who hid the bodies away in the crawl space also made the door they found in the back of the closet. They cut the small door to be able to get access to the crawl space to hide the bag. Then, in an effort to keep the door from being conspicuous, they then built the closet in front of it."

It is, she acknowledges, only speculation that flames the imagination and passes the time as everyone waits for real answers.

* * *

In a more perfect marriage of criminal investigation and journalism, there would, at this point in the story, be some degree of resolution, some insight into the behavior and motive that led to the horrifying deaths and disposal of three innocents. Whoever's responsible would have been identified and arrested, charged, and arraigned, and a trial date would have been set. His or her—or their—troubled life histories would have been thoroughly investigated and made public in print and on Action News at 10. There would have been congratulatory press conferences and some sense of relief on the part of those wrongly branded suspects.

And, most importantly, we would be able to identify the victims as something more personal than "three mummified newborns."

Realistically, no such occurrences are likely anytime soon. If ever.

Out at the end of County Road 153 and in the offices of Brownwood's newly-built Law Enforcement Center, the questions continue to far outnumber the answers. And there is no satisfactory end in sight. Despite the talent and techniques of the forensic scientists and law enforcement officials, there is an unspoken but real fear that closure might never come to a case that is too old and too cold. Too strange. Even those working long hours to see that it is solved privately wonder at the long odds they face.

And that, along with the lost and disrupted lives, community fear and anger, confusion and frustration, only compounds the tragedy, adding another shade of darkness to the mystery.

"It is for all those reasons," says Ranger sergeant Hanna, "that we're going to solve this case. We have to."

◆ *Dallas Observer*, November 2003

POSTSCRIPT:

It was not weeks, but eight months before Dr. Gill-King announced his findings to the investigating authorities. The case, he said, had "all the trappings of a bittersweet Gothic novel"—but he could provide few answers. The babies, he concluded, died twenty or more years ago, possibly of a rare blood disorder. He could not, however, determine if they were related. The doctor did find that the mummified body slightly larger than the others was a male. The two smaller skeletons, he says, may have been twins.

And there was a possible clue to the time when at least one of the children died. It had been wrapped in a sheet that hasn't been marketed since the early 1960s, featuring the likeness of cartoon character Dennis the Menace.

Shot In the Dark

It began with a seemingly harmless joke, the kind good ol' boys in the rural north Texas community of Whitewright traditionally enjoy.

Down at the Quick Check, a popular early morning coffee stop, someone placed a donation jar on the counter, attaching a hand-written sign that whimsically urged contributions to a fund that would help purchase a badly needed four-wheel drive vehicle for the local police department.

No one is sure whose idea it was, but the event that generated it is clear. On a cold, damp evening back in late November of 2000, a fleeing driver led officers on a wild and winding chase along the scrub brush of Grayson and Fannin Counties' backroads. At some point, however, the police patrol cars—one from Whitewright, another from neighboring Bells—got stuck in mud, and the white pickup they had been pursuing got away.

It didn't take long for word to spread through Whitewright, population 1,740, that the police had to phone for a tow truck to come to their rescue. By the next morning, good natured ribbing greeted 53-year-old Corporal Jim Lamance, a late-in-life member of the four-man police department who had been driving one of the cars that night. Soon, the "donation" jar was in place. By all accounts, Lamance didn't find it at all amusing. More embarrassed, he was angered by the coffee shop jibes directed his way.

Still, by most locals the matter was viewed as innocent fun—until a few weeks later when another chase ended in a bizarre midnight gunfight that left Lamance, just two years into his law enforcement career, slumped in his patrol car, dead from a single gunshot wound to the face. In the early hours of December 23, the warmth and merriment of the holiday season quickly turned cold and somber. Instead of the anticipated Christmas celebration, the Lamance family was preparing for a funeral, a well-liked farmer and manufacturing plant worker had been arrested and was being held on a million dollar bond, and Whitewright was becoming a community divided.

Now, three years later, after details of the tragic story have repeatedly changed, bitter accusations have been exchanged, and two controversial trials have been conducted, it remains so.

Peel away the layers of grief and suspicion, legal sleight-of-hand, vicious rumors, and shrill-voiced disappointment in the judicial system, and the unanswered question remains: Who killed Jim Lamance?

Investigating authorities concluded Richard Carl Hicks, the same man Lamance was chasing along the maze of rural backroads for the third time in a matter of weeks, fired the fatal shot. Hicks, who freely admits his involvement in two previous chases, insists he had nothing to do with the officer's death and was, in fact, at home in bed when the tragedy occurred. A highly regarded Dallas forensic pathologist, after reviewing the evidence, came forward with an alternate scenario too horrifying for the Lamance family to even consider. Yet in May, 2003, a year after a jury acquitted Hicks of capital murder charges in state court, a federal judge ruled that the evidence against him was more convincing than the jurors had believed.

In April, 54-year-old Hicks began serving a fifteen-year federal prison sentence, convicted not of murder but, instead, of violation of a protective order that was sworn out against him by his former wife three years earlier. It had nothing directly to do with the death of Jim Lamance, yet in the minds of many, it had everything to do with a manipulative legal system's embittered determination to see Hicks punished for a greater crime it was convinced he committed.

Thus it is a tangled story that is woefully lacking a satisfactory resolution. Friends and family of Lamance continue to grieve, as do those convinced that Hicks has been unfairly treated by authorities who managed to find a way to circumvent the legal issue of double jeopardy. Too, the police, sheriff's department officers, and Texas Rangers that investigated the case have been roundly criticized. Even by the man who ultimately decided Hicks' fate. From the bench during Hicks' sentencing hearing, federal judge Paul Brown stated that "there's no question that it [the investigation] could have been handled and carried out better" and that "certainly it won't be written up in any textbooks."

No winners. Only lives lost and ruined. Police placing black tape over their badges in honor of one of their own; friends of the accused wearing yellow ribbons to demonstrate their support. All because of the lingering echo of questions about what actually occurred on that dark and tragic December night. The answers remain as elusive as windblown smoke, depending on whose story you choose to believe.

* * *

Only once in recent history has the outside world taken much note of little Whitewright, 65 miles northeast of Dallas. That came in the mid-'80s when word began to spread that a quiet and reclusive hardware store manager named Joe Tom Meador had stolen millions of dollars worth of

German art treasures while serving as a forward observer for an Army artillery unit during World War II. The famed Quedlinburg church collection, hidden away in Marz Mountain caves for wartime protection, was looted by Meador and secretly mailed back to his home. There the priceless pieces remained for four decades, long after their thief's death, until investigators tracked them down almost a half century later and the German Cultural Foundation negotiated an estimated $3 million deal with Meador's heirs to buy back the items.

Today, however, the scandal of Joe Tom Meador and his stolen stash of gold and jeweled treasures is old news. Now, at the Dusty Saddle, a dark and jangly beer joint on the edge of town, it never takes long for the conversation to get around to the death of local officer Lamance and the imprisonment of former patron Hicks. There, just a half mile from the block-long downtown area that houses the bank, a home-cooking cafe, several antique shops, a renovated movie theater, and an auto parts store, news travels fast. If you want to know what's going on in town, forget the weekly *Whitewright Sun* or the six o'clock news out of nearby Brenham or Sherman. Just stop in for a cold Bud or a game of 8-ball and listen.

A construction worker, settled into his regular late afternoon place at the bar, assures that there is no tidbit of local fact or gossip that doesn't makes its way to the Dusty Saddle with lightening speed. "Hell," he says, laughing, "I graduated high school, went to two years of college and served in the military, and never learned as much as I have sitting right here."

On a recent afternoon, a quick poll of the dozen customers hiding from the 95° heat indicated that there wasn't a single person in the place who believed that Hicks, who spent every day of his life—except the two years he was in the service—in Whitewright, shot and killed anybody.

"My husband and I have known Richard for years," says local resident Lea Head. "He's one of the most honest people you'll ever meet. He's a good, plain, God-fearing man who would be the first to admit it—if he'd done what they accused him of." To emphasize her point, she notes that it was Richard's demand that his son tell the truth when called to testify that played a major role in his being sentenced to serve federal prison time. But, more about that later.

While friends and supporters proclaim his innocence with a fervor that borders on the evangelical, they are equally quick to admit he had a drinking problem that had grown worse since his wife Sandra filed for divorce. "I fussed at him about it constantly," says his mother, Geraldine. "After the divorce, he started spending more and more time at the Dusty Saddle. He'd come home and call me late at night, just wanting to talk. I kept telling him he had to stop drinking and get on with his life." So did his father, Glenn. "I never saw him take a drink of whiskey," he says, "but he was drinking way too much beer."

Friends at the Dusty Saddle agreed. And since it was well known that the local police routinely patrolled the private club's parking lot, ready to stop departing drivers they suspected of being intoxicated, it was a good bet that Hicks was destined for legal troubles. His record soon included one DWI and a couple of arrests for public intoxication.

And the chases he had led the police on became part of Dusty Saddle folklore. There was, for instance, the night when, after speeding along the caliche roads that border the flatland grain fields of the countryside and losing those chasing him in the process, Hicks had returned home, pulled into his driveway, and simply sat in his pickup, awaiting the inevitable arrival of the police. He was sound asleep—or passed out, depending on which version of the story you choose to believe—when Jim Lamance and his brother Kevin finally arrived. "I knew they'd be coming," Hicks later told friends, "and I didn't want them busting my front door down. So, I waited outside for them."

Too, he freely admitted it was him the police were chasing on the night their patrol cars got stuck in the mud.

Though hardly Public Enemy No. I, Richard Hicks was no candidate for sainthood. By his own doing, he'd made himself a closely-watched target of the Whitewright police. "He called me one evening, just a couple of days before the shooting," says friend George Varner, "and suggested we go have a beer. When I told him I'd meet him [at the Dusty Saddle], he asked if I'd come by and pick him up. He said that every time he left the house the police followed him."

Still, it all seemed like pretty typical life in small town Texas—until the early morning hours of December 23, 2000. Too late, it became evident that the perfect storm had been forming.

* * *

Kevin Lamance, 43, recently graduated from the police academy and serving as an unpaid reserve officer, was riding with his brother when they passed the Dusty Saddle and noticed a new white pickup parked on the east side of the small building. "Looks like Richard Hicks has bought himself a new truck," the younger Lamance remembers commenting.

The time was 5:30 in the afternoon. Several times during their evening shift patrol, he recalls, he and his brother noticed the pickup still parked at the members only club. It was, according to police records, nearing 1 a.m. when the Lamances saw the truck weaving along the highway. Making a U-turn, Cpl. Lamance, believing the driver was likely intoxicated, turned on his deck lights, began following, and attempted to pull the pickup over. Instead, the driver sped away and the officers pursued. Eventually, the high-speed chase left the Grayson County main roads and continued along the darkened one-lane Fannin County Road 4510.

The younger Lamance brother says they were following the pickup at a distance of approximately 40 feet when it suddenly made a left turn into an open field bordered by Bois d'Arc Creek and came to a stop over 200 yards away. The officers parked on the dirt road and radioed the Fannin County Sheriff's Department for assistance, describing the pursuit, giving their location, and stating that they believed the driver to be Richard Hicks.

Just moments later, Kevin Lamance recalls, he heard a rifle shot and felt the rush of a bullet past his face. He and his brother simultaneously ducked down, and the elder Lamance quickly called in a "shots fired" message. "I heard a second shot," Kevin would later recall, "and suddenly felt the [patrol] car rolling forward." It was as he reached over to put it in gear and stop the movement that he saw his brother slumped over the wheel. "I knew he had been shot," he says.

In the darkness, it was impossible to see clearly, but a fatal shot had entered the right eye of Cpl. Lamance, exiting the back of his head. A coroner's report indicated that the shot had ruptured the eye, nearly pulpified the brain, and fractured the officer's skull.

The recording of Kevin Lamance's call to the Fannin County Sheriff's dispatcher is chilling: "Oh, God, get someone here quick. He's been hit in the head . . ." Then, he's heard to say, "He [the shooter] is taking off back toward his house . . . get somebody after him." Though he admits neither he nor his brother ever actually saw who the driver of the pickup was that night, the "he" Lamance referred to was Hicks.

The reserve officer says he then attempted to draw his weapon but nervously dropped it in the floorboard. After a frantic but unsuccessful search for it, he attempted to unholster his injured brother's service revolver but was unable to do so. Finally, he found his own 9 millimeter handgun, exited the car, and began shooting in the direction of the fleeing pickup. He'd fired at least a half dozen shots before the truck exited the field and disappeared over a small bridge. One of Lamance's shots, it would later be determined, had lodged in the hood of the patrol car.

After the truck disappeared, Lamance says he went to the driver's side of the car to help his brother. "He was choking pretty bad, and I pulled him out of the car and laid him down. I held his head up because he was having a hard time breathing," he says.

* * *

In the pre-dawn hours, with Department of Public Safety helicopters flying overhead and officers from two sheriff's departments and several neighboring police departments surrounding Hicks' rural home, he was arrested. After firing tear gas and concussion grenades into the brick house, members of the Grayson County Sheriff's Department's Special Response Team entered to find the suspect in his bedroom, clothed only in his underwear, putting out a small fire on the carpet caused by one of the incendiary grenades.

During a recorded interview later conducted by Texas Ranger Lee Young at the jail, Hicks was asked if he'd recently fired a gun. "No," he replied. Did he know why he had been taken into custody? "No," he again replied.

Meanwhile, just a few miles away, the crime scene investigation was underway. In the muddy field, over two hundred yards from the road, Fannin County deputy Mike McClellan found tire tracks, boot prints, and two spent 30-30 shell casings that would ultimately be matched to a rifle found in Hicks' home.

Thus, as a funeral for Lamance was being held, his accused killer began a fifteen-month stay in jail, indicted for capital murder and attempted capital murder, agonizing over two shots in the dark that had ended one life and promised to crush another. They were not, Hicks repeatedly told family and friends, fired by him. "The first time I visited him in jail," says his father, "I asked him straight out if he did it. He said, 'Daddy, I didn't shoot that policeman.' Since that day he's never said anything different."

However, it wasn't until his trial in the spring of 2002 that the tragic story took a new twist, raising many of the questions that linger to this day.

* * *

On that December 22, Richard, accompanied by long-time friend Waymon Anderson, traveled to Oklahoma, where Hicks purchased a new white GMC pickup. Returning to Whitewright shortly after 5 p.m., Hicks checked on his cattle then stopped on his way home to visit his parents who live only a half-mile away. "It was 5:30 when he got here," says father Glenn. "I take my insulin shot at that time every day. That's what I was doing when he walked in."

The elder Hicks recalls walking out to the driveway to look at his son's new truck. In t he cab, he recalls, there was nothing but a tin of Copenhagen snuff and a Coca-Cola can. "He stayed maybe thirty minutes, then went home."

Thus, as Hicks' lawyers would eventually point out to a jury, the white pickup the officers said they had initially seen parked at the Dusty Saddle at 5:30 could not have belonged to Richard Hicks. It was then that Kevin Lamance's recollection of the events leading up to his brother's death began to change. Actually, he would eventually testify, he and Jim had not gone on duty until 7 p.m., thus it was more likely that they'd first seen the truck around 7:30.

At 7:30, however, 22-year-old Casey Hicks, driving his father's newly-purchased truck, was pulling into the parking lot of the Bonham Wal-Mart, 25 miles away, to pick up girlfriend Pamela Skinner, who was getting off work. Skinner would later testify that they drove directly to Hicks' home where they talked with Richard for some time. He was still there, she recalled, when they left sometime later in Casey's pickup.

Meanwhile, several patrons of the Dusty Saddle who had been at the club between the hours of 4 and 8 p.m. said they had not seen Hicks there. "My husband and I had agreed to meet there that night," remembers Lea Head. "We arrived in separate cars, and I stayed a while then drove on home. Johnny [her husband] was leaving at 10:15 and met Richard as he was coming in the door."

And with that, Kevin Lamance's recollection changed again. He would remember that it was actually around 10:15, shortly after his brother had written a ticket to a local driver, that they first noticed the pickup in the parking lot.

Dusty Saddle bartender Carey Mitchell says that Hicks did, in fact, arrive shortly after 10 p.m. and remained until her midnight closing. During that time, she testified, she did not serve him enough beer to cause him to be intoxicated. It is tradition for the last customer to stay while she cleans and locks up. Richard did so, leaving the club with her.

Hicks would later tell friends that he'd then driven directly home and gone to bed. He was sleeping, he explained, when he awoke to the smell of burning carpet caused by the SRT's flash grenade.

Thus began what veteran Sherman attorney Mike Wynne, who had represented Hicks on his earlier DWI case, calls a prosecutorial "runaway train." With limited experience in criminal law, he sought the help of Bob Jarvis in defending Hicks against the new charges. A prosecutor for legendary Dallas district attorney Henry Wade in the early '80s and Grayson County D.A. for twelve years, Jarvis had just recently lost a bid for reelection and was preparing to enter private practice. As he began reviewing the evidence against Hicks, he quickly came to the conclusion that the case he agreed to help defend was one built on lies. "There's no other way to describe it," he says.

Fannin County Attorney Myles Porter disagreed and proceeded with plans to try Hicks for capital murder.

It would, however, be far more than changing stories and faulty memories that were ultimately the target of attack by the defense lawyers. "I began making a chart of all the things that weren't right," says Jarvis. In addition to the changing time frame offered by Lamance, the list was lengthy.

Forensic experts had been unable to conclusively match soil samples taken from the field where the shooting occurred to that on Hicks' impounded truck. In fact, though the field had been muddy that night, there was nothing but what experts described as "road film" on the truck. Tracks in the field could not be matched to the tires of Hicks' truck. There was indication that the fleeing truck had run over several large, water-darkened logs that had floated up from the nearby creek, yet no matching particles were found in the tire treads or on the undercarriage. Two pairs of boots taken from Hicks' home after his arrest could not be matched to the footprints found in the field. A gunshot residue test, used to determine if someone has recently fired a weapon, had been administered to Hicks shortly after his early morning arrest and was negative. No fingerprints were found on the 30-30 casings located by Deputy McClellan the following day or on the rifle taken from Hicks' residence.

Then there was the matter of the fatal long-distance shot. Investigators had measured the distance from where the pickup was parked to the Lamances' patrol car at 217 yards. "This incredible shot," says Jarvis, "was made in the pitch dark. There was a slight rise between the truck and the patrol car, making it impossible to see anything but the top of the car parked on the road."

Both windows of the patrol car were only partially rolled down at the time of the alleged shoot-out, yet two bullets had to have entered the driver's side—one whizzing past Kevin Lamance's face, the other striking his brother—and exited the passenger window without leaving a trace. Neither bullet was ever found by crime scene investigators.

Edward Hueske, a firearms expert and criminal justice instructor at the University of North Texas, later attempted to duplicate the fatal shot on a firing range. In daylight and under ideal conditions, he managed to hit a 10-inch target only once in nine tries. "I can't say doing it [firing the shots credited to Hicks] is impossible, but it is very difficult; pretty remote."

Still, according to the DPS forensic lab tests, the Remington shell casings found in the field were a match to the Marlin 30-30 taken from Hicks' home at the time of his arrest. "Actually," says Glenn Hicks, "the rifle was mine. I'd bought it and a partial box of shells from a friend for $100. At the time, I was having trouble with wolves coming around the place." He'd loaned the rifle to his son and grandson, he said, when they were invited to go wild hog hunting in the fall of 2000.

If the authorities were so certain that Lamance died from a rifle shot, the elder Hicks, sitting in his living room, wonders why Texas Ranger Young twice visited his home to ask if Richard owned a 9 millimeter handgun. "He got on the [witness] stand and swore he never asked me that," Glenn Hicks says, "but he sat right in that chair on two different occasions and asked me."

The testimony of Dr. Linda Norton, a Dallas-based forensic pathologist, provided a likely answer.

She believes the long-distance rifle shot theory is the result of what she calls a "preposterous" investigation of the crime. Most often a witness for the prosecution, she agreed to review the evidence of the crime for Jarvis and Wynne and came to the conclusion that Jim Lamance's death was not a murder, but rather the result of a tragic "friendly fire" accident.

It was, she testified, a bullet from Kevin Lamance's handgun that killed his brother.

"I could find no case in history where a 30-30 fired from such range ever hit someone in the head," she says. "I also found it preposterous to think that a bullet could enter through a half-open window and exit the opposite (half-open) window." She points out that the inexperienced medical examiner who conducted the autopsy had difficulty even determining which was the entry wound and which was the exit wound and only included the fact the death had been caused by a "high-powered rifle" because authorities who delivered the body to the medical examiner's office had told her the shot came from a 30-30.

Additionally, while examining the autopsy photos, Dr. Norton detected what she determined to be "stippling," small specks of gunpowder residue that indicated the fatal shot had come from close range, not a distance of 217 yards.

"The physical evidence is just not consistent with [Kevin] Lamance's testimony that his brother was slumped over the steering wheel," she testified. Her recreation of the nightmarish event has driver Jim Lamance standing outside the police car when his brother, having exited the other side of the vehicle, began shooting.

"The individual [Kevin Lamance] panicked. He began to fire wildly, and his brother probably looked over at him and was shot in the eye," she says.

After hearing Dr. Norton's testimony, it took the jury less than three hours to acquit Hicks.

Sherman Herald Democrat reporter/columnist Jerri Whiteley spoke for many when she wrote, "I don't know who shot Whitewright officer

James Lamance. For that reason, I don't know if the verdict allowed a guilty man to go free or if it finally sent an innocent man home."

* * *

Finally free on a reduced bond of $20,000, Hicks—jobless and deeply in debt because of almost $300,000 in legal fees—returned home to a celebration staged by family, friends, and former coworkers. Though there was brief speculation that Port was contemplating a second trial for the attempted murder of Kevin Lamance, nothing ever came of it. There was also the suggestion that the angered Lamance family was planning a wrongful death civil suit against Hicks. Soon, that too seemed unlikely.

"For a while everything got quiet," says Jarvis, "until we began to hear that several of the same people who had testified in the state trial were being summoned to a federal grand jury." When he heard that, he knew full well what was coming.

During Hicks' state trial, his son, Casey, was called to the stand as a witness. In an effort to demonstrate for the jury that his father was hardly an expert marksman, the youngster mentioned occasional hunting trips they'd been on two years earlier. Innocent and insignificant as the testimony might have sounded at the time, it set in motion a plan that eventually resulted in new charges being filed against his father.

After his divorce, Hicks had driven to his ex-wife's home in April of 2000 and allegedly fired a shot in the direction of the house. Though no one was injured and no bullet hole discovered, his wife immediately sought a protective order against him. Among the numerous restrictions placed on Hicks by court order was that he "could not possess firearms or ammunition."

Thus on a rainy Thursday in October of 2002, ATF agents appeared at his home and placed him under arrest—despite the fact the two-year order had expired. "It was pretty clear," says attorney Jarvis, "that this was far more than an arrest for violation of a protective order. That was obvious the minute we read the indictment and saw that one of the allegations was that during the time the order was in effect, Richard had been in possession of two 30-30 casings found in the field after Jim Lamance's death."

What the state had failed to do, the federal system was going to attempt. Jarvis and Wynne immediately began preparing for a retrial of the alleged murder. And, interestingly, the prosecutorial bar would be lowered during the federal proceeding. In state court, a conviction can result only if a jury finds the defendant guilty beyond a reasonable doubt. In the federal system, guilt is determined when the jury is convinced beyond a preponderance of the evidence

While the maximum punishment for the new crime Hicks had been charged with is generally a year or less in jail, often probation, federal prosecutors asked the judge to employ the little-known procedure of "cross-referencing" the sentencing guidelines if it was proved that one crime (the restraining order violation) led to another (the murder of Jim Lamance). By using the procedure, the judge could assess a penalty that ranged from fifteen years to life in prison.

"The [protective order violation] statute was put in place to protect the spouse from abuse," defense attorney Wynne says, "not to go after someone already acquitted of capital murder. At no time did Hicks' ex-wife ever make any complaint about him violating the order."

Still, a guilty verdict on the federal charges came quickly, helped along by the testimony of Hicks' son, who again told of the hunting trips. "It was a hard thing for him to do," says George Varner, "but he said his daddy had insisted that he tell the truth when he took the stand. That tells me all I need to know about the character and honesty of Richard Hicks."

The two-day sentencing hearing that followed, however, had nothing to do with protective order matters. Instead, U.S. Attorneys Arnold Spencer and Jaime Pena did exactly what Hicks' lawyers had anticipated. Many of the same faces that had appeared on the witness stand during the state trial were back. Kevin Lamance retold his version of the tragic event. And Dr. Norton again argued that Jim Lamance's death had resulted from a shot fired by his brother. Meanwhile, Dr. Lynn Salzberger, who had conducted the criticized autopsy, testified that she had seen no gunpowder residue on the victim and remained firmly convinced he had been shot with a high-powered rifle from long range.

The defense's efforts to have the victim's body exhumed in an effort to settle the issue had earlier been denied.

♦ *Dallas Observer*, June 2003

Family Secret

The troubling secret languished for a half century, hidden and purposely ignored, as mother and son chose to protect each other from what each considered a dark truth the other couldn't accept.

When young Herb Vest asked how his father died, his mother routinely answered that the young ex-serviceman she'd married in 1943 had been the victim of a sudden heart attack. Her answer was always dismissive, a clear signal that it was a subject on which she did not wish to dwell. And so her gangly, North Texan, teenaged son, who would one day earn millions as CEO of his own investment securities firm and be recognized by Ernst & Young as Entrepreneur of the Year in 1999, knew his mother was not telling him the truth. He'd known by the time he was 11—since the day he and a friend discovered a stack of yellowed letters to his uncle while playing in the attic. One of the letters discussed the death about which no one talked.

And so, for all those years, there was the secret within a secret, a strange and unspoken bond that tethered mother, son, and the distant memory of Harold "Buddy" Vest, who died at 25.

Now 80, Ruth Vest Powers sits at the dining room table in her son's plush Dallas home on the edge of Preston Trails Country Club, remembering a day in the late '90s when she finally decided it was time to respond honestly to his questions. She does not credit any sudden epiphany, no demand from an inner voice, nor a gripping need for conscience-clearing. It was simply time, she says. "For so many years," she recalls, "I had this terrific fear that Herb would find out. I just couldn't tell him, couldn't plant that kind of seed in his mind. Then, suddenly, one afternoon I telephoned him and asked that he come over to my house and talk."

What she finally wanted to tell him was that his father had committed suicide.

On that same day, Vest admitted he'd known since reading his uncle's letters as a young boy. He confided to her that, in 1966, when he was a new Army inductee passing through Gainesville en route to Fort Benning, Georgia, he visited the local library to find and read the newspaper account of his father's death. What he didn't know—what he wanted desperately to learn—were the details of what occurred inside his father's Gainesville cabinetmaking shop on that bizarre night, June 27, 1946. The answers his mother provided would haunt him, prompting a torrent of additional questions, lending greater mystery to an event that today borders on obsession for the 59-year-old self-described "bulldog," who admits he will "either find out what really happened or die, whichever comes first."

With the help of a dogged private investigator, authorities in Cooke County, a highly regarded forensic anthropologist, and a mysterious letter sent by someone who signed her name "M. Smith," Herb Vest now determinedly moves toward the day he will prove to himself, his mother, and the rest of the world that his father was, in fact, murdered 58 years ago.

"What he is doing," Ruth says of her son's effort, "is one of the greatest gifts he's ever given me." She, too, wants the world to know that Buddy Vest, whom she describes as "one of the most handsome young men you ever saw," did not take his own life.

She is now convinced that her husband was the victim of a senseless and sadistic murder. So is her son. Now, all that remains is the daunting task of tracking down the proof.

* * *

Pretty, auburn-haired Ruth Blakely had just left her teenage years behind in the spring of '42 and was growing restless, weary of the rural confinement of little Henrietta, Texas, where her father served as mayor. Thus, when her older sister, whose husband had been drafted into the Army and stationed at Fort Custer near Battle Creek, Michgan, invited her along on a visit, she eagerly accepted.

There, during a stop at the base PX, she met Harold Eugene "Buddy" Vest. Today, decades later, she remembers it as love at first sight. Vest, tall and slender, was witty, well-mannered, and had a great sense of humor. Born in Chicago, son of a carpenter, he'd dropped out of school at fifteen and worked as an apprentice cabinetmaker in a shop in the shadows of Wrigley Field until he was drafted.

The things he wanted most in life, he soon confided to the young Texas girl, were to start his own cabinetmaking business and for her to be his wife. Two months later, that spring, Vest was granted leave and traveled to Henrietta, where he and Ruth were married. Following a one-night honeymoon in nearby Wichita Falls, she returned to Michigan with him to live while he was stationed stateside. She gave birth to their son a year later.

When her husband was shipped out to Europe, Ruth and her baby returned to Henrietta to live with her parents while awaiting Buddy's discharge. His military service complete, he took a train to Texas, purchased a small frame house in Gainesville with a G.I. loan, and soon fulfilled his dream of opening his own cabinet shop on the city's main street.

Herb Vest learned these facts as he grew to manhood. "All I really knew," he says, "was that my father was a happy man, didn't drink or gamble, had a new baby and a new business, and no problems that anyone was aware of." It was hardly the profile of a man contemplating suicide.

What Vest had waited a lifetime for his mother to share were details of his father's death, which occurred just four months after he settled in the North Texas community.

The story began, as most nightmares do, in the darkest hours of the night:

Well past midnight, Ruth recalls, she wakened to realize her husband, who had told her he would be working late, still hadn't returned home. In the kitchen, she saw the acorn squash and roast she'd prepared for him before going to bed remained untouched.

Without car or telephone, she gathered her 22-month-old baby into her arms and walked to the house next door. "I didn't know the people," she says, "but I went over and knocked on the bedroom window to ask this lady if she could give me a ride down to my husband's shop."

The neighbor agreed without hesitation, and soon the two women and the baby arrived at Buddy Vest's shop on California Street. "The lights in the front of the store were out," Ruth remembers. Today, she can only assume the door was unlocked, since she and her neighbor were able to enter and walk toward the back of the small building. In a far corner, where plywood walls lent privacy to a makeshift restroom, they could see thin rays of light.

Ruth, her baby still in her arms, approached the restroom door only to find it locked from the inside. While she has no specific recollection of doing so, she's certain that she must have called out her husband's name and heard no answer.

"When we parked in front of the shop," she says, "we'd noticed a young man in a sailor's uniform standing by the road hitchhiking. We went out and asked if he could help us."

The sailor pried the restroom door open enough to see the horror inside. Shielding the women from the sight, he told them to call the police.

"My neighbor drove me to my sister's house," Ruth remembers, "and I woke her and her husband to tell them there was something terribly wrong down at the shop. It's strange how certain things stand out in your mind and other memories are completely lost. What I remember is my brother-in-law standing in the living room in his shorts, a panicked look on his face, as he hurriedly pulled on his pants. He left immediately with my neighbor, who volunteered to drive him to the shop."

What he found was tragic: Buddy was dead, hanging by his neck from the restroom wall with a thin leather machine belt. His ankles were tied with rope and affixed to an eye screw in the wall. Another rope around his waist bound his left arm to his side.

He wore only a woman's girdle and panties.

Such grotesque details were kept from his widow. The police never questioned her. Her father, who had rushed to Gainesville immediately after learning what had occurred, at first only hinted at the ruling the local Justice of the Peace would ultimately make.

"The day after my husband's body was found," Ruth says, "my father asked me if he had seemed at all despondent. And, while it made no sense to me at the time, he wanted to know if I had ever put any of my underclothes in the 'rag box' Buddy had down at his shop." It was common in those times to keep discarded and worn-out clothing to use for cleaning and dusting.

By the time a funeral service was held at the Henrietta First Baptist Church, Ruth knew only that her husband had killed himself. But, thanks to her father's considerable influence, the newspaper account of Buddy Vest's death contained no details about the state in which the body had been found. In fact, Ruth herself only learned the strange details two years later, during a conversation with her sister.

In a time when people trusted authority figures more easily, the distraught widow took what she was told at face value. "I had no choice but to believe that my husband had taken his own life. I couldn't understand why he would do it, but there was no other way to explain what had happened."

Only in retrospect does she remember her father expressing a fleeting hint of doubt. "The next day, after he had talked with the police, we were in the yard outside my sister's house, and he told me that it appeared Buddy had hanged himself," she remembers. "But, then, he made a comment that I never completely understood. He seemed really perplexed—almost as if he was talking just to himself—when he said, 'At any time he could have touched the floor with his feet.'"

In the days immediately following the tragedy, another strange event occurred that defied explanation. Weeks after her husband died, Ruth read a brief notice in the Wichita Falls newspaper that a patient named Harold F. Vest of Henrietta had been admitted to a hospital there. When her father visited to check admission records, nothing indicated what the patient with the name remarkably similar to his son-in-law's had been treated for or when he was released. Nor did anyone by that name live in Henrietta.

Even while resigned to the fact her husband died at his own hand,

Ruth found herself wondering if perhaps someone might have stolen his identification. Only then did she realize she'd never received Buddy's wallet or any personal effects from either the investigating authorities or the funeral home. Nor would she ever.

* * *

Long interested in Texas history, Herb Vest attended a lecture in the summer of 2002 on the infamous Gainesville hangings of forty Union sympathizers. He listened as the speaker talked about the sinister motive for the 1862 event, telling how, at that time, Confederate Texans viewed Northerners with great disdain.

The lecture stayed with Vest, eventually giving rise to a theory about his father's strange death. Maybe it was a reach, but was it possible, he wondered, some of Gainesville's residents resented the fact Buddy Vest came to Texas from Chicago? Had the hatred manifested by what would come to be known as The Great Hanging in Gainesville lingered, perhaps claiming his father as a latter-day victim?

It was time, Vest decided, to go in search of the truth. The stepfather who raised him passed away in 1996, eliminating Vest's worry that his lifelong concern about how his biological father died might somehow offend his stepfather. Thus, in September of 2003, Vest contacted Danny Williams, a friend and private investigator who had done work for him for over a decade. His assignment: travel from his Addison headquarters to Gainesville and find out how Buddy Vest died.

In his 26 years as a private investigator, Williams says, he's never been involved in a case so intriguing, challenging, and troubling.

At the Gainesville police department, he found no records of any investigation into Buddy Vest's death. "At the very least," he says, "there should have been some kind of written report by officers called to the scene, detailing what they found. But there was nothing." Nor was he able to find any living members of the eleven-man police force that served the city at the time. At the Cooke County courthouse, things got even more perplexing. On record was not one, but two death certificates, both bearing the signature of then Justice of the Peace L.V. Henry. On one, the cause of death was entered as "asphyxiation by strangulation," but it made no mention of suicide. The other cited "suicidal hanging." On one of the documents, Henry's signature was clearly a forgery.

Cooke County District Attorney Janelle Haverkamp, a lifelong Gainesville resident, is certain of it. Early in her career, she worked with Henry and recalls that an accident had rendered his right arm and hand useless. "He taught himself to write left-handed," she says, "and his handwriting was very distinctive. One of the death certificates was clearly filled out and signed by someone else." Gainesville resident Dan Flint, a former Leazer-Keel Funeral Home employee who assisted in removing Buddy's body the night it was discovered, has signed an affidavit in which he notes that he had been very familiar with Judge Henry's handwriting and that the name written on the death certificate shown him was "not the signature of Justice of the Peace L.V. Henry." Jim Hatcher, a former law partner with Henry, provided a similar affidavit.

And current Justice of the Peace, Dorthy Lewis, adds yet another element of mystery. "In those days," she says, "all death certificates were typed." The one that bears the forged signature, she notes, was done in longhand.

At Williams' request, Judge Lewis sent a clerk in search of the long stored-away inquest report. The index of the three-inch thick 1940s Death Records book lists no inquest for the Vest death. Only after the clerk methodically went through the entire volume, page by page, was she able to locate the brittle, yellowed document.

Finally, Williams was able to read a detailed account of what investigators found when they arrived at Buddy Vest's cabinet shop on that early June morning. The inquest record describes the thin leather belt wound around Vest's neck and attached to three nails that had been hammered into the restroom door, the small ropes that bound his ankles and one arm, and the fact the "body was clad in socks and ladies panties and a womans lastex [sic] girdle." A small block of wood, on which the victim presumably stood at some point, was found a few inches from the body. An open knife, the report indicates, lay near a drain in the floor.

"It convinced me there had been no suicide," Williams says.

Yet even the revealing document begged new questions. It lists the victim's first name as Richard rather than Harold, and the address of the cabinet shop is incorrect. And the lower portion of the report, where the author's signature would traditionally be affixed, has been neatly torn away.

Armed with a copy of the report, the methodical Williams sought the opinion of several experts on auto-erotic asphyxiation, a form of sexual gratification wherein a person chokes him- or herself during masturbation. Each assured him they had never heard of a case where a victim's feet were tied to a wall. Nor, for that matter, did any data indicate such a sexual practice was even known as far back as the '40s.

The investigator found more questions than answers. What answers he did find convinced him that he was actually investigating a homicide and that there had likely been, for some reason, a cover-up. "There is no question in my mind," he now says.

Williams phoned the man who had hired him. "Herb," he said, "this is a murder."

But how to validate his belief? Where to go next with a case colder than cold? He'd even knocked on the doors of many of Gainesville's aging citizens, had wandered among them at local restaurants, randomly asking questions but getting no answers. He was at a dead end.

Encouraged by Williams' findings, Herb Vest, the "bulldog," refused to accept conjecture or speculation. He wanted proof and was now convinced it existed, perhaps in some faded memory that only needed prodding.

* * *

In a Sunday edition of the *Gainesville Daily Register*, Vest placed an ad offering a $10,000 reward to anyone with information on his father's death. It was a long shot, and two weeks of silence followed. Williams, convinced of failure, began considering an unorthodox plan to have flyers requesting information printed and hand-delivered to every residence in Gainesville.

Then, late last October, a three-page letter, typed and single-spaced, arrived at his office.

Signed only "M. Smith," it tells a strange tale of flirtation and a lover's jealousy that erupted to cause Buddy Vest's death. "I thought at first that it might be a hoax," Williams admits, "so I took it—along with information from the inquest record—to several forensic psychologists for evaluation." After studying the letter, each concluded that the writer had, in fact, likely been present in Buddy Vest's shop the night he died.

"This," M. Smith writes, "is a bizarre story, and I guess I need to tell it to someone."

In the letter, she describes herself as having been an attractive young woman who, in those days, partied, drank, danced, and "could have just about any man I wanted."

"I first saw Buddy in the lumber yard in Gainesville. He was the most handsome man I'd ever seen…beautiful eyes and complexion. I was completely smitten by him." In time, she made a point of being at the cafe near his cabinet shop whenever he arrived for lunch, even occasionally stopping into his shop on the pretext of being interested in learning how to work with wood. "I enjoyed flirting with him," she writes.

The flirtation, she admits, was one-sided. In brief conversations she and Vest shared during her visits to his shop, he regularly spoke of his wife and young son.

Still, she writes, on that June evening, aware that Vest was working late, she "put on [her] best party dress, fixed [her] hair, and went to see Buddy at the cabinet shop right after dark."

"Now," she continues, "for the ugly part." In the well-constructed and articulate letter which she says she wrote numerous times before deciding to mail it, she tells of an affair she was having with a married and very jealous Gainesville police officer to whom she refers as "Jim"—though she insists it is not his real name.

Shortly after she arrived at Vest's shop, her boyfriend and two of his friends burst into the store. She writes: "Jim went berserk. He pulled a gun and said he was going to kill us [her and Vest] both."

The story M. Smith weaves is straight out of a modern day television crime drama. Her enraged boyfriend, convinced she and the cabinetmaker were involved in a sexual relationship, grabbed her by the hair, pulled her head back, and stuffed the gun barrel into her mouth. When Buddy Vest yelled for the intruder to stop and let the woman go, insisting that there was nothing romantic going on between them, "Jim" instructed his companions to tie Vest up. They stuffed a handkerchief into his mouth to silence him.

According to the letter, "Jim" struck Vest several times then ordered his accomplices to remove Vest's clothing. M. Smith was then made to remove her undergarments. Laughing, the intruders put the panties and girdle on the bound and gagged cabinetmaker.

The author of the letter writes that, before the night ended, her boyfriend repeatedly sodomized her and she overheard a plan to either tar-and-feather Vest or kill him and hide the body. She remembers hammering sounds from inside the restroom, someone asking if anyone had a knife he could use to cut some rope, and one of the men removing a belt from a machine saw and taking it with him into the restroom. While she writes that she was not in a position to actually see what was happening inside the corner restroom, she recalls one of the men saying, "That will hold the sonuvabitch; he can't get down from there."

Finally, she writes that "Jim" took her home, leaving the others to stand guard over Vest until he returned. He threatened to kill her if she ever mentioned what happened.

Not until one of the accomplices stopped by her home the following day did she learn Buddy Vest was dead. She claims she was told that if anyone spoke of what happened at the cabinet shop, they would all be sentenced to die in the electric chair. "I am so truly sorry...I will go to my grave knowing that I caused [his] death," M. Smith writes.

Today, two of the men mentioned in the letter, including "Jim," are dead. A third, she writes, "is still living but his memory is not good."

She closes the letter by insisting that, since family members of the three assailants are still alive, some still living in Gainesville, she is reluctant to come forward, even while wondering if it might be possible to earn the reward "without exposing my identity." She suggests payment could be sent to her in an envelope addressed to her via General Delivery at the Gainesville post office.

Instead, Vest and Williams waited several weeks—thinking the woman might come forward—before responding with a letter promising to up the reward to $25,000 if she came forward and provided additional information, including the real names of the men described in her letter.

To date, "M. Smith" has not replied.

She did, however, provide forward movement to the investigation. Her letter, combined with the inconsistencies in the death certificates and the missing portion of the inquiry report, satisfied Justice of the Peace Lewis in January that there was enough probable cause to order the exhumation of Buddy Vest's body for examination by noted University of North Texas forensic anthropologist Dr. Harell Gill-King and Dr. Joseph Guileyardo, a Dallas forensic pathologist. District Attorney Havercamp, while signing off on the request, also felt she'd seen enough evidence to order an investigation into the cause of Vest's death.

Noting that there is no statute of limitations on murder, Haverkamp says it is now possible a criminal investigation might be opened. And, adds Judge Lewis, "I believe there are people still here [in Gainesville] who, if they would come forward, have information that would shed light on this case." Danny Williams agrees: "I refuse to believe that one of the four people who were there that night didn't talk to someone about what occurred." His recent research revealed that of the 30,000 who live in Gainesville, 1,800 residents are over the age of 70. Soon, a letter requesting their help will go out to each of them.

* * *

On a recent April morning, Ruth Vest Powers sat alone in an automobile parked on the edge of Henrietta's Hope Cemetery while in the distance earth-moving machinery dug into the grave where the body of her first husband lay buried for 58 years. Herb Vest, calm at first, seemed to grow agitated, pacing endlessly while the workmen performed the task he was funding. Members of the media, whom he alerted, mingled near the grave site, shooting film, snapping photos, and scribbling in notepads.

"It was a difficult thing to watch," recalls Judge Lewis, who had never before ordered an exhumation. "After a while, I went over to Ruth and sat with her, telling her that I knew what we were doing was difficult but that I hoped it might eventually bring her some peace."

"It's just not one of those things you ever expect to do in your lifetime,"

Ruth replied. "But I had to come because I feel so badly for my son. He's had to live with this for so long.".

After an hour, a crane lifted a badly rusted metal vault containing the casket. Taken to the warehouse of a Henrietta funeral home, it was examined by the judge and the forensic experts, sealed in sheets of plastic, and prepared for delivery to Dr. Gill-King's Denton laboratory.

There, depending on the condition of the body, he will conduct a search for any physical evidence that might point to the possibility of murder. Dr. Gill-King, who has a policy of not speaking with the media while working on a case, has told Judge Lewis he plans to search for bruising, abrasions, or even broken bones, as well as any possible trace evidence that might corroborate the suggestion that Buddy Vest was, in fact, assaulted.

He's given neither Cooke County authorities nor Herb Vest any suggestion of how long he'll need to complete his examination.

And so the half-century-old wait continues. For Dr. Gill-King's findings. For the possibility that "M. Smith" will eventually come forward or that her true identity might be discovered.

"If there are those who have first-hand knowledge of how my father died, all I want to do is talk to them," Herb Vest says, "to have them explain to me what happened. If M. Smith were to walk through the door today, I would hug her."

If, in fact, one of the men who burst into the cabinet shop that long-ago night still lives, Vest says he would argue against any manner of prosecution. "In the unlikely event the D.A. was determined to take the matter to court, I'd agree to pay for the man's defense if he would cooperate with our investigation and be truthful about what happened," he says. D.A. Haverkamp says charges are unlikely. If, she says, the information in the Smith letter is correct, there is little chance the surviving perpetrator would be competent to stand trial.

His quest, Vest insists, is not about revenge. Only the truth.

◆*D Magazine*, August 2004

Madness at Mount Carmel

They locked themselves away in a rambling, ever-growing complex that for years sat quietly in the pastoral countryside ten miles north of Waco. The structure, located on a 77-acre parcel of land, houses an estimated 100 members of the religious sect which calls itself the Branch Davidians, a splinter group of the Seventh Day Adventist Church.

In times past, the residents lived a quiet, isolated life of prayer, Bible study, and hard labor—all while dutifully preparing for the end of the world they believe will soon come. They tended their vegetable gardens and small herd of Holstein and Jersey cows, made their own clothing, home-schooled their children, and eschewed such worldly luxuries as indoor plumbing. Even in nearby Waco, a city of such religious bent that it is often referred to as "Jerusalem on the Brazos," the Davidians were generally judged a harmless oddity. Such had been the attitude of the community since the Davidians settled in their area in the mid-1930s.

However, in the aftermath of a deadly raid by agents of the U.S. Bureau of Alcohol, Tobacco, and Firearms—a by-product of an attempt to serve search and arrest warrants for possession of illegal firearms and explosives—they and their messianic leader gained worldwide attention. Their once private lives became headline news from New York to London, Sydney to Tokyo. They captured the fascination of those who view *Good Morning America*, *Nightline*, and tabloid TV's *A Current Affair*. Reporters from around the globe stationed themselves just down Farm-to-Market 2491, waiting, watching, and wondering what this modem day religious war is all about. And just who the people are barricaded inside the building built from their own sweat and dedication.

In the days since the bloody siege began on the last Sunday morning in February, they have been described as heavily armed, law-breaking, religious zealots whose firepower and fanaticism pose grave danger. Their leader, 33-year-old Houston native Vernon Howell, now known as David Koresh, has been labeled as crazed, charismatic, and highly manipulative—a self-proclaimed Lamb of God who said he alone holds the divine power to open the apocalyptic seven seals named in the Book of Revelation.

ATF spokespersons, in the wake of the 45-minute firefight that claimed the lives of four agents and saw 16 others wounded, have suggested that a telephone call just moments before their arrival may have alerted Koresh, thereby turning the plan into a disaster. Yet, in a series of confusing, evasive press conferences following the tragedy, no one has been able to explain the lack of any attempt to serve the warrants peacefully.

Rather, the official focus has been on the perception of evil and potential terror now barricaded behind the walls of the rambling building to which they refer as "the compound."

Following an eight-month investigation of the activities of Koresh and his followers, including infiltration of the group by an undercover ATF agent, authorities determined the ever-growing arsenal stored in the Branch Davidian headquarters included illegal firearms and explosives. Additionally, reports from ex-Davidians made claims of physical and sexual abuse of children by the cult's leader and that Koresh had as many as fifteen wives among his followers.

Then, as post-raid criticism of the ATF's tactics mounted, federal officials began leaking stories to the media that the Davidians were stockpiling arms for a planned assault on the city of Waco that would "make the Los Angeles riots look like child's play"—though no one seemed able to explain why the Davidians would do such a thing—or that a mass suicide the likes of Jonestown would have been eminent without federal intervention.

At press briefings, stories changed daily. First, Dan Hartnett, associate director of the ATF, explained the raid was planned for Sunday morning out of concern for the safety of the Davidian children. "Intelligence had indicated that the women and children would be isolated from the men at that particular time," he said. A day later, while describing the scene as officers approached, he noted everything "seemed normal" as "children played in the yard."

As the standoff wore on, federal authorities added new accusations: The Davidians were reportedly dealing drugs from the compound. They were active participants in a network of illegal arms dealers. They were laundering money.

What was going on in the McLennan County countryside, then, was clearly judged illegal, immoral, and potentially dangerous. Yet in the wake of the tragic death toll—which climbed dramatically once it was learned how many sect members residing in the compound lost their lives in the bloody Sunday attack—criticism and dismay replaced the initial shock that swept through Waco.

Not only did locals wonder how such insanity could be visited on their quiet Central Texas lives, but they began to ask why. Many pointed out that the Davidians they knew for years were the same quiet, non-threatening, polite men, women, and children they encountered while shopping at K-Mart and Sam's Wholesale, in bank lobbies, downtown businesses, and local eateries.

Even back in 1987, when a power struggle for leadership of the sect erupted in gunfire at Mount Carmel and resulted in the indictment of Koresh and a half dozen of his followers, locals generally passed off the event with shrugs and bemused smiles.

It occurred at a time when the Davidians were still led by George Roden and the then dilapidated encampment was known as Rodenville. Struggling to maintain his leadership role against charismatic Koresh, Roden visited a nearby cemetery and exhumed a casket containing the body of a woman who had reportedly been buried for a quarter century and issued an insane challenge to his rival: whichever man could raise the woman from the dead would reign over the McLennan County Davidians.

Records show Koresh went to the authorities to complain of Roden's grave desecration. McLennan County Sheriff Jack Harwell, who had been hearing strange stories from the sect's headquarters most of his life, explained he would need more evidence before launching an official investigation. He suggested Koresh return to Mount Carmel and take photographs of the casket to prove it did, in fact, contain a body.

When Koresh and six of his followers arrived, all armed with rifles, gunfire broke out quickly. And, while no one died in what amounted to a modern day Texas land war, attempted murder charges were leveled against Koresh and his raiders. Arrests were made quietly and peacefully after Sheriff Harwell phoned Koresh to say that deputies were en route to arrest them and claim their weapons.

In 1988, a mistrial was declared after jurors could not reach a verdict, and Koresh was set free. The other six Davidians were found not guilty. Officials, having determined that none of the weapons they confiscated were illegal, returned them along with 3,000 rounds of ammunition.

J. L. Crawford, an investigator in the McLennan County District Attorney's office at the time, made a half dozen visits to Mount Carmel in the aftermath of the power struggle and talked at length with Koresh and many of his followers.

"What I found were some beautiful people," Crawford said. "They're quiet, they're healthy, and will walk around the block to avoid any kind of argument. If someone criticizes them or insults them, they smile and walk away.

"While most of the people here in Waco view them as strange, I've never heard anyone say they felt threatened by them. They pay cash for what they buy, they do their banking in town, live simply, and take care of each other."

And, while federal officials insist that Koresh forced members of the sect to turn over all their money and possessions to him, Crawford said his earlier investigation revealed most members were in control of their own money.

"Now, because their beliefs are different, everyone is calling them crazy," Crawford said. "So what if they are? There's nothing in the Constitution that makes that a crime."

From as far away as Houston came echoes of Crawford's sentiments. Severely chastising federal officials for their actions and the manner in which they attempted to serve the warrants, Houston city councilman John Goodner observed, "I find their [the ATF's] actions totally unacceptable. From what I've heard and read, the whole matter was badly handled. We have a lot of freedoms in this country. Among them is the freedom to be absolutely nutty if you want to be."

Too, said Crawford, the Vernon Howell, a.k.a. David Koresh, he knew is hardly the Texas version of Charles Manson that authorities and the media described. "Oh, he's got charisma," Crawford admitted, "but the man I know also has a tremendous ego problem. In fact, he struck me as a person who needed constant reinforcement. We sat in my office for an hour after his trial, and he kept asking me if I really thought he was guilty, if I thought he was a bad person. He wanted my assurance that I didn't think badly of him.

"George Roden scared me. Vernon Howell didn't in the least."

Attorney Gary Coker, who represented Koresh in the 1988 trial, admitted that his former client is "a little weird," but hardly the maniacal doomsday prophet the authorities and the media describe. "The people who live out there," Coker said, "are not violent. They're peace-loving. They're vegetarians. They don't even drink or smoke."

"They never really bothered anybody," added long-time Waco resident Richard Cornelius. Kenneth Ellis, who lives near Mount Carmel, agrees: "I think the sneak attack was wrong. This is America. They should have given them the chance to surrender. "

When asked during a news conference why the ATF had not simply waited until Koresh was away from Mount Carmel to arrest him, Hartnett said such a plan was impossible since Koresh had not left the compound for months and had told followers that he would not leave it again.

Shortly after Hartnett's statement was made public, Angela McDaniels, a waitress at a Waco restaurant, recalled serving Koresh and several other

Davidians just weeks earlier. "They had cheese nachos and iced tea," she said, "and were very nice." Margaret Jones, an acquaintance of Koresh, said she saw him in a Waco store as late as the end of December. He was also seen at a gas station not far from Mount Carmel about the same time.

"All those people were doing," said Waco resident and local tavern owner Dennis Moore, "was defending their property. We've always referred to their place as a religious commune. Now, everybody's calling it a cult."

Bob Foster, editor of the weekly *Waco Citizen*, found the entire matter disturbing. "If someone cam storming into my house on Sunday morning, I'd feel I had the right to protect myself."

The members of the Branch Davidians, many Waco residents insisted, were hardly society's flotsam. The sect's international, multi-racial membership even included Harvard-educated Waco attorney Wayne Martin.

"Martin is an excellent lawyer," said State District Judge Bill Logue. "He's always been an above board, moral kind of guy who handles his matters here very proficiently."

Members of the Waco legal community were surprised and saddened to learn that Martin remained inside the complex.

Vic Feazell, former McLennan County District Attorney now in private practice in Austin, said that an understanding of the Davidians' beliefs and philosophy is necessary to understand their response to the Sunday assault.

"They're protective of what is theirs," he said. "They're protective of their land, viewing it as Muslims do Mecca and Jews view Jerusalem."

The storming of the compound by ATF agents, he said, "was a vulgar display of power on the part of the feds being met with fear and paranoia on the part of the Davidians. It was a sad day for the Davidians and a sad day for our government."

"When we arrested them [following the aforementioned 1987 incident]," Feazell, himself an ordained minister, said, "we treated them like human beings. They were extremely polite people. Following the trial— although we didn't agree with everything they said or believed—several members of our staff were pretty sympathetic toward them."

"They are people who just wanted to be left alone," observed one former Waco resident who asked that her name not be used. "Their lifestyle is very much like the Amish. They raised bees and sold honey; they lived very peacefully. They've chosen to arm themselves in the same manner all 'survivalists' do—for protection against outsiders who might try to take their home, their food, their belongings in the event of the apocalypse."

The idea of Koresh and his followers planning an attack on the 104,000 citizens of Waco, she added, "is absolutely absurd."

While many of the accusations made against the Mount Carmel complex were only answered once the siege ended, evidence increasingly indicated at least some claims and concerns were groundless.

Federal officials and the media relayed accusations by ex-sect members that children living in the compound were abused. Of the 21 children, ranging in age from five months to 12 years old, who were sent from the compound and turned over to Child Protective Services, none appeared to have been abused or neglected, according to Services supervisor Joyce Sparks.

"The children are in remarkably good psychological condition, considering what they've gone through," she said. "They appear very healthy, are well behaved and well educated." The older children, she pointed out, care for the younger ones, reading to them, playing with them. Before each meal, the youngsters joined hands and prayed.

Several, she said, talked about taking cover beneath their beds when the shooting began that Sunday morning.

When the children were turned over to authorities, they carried with them notes written by their parents, giving their names and favorite foods. Each child also carried a small bag containing personal items, such as books and toys.

One youngster left the complex carrying a cardboard box containing six mixed-breed puppies. An attached note explained that they had not yet been weaned from their mother, which had been shot and killed in the Sunday gun battle. When a Waco TV station broadcast word that the orphaned puppies needed homes, local residents responded and claimed them in less than thirty minutes.

The mid-week arrest of two women who voluntarily left Mount Carmel, one to deliver a taped message from Koresh to the FBI, the other to accompany the children, resulted in another avalanche of governmental criticism. Margaret Lawson, 77, and Catherine Mattson, 75, were shackled, handcuffed, and taken to court, where they faced charges of conspiracy, murder, and attempted murder.

Federal officials insisted to the press that they were convinced the women had been directly involved in the gun battle. What they did not mention was the fact Mattson, a 20-year resident of the Davidian facility, is legally blind, having undergone five eye operations in recent years.

While charges against the two women were dropped a day later, authorities said they would remain in custody as material witnesses. Attorney Coker, pleading to the court for Mattson's release, was told that she was a "flight risk."

"This woman," the appalled lawyer said, "is 75 years old, blind, doesn't even know how to drive a car, and has no money. What kind of flight risk can she possibly be? All she wants is to return to her home."

His request for her release fell on deaf ears, and both she and Lawson remained in jail.

As the standoff continued, so did the criticism of the manner in which it all began.

In Dallas, a group of demonstrators marched in front of the federal building, decrying the storming of the Davidian compound. One carried a placard asking, "Is Your Religion ATF Approved?" Said protester Karen Tegtmeyer, a Dallas computer programmer, "It is not against the law to have religious views, and it's not against the law to protect yourself."

Retired Colonel Charles Beckwith, founding commander of Delta Force, an elite and highly trained military attack group, publicly labeled the ATF's assault on the Davidians "a disgrace to this country." Col. Beckwith, who said he wrote a letter to the White House about the matter, noted, "I certainly wouldn't have gone in there with guns blazing. That's crazy."

In Washington, FBI officials acknowledged they, too, received accusatory letters about the Waco sect's activities last spring and had conducted an investigation that did not confirm any criminal behavior on the Davidians' part. Director William Sessions made it clear to reporters that his agency had "no involvement in this particular operation at all" before it was called in following the deaths of the ATF agents.

Treasury Secretary Lloyd Bentsen, whose department oversees the ATF, lauded the bravery of the agents involved in the operation but then added that the organization's actions would be reviewed and the effectiveness of the operation evaluated.

A dark, growing sadness blanketed the story as it unfolded—sadness for lives lost needlessly by what appears to have been an ill-conceived, poorly conducted, and overly aggressive plan, sadness for the thinly disguised attempts of federal authorities at damage control in the aftermath of the raid, and sadness for a strange group of people accused of sins as yet unproven.

It is a tragic, ugly story, regardless of the vantage point from which one views it.

◆ *San Antonio Current*, March 1993

* * *

In New York, the *Time* magazine powers-that-be determined that it would be in the publication's best interest to maintain an around-the-clock vigil of the slowly unfolding story. At least one reporter would remain in Waco, gathering whatever new information he might uncover, ever ready to summon other members of the reporting team at the slightest hint of any major development.

After weeks of standing sentry, I informed Houston bureau chief Dick Woodbury that it would be necessary for me to take leave of my post for a day. Months earlier, I had agreed to speak to a Monday gathering of high school students in Olney, Texas, and saw no reason to cancel. It appeared, after all, that the standoff was destined to go on indefinitely. Dick agreed to cut short his own brief visit home and spell me in Waco.

Minutes after I had outlined the pluses and pitfalls of life as a journalist to the Olney students, a teacher appeared and frantically summoned me to a nearby coffee room. There, amid a crowd of silent watchers, a television showed live footage of the Mount Carmel complex in flames.

By late afternoon, I was back in Waco.

As frustrated reporters worked for the next several days to pull together details of the unbelievable end to the 51-day standoff, government officials finally agreed to allow a small group of media members near what was left of the Davidians' home. A select pool of reporters would make the trip, note what they saw, then return to pass along their observations to the still-growing body of journalists.

I was among the half dozen escorted to the scene by Department of Public Safety officials.

Later that evening, after sharing my notes with reporters from throughout the world, I sat alone in my motel room, contemplating the grim, surreal aftermath. Nothing I'd ever witnessed had so affected me.

Sometime just before midnight, a long distance call from Dublin, Ireland, interrupted my somber thoughts. An editor with *The Irish Independent* had somehow learned of my trip to Mount Carmel and asked if I would write my impressions for his paper. Bone weary of the whole sad affair, my first inclination was to decline. Then, however, it occurred to me that, by putting my thoughts in writing, I might somehow purge the disturbing sights and sounds of the afternoon from my mind.

And so, into the night, I wrote . . .

Last Rites for Mount Carmel

The same Texas prairie wind which had whipped angry, deadly flames through a makeshift structure some had begun to call "Ranch Apocalypse" continued to blow. Yet now the sky was suddenly blue and cloudless as a small group of journalists finally gathered for a closer look at the smoldering remains of what the world had come to know as the Branch Davidian compound.

Now, however, the wind whipped only the tiny orange flags mounted on thin strands of wire, marking the locations of charred, faceless bodies of men, women, and children who were once members of a strange and devout group of people who had called this place home.

The three-story building, ravaged by fire on Monday as a 51-day standoff against federal authorities had finally come to a horror story end, was reduced to a field of ashes no more than two feet high.

As the small entourage of newspeople watched from behind a yellow stream of crime scene tape, dozens of camouflage-dressed workers went about their grim task, searching the debris for additional remains to add to a body count which had grown hourly.

In the middle of the wreckage was a cinder block vault, which had survived an earlier Mount Carmel fire in the pre-David Koresh days, now standing as a landmark centerpiece of the violence and destruction. Atop the structure which originally housed printing equipment owned and operated by an earlier generation of Davidians, nine orange flags flapped in the wind, signaling the greatest concentration of bodies. Two, then three, investigators climbed a ladder leaning against the 10-foot high structure and carefully made measurements, documenting the exact location of the charred remains.

The barrel of a rifle, still mounted atop a tripod, was clearly visible. What the silent reporters could not see were that weapons were still clutched in the hands of several of the dead. Two bodies, an adult woman and a child, were entwined. A protective mother and her innocent child.

Inside the vault—which military-minded officials insisted on referring to as "the bunker"—was what investigators described as "a million rounds" of unspent ammunition. And more bodies.

Just a few feet away, wisps of smoke continued to rise from the ruins, making the scene highly dangerous for those working among the aftermath of the carnage. Only hours earlier, in fact, an explosion near the vault had blown debris 10 feet into the air, forcing FBI explosive technicians to halt work while they screened the area for potential danger. An hour had passed before they allowed the grim work to continue.

Despite the presence of an estimated three dozen FBI, ATF, and Texas Rangers investigators, there was a hushed, almost surreal atmosphere to the manner in which they went about their job. There was little evidence of conversation; movements were almost mechanical, every step carefully taken.

When two agents left the ruins, carrying a black rubber body bag in the direction of a small tent erected on the edge of a nearby pond, they did not appear to speak to each other. Placing the bag alongside a growing row of others, lined up side-by-side, the two men turned and slowly walked up the gentle incline leading back to the fire site, still silent.

It was a scene reporters saw repeated three times during their half hour observation. Just before DPS officials escorted them away from the area, a body was carried out the door of the concrete vault, wrapped in one of the white sheets provided by the Tarrant County Medical Examiner's office.

That brought the number of bodies removed to seven—a small, grim preamble to the count that was destined to grow far higher.

There was precious little that remained of the rambling tan building with its gray composition roof, a structure that had become such a familiar sight on front pages and evening news broadcasts throughout the world. At one end, the rusted water silo, remodeled by Koresh and his followers to serve as a storage facility, still stood as a mark of the northern boundary of the compound. On the opposite end, a carousel once used for walking and training horses stood above the ashes like a blackened, gnarled metal spider. Throughout the ruins one could see metal fixtures protruding from the aftermath of the deadly inferno: a set of bed springs here, what appeared to be a stove or kitchen pantry there, all fire-blackened and misshapen.

Adjacent to the vault there was evidence of the Davidians' resolve and ability to remain inside for weeks, perhaps longer, had not the fiery conflagration come. Hundreds of gallon-size cans, labels burned away, were piled against one wall. Investigators confirmed that they were part of a food stockpile—canned fruits and vegetables—the survivalist community had long been storing away for the apocalypse their leader had prophesied.

Even in the overwhelming devastation, there remained scenes of the serenity the Davidian countryside had afforded its residents. The two small, shallow ponds located near what was once the front entrance still provided life-giving water to bordering willow trees. A small rowboat, overturned on the bank, awaited fishermen who would never again come. In a nearby rain-greened pasture, cattle lazily grazed, oblivious to the tragedy.

A few hundred yards away, parked beneath a stand of mesquite trees, sat Koresh's black '68 Camaro which he had so often spoken about to FBI negotiators. Near it was the wreckage of what appeared to be an early model mobile home, tangled and dented, no doubt by tanks that had pushed it away from its previous location near the front entrance. An old Silver Eagle bus stood immobile, both front tires flat. Nearby were a number of other vehicles owned by the Davidians, none apparently damaged.

Not far from the silo, on the opposite end of the block-long compound area, however, sat the remains of a red automobile so badly damaged that it was impossible to determine its make and model. Little more than a tangle of metal, it sat just off the deeply rutted path that had been worn by military vehicles that had been circling the Davidian residence day and night for the duration of the standoff.

Nearby, its nose pointed toward the pond, sat the old white bus so often seen in still photos and long range TV shots during media reports from Waco.

Across the dirt road which borders the front of the Davidians' property, two small frame houses—one of them briefly the residence of undercover ATF agents assigned to the case— were also ringed with crime scene tape. On their small concrete porches were piles of sandbags, evidence they had later become the posts of FBI sharpshooters during the siege.

One was stricken by the sparse evidence remaining that on this rural site there once stood a massive, maze-like building. And that within its walls over 100 people lived and listened to their leader preach his doomsday messages.

Where a dormitory and music room, a cafeteria and kitchen once stood, there were only flagged stakes marking the gridwork patterns for the investigation that is likely to go on for weeks, perhaps months. Gone were the tricycles and go-karts once parked outside, signals of happy, carefree childhood.

Absent, too, were the rolls of concertina wire which authorities had placed around the compound.

Where the white and blue Davidian flag once flew, a Texas state flag had been hoisted to half-mast. Immediately beneath it was an ATF flag bearing four stars in memory of the agents who lost their lives in the February 28 gun battle which set all this madness in motion.

Nowhere was there any evidence of a memorial to the Davidian dead.

Despite the activity, it was the almost hypnotic quiet that grabbed one's attention. It was as if the questions being asked by the highly-trained crime scene investigators, arson inspectors, and medical examiners were being posed in whispers.

Standing on the edge of that dusty Double E Ranch Road, silent, grim-faced reporters took notes, occasionally discussing observations with each other. For Mark England of the *Waco Herald Tribune*, coauthor of a highly critical series of articles on Koresh and his followers, which had begun just a day before the February raid, there was a feeling of disorientation. "Without the mammoth compound looming across the horizon," he later wrote, "nothing looked familiar."

And, he noted, he thought of the children. As did we all.

Standing there, I felt a sense of emptiness unlike any I've ever experienced. For the moment, all the blame-placing and finger-pointing that was ringing from Waco to Washington didn't matter; arguments over religious philosophy and FBI tactics seemed unimportant, as did the millions in taxpayer dollars the standoff had cost. All those things a reporter is supposed to be ever cognizant of were momentarily lost in an agonizing wave of sadness and reflection.

I found myself thinking back to a scene which had been played out in a time that suddenly seemed long ago.

It was in that first week of the standoff that a number of children had left the complex, released to authorities by Davidian parents. Among those who emerged was a bright-faced, handsome little boy with a message pinned to his blue jacket: "Remember," the note read, "that Mommy and Daddy love you." In his arms was a cardboard box; in it were six puppies not yet weaned from their dead mother, which had been killed by ATF gunfire.

It is that hard-etched, bittersweet memory, somehow suddenly revived by the smoldering ruins, that I shall not outlive.

♦ *The Irish Independent*, April 1993

POSTSCRIPT:

Once investigators and medical examiners completed their work, they determined 81 people—men, women and children—died in the inferno. Still, the tragic story did not end. In June of 1994, U.S. District Judge Walter Smith levied 40-year prison sentences on five Davidians who escaped the blaze. Others received sentences ranging from three to 15 years.

In a brief statement to the media, the judge, who had issued the initial search warrant that set the event in motion, called what had transpired at Mount Carmel "an American tragedy of epic proportions."

Secrets of Ashland Farm

Sheltered in ancient oaks, ash, and silver maples, with the Blue Ridge Mountains a distant backdrop, it is one of the crown jewels of northern Virginia horse country, the envy of an elite rural neighborhood that includes such residents as the Kennedys, the Cookes, and the Mellons. Historic Ashland Farm is more than 300 acres of rolling emerald pasture land dating from 1724. Its centerpiece, a rambling two-story stone mansion once used as a hospital for wounded Union soldiers, sits at its highest point, in full view of admiring passersby traveling westward from Warrenton Township.

Sleek, well-groomed thoroughbreds graze along a manicured hillside, and idle geese ring the bank of a pond. It is Currier-and-Ives idyllic, seemingly far more valuable than the Fauquier County tax assessor's estimate of $3 million. When billionaire arms dealer Sam Cummings was looking for a home for his animal- and privacy-loving twin daughters, who were anxious leave their Monaco and Switzerland upbringing behind and quietly settle in the United States, he found Ashland Farm perfect. It had pastoral style and class—even an intriguing sense of romantic mystery.

Legend says a Union paymaster buried the army's payroll somewhere on the property. A century and a half later, the cache remains hidden, a secret still guarded by Ashland Farm.

Today, however, the buried treasure story pales in comparison to a modern day question, one that has been whispered along the sidelines at the Great Meadow Polo Club, argued in booming voices in the century-old courthouse in Warrenton, and posed by reporters who run the journalism gamut—from *The New York Times* to tabloid television shows.

What happened on a warm Sunday morning last September between reclusive heiress Susan Cummings, 35, and her polo-playing Argentine lover, Roberto Villegas, 38? What dark secrets set the stage for Cummings' 911 call stating that a four-goal polo professional, whom many thought she would one day marry, lay dead on her kitchen floor?

At first blush, it seems a story stolen from the imagination of romance writer Danielle Steele: The attractive but painfully shy heiress who insists that her name be pronounced "Su-zahn" and who finally finds the love and happiness that eluded her in the faraway lands of the rich and famous. Her hero is a talented, fun-loving polo player who escaped the rural poverty of Argentina to ply his profession at horse farms and polo fields across the United States.

If, indeed, opposites attract, the relationship of Susan Cummings and Roberto Villegas is a textbook example. Handsome and outgoing, he had grown up a farmhand's son in the Argentina province of Cordoba, where young boys with athletic dreams hope to excel at soccer or polo. Cummings and her fraternal twin sister, Diana, were born in Monaco, schooled in France, and raised in Switzerland and Monte Carlo. Their adolescent playground was the French Riviera.

If the elder daughter of Sam Cummings and his Swiss wife, Irmgard, had a driving interest, it was animals. Though she earned a bachelor's degree in arts and humanities at Mount Vernon College in Washington, D.C., those who knew her then insist that, if not for her financial independence, she might well have become a dedicated veterinarian. Her dream was less demanding—to live a quiet country life surrounded by her animals. Her father was quick to make that dream come true.

On frequent trips to his Midland, Virginia, munitions factory, Sam Cummings became enamored of the picturesque landscape and decided that Ashland Farm would suit his daughters, who had long been lobbying to live in the United States. He purchased the multimillion dollar estate in 1984, and the sisters, with their dual American and British citizenships, became residents of Fauquier County.

However, they did not bother to immerse themselves in the social swirl of their new locale. No one seems to recall the Cummings sisters participating in the endless parade of parties, gatherings, and charitable activities. For Susan Cummings, an acquaintance says, a day out was a trip to the feed store and the tack shop or a stop at the local SPCA to see if any new castoffs needed a home.

In every way, Cummings is a contradiction to the region's social norm. The heiress has no servants and employs just a few part-time hands who assist with the horses and cattle kept on the grounds of Ashland Farm. Although those who know her remark on her "striking elegance," Cummings prefers to wear jeans, boots, and flannel shirts.

"The first time I was ever in her home," says a woman who occasionally rode with Cummings on hunting pairs, a favored cross-country training event for fox hunting, "I was surprised at how sparsely it was furnished. It was as if she had decided to live in just a few rooms of this grand old house."

What is abundantly clear to the occasional visitor, however, is the keen interest in guns that Cummings shares with her father. An entire room is filled with weapons of all sorts, from ancient muskets to the latest handguns, all displayed museum-style. Noting that Sam Cummings trained Susan to be an excellent shot, Villegas often joked to friends that he hoped she never woke in the middle of the night and mistook him for a burglar.

Guns and spare furnishings aside, what strikes most visitors is that Cummings' twin resides not in the main house but in a nearby guest cottage.

"Both Susan and Diana are ladies with a great deal of dignity," says John Pennington, a Warrenton businessman who has known them since they arrived in Virginia. "I think their father realized that they wanted a relatively simple life, and he made that possible for them."

Louisa Woodville, who boarded her horses at Ashland and rode with Cummings, saw little of the Continental upbringing in her friend's lifestyle. "She's just a lovely, gentle person," Woodville insists.

Another observer tells a story of how the two sisters, once faced with ridding their property of pesky groundhogs, brought in a local trapper to humanely capture the pests and release them elsewhere.

As one talks with those who consider themselves friends of Susan Cummings, the same persona emerges time and again: shy and gentle, she has a deep and abiding affection for animals and a certain elegance and aloofness in her carriage. But beyond that, the world in which the wealthy heiress has lived most of her adult life is no easier to locate than the long-buried Union soldiers' payroll.

Villegas' story, on the other hand, is told with gusto and a wide range of superlatives by his many friends. It begins with the fact that his route to the Virginia horse country was difficult and hard-fought. "The beauty of Roberto," says Bill Ylvisaker, founder of the Palm Beach Polo and Country Club, owner of nearby Cotswold Farm, and one-time mentor and patron to Villegas, "was that he had pulled himself up by his bootstraps. In every sense of the word, he was a self-made man. I had great respect for him."

Villegas began playing polo at fifteen. A job as a stable hand led to his first lessons, and five years later, he accompanied a fellow Argentine to the United States in search of work as a groom, hoping to take the first step in the direction of the American Dream. He was, he knew, a talented polo player, and he eagerly sought to prove his abilities. It didn't take long. In short order, Villegas served his apprenticeship and gained entry into that society of Argentines who travel from polo club to polo club throughout the United States, wintering in Sarasota and Palm Beach and summering in Texas and on the Eastern seaboard. Roberto Villegas quickly established a reputation as a gifted horseman and player and ultimately rated top honors on the club circuit. Among his peers, he was a better-than-average journeyman, earning the $4,000 per month that a four-goal club pro generally commands.

Things only got better when he settled in Virginia, playing for Ylvisaker's Cotsworth Farm team. "He lived on my farm [near Middleburg] for two years," says Ylvisaker, "and we became very close. We worked out together every morning, and I delighted in his company. In addition to his talent as a polo player, Roberto was a fine gentleman who was well liked by everyone he came in contact with."

Richard Varge, president of the Great Meadow Polo Club, says Villegas' grace and style breathed new life into the club's arena polo competitions. A downsized, faster version of the game played on a smaller field with three riders to a team instead of four, arena polo had long been a regular Friday evening event at Great Meadow during the summer months. Over the years, however, it became more of a social event than an actual competition, rarely attracting more than 100 spectators. The fact that attendance had grown to more than 1,000 was, according to Varge, due to Villegas' talent.

"People came to watch him play because he was such an exciting athlete. Before he began playing, our matches were very amateur. But with him on the field, making one spectacular play after another, everything rose to a new level," Varge says.

While teammates and opponents admired his abilities, Villegas hardly viewed himself as the star of the show. "I never saw any indication that he let his own ego get out of control," recalls Varge. "He was playing for the sheer fun of the game, enjoying himself and the people around him. During matches he was always very protective of the others on his team, and I'd say he was something of a mentor to half the young players around here."

Once the matches concluded, he was apt to take over as chief cook at the traditional *asado*—an Argentine barbecue—that followed. "Roberto was a very friendly person," Varge adds. "He had as much time for the farm boy hoping to learn the game as he did for the patrons and tournament sponsors." According to several, he also found time for the young women who regularly attended the matches, parading the sidelines in their miniskirts and high heels. His muscular body, dark wavy hair, and mischievous smile did not go unnoticed by the polo groupies who traditionally made the visiting "Argies" their amorous targets. Vallegas' popularity spread well beyond the boundaries of the polo arena.

* * *

Though some in the media have suggested otherwise, Susan Cummings was hardly a polo groupie. Rather, she simply arrived at the Willow Run Polo School in the spring of 1995, announcing to its Argentine manager, Jean Marie Turon, that she wanted to learn the game.

It quickly became clear that Cummings had finally found a pursuit that would not be merely another of her passing fancies. Since moving to Ashland Farm, she had shared her sister's fascination for fox hunts, jumping, and show horse competitions, but her passions faded quickly. For a time, she became preoccupied with art.

Polo, however, was different. "She came to ride almost every day," says Turon. "Our lessons are broken up into groups, and often she would finish in one group and jump right into another."

Although never an instructor at Willow Run, Villegas enjoyed spending time there, talking and playing cards with fellow Argies and offering instruction and encouragement to those eager to learn his sport.

In a community with a long and well-documented history of local women falling in love with handsome Latin athletes, it should not have been any real surprise that shy, single Cummings began spending a good deal of time in Villegas' company. Initially, however, most assumed she looked to Villegas to help her quickly reach a competitive level of polo.

It soon became clear, though, that another polo romance was bursting into bloom. "It was kind of sweet, really," says Betsy Branscome, local horsewoman and equestrian editor of the *Fauquier Times-Democrat*. "Every time I went out to a match, I would see them holding hands, always together." But, like most, Branscome thought it an odd coupling. "For the ten years or so that I've known Susan, we've never had what I would call a real conversation. Once you get past 'How are you?' and 'I'm fine,' that was about it. On the other hand, Roberto was one of those who never met a stranger. He loved being around people, having a good time, partying, and laughing it up."

Thus, not Cummings' wealth, but her association with its star player gained her entry into the social world of the Great Meadows Polo Club. "Roberto opened a whole new world to her," a club member says.

Few were surprised when she announced her eagerness to field an Ashland Farm team and that she had persuaded Villegas to be her pro. What did seem extraordinary was the business arrangement the couple struck: Villegas received no monthly salary, and instead of hiring a groom, Cummings and Villegas tended the chores themselves. In exchange, Villegas lived with Cummings at Ashland Farm and had no expenses to speak of. Clearly, the deal mixed business and pleasure. If the new polo patron at Ashland was determined to field her team in an uncharacteristically penny-pinching manner, whose place was it to criticize?

By most accounts, Villegas was happy with their arrangement. Two years shy of 40, he had set aside any aspirations to join polo's premier rank. Playing at the club level and enjoying the game for the pure pleasure it offered were quite enough. He told friends he was ready to settle down, maybe even get married.

Through the summer of '95, it looked as though that might happen. "He and Susan were so attached to each other," remembers Varge, "that we kidded him a great deal about already being married." When Cummings noted that his endless love for *asados* had begun to takes its toll on his once-trim waistline, Villegas immediately went on a diet. When he approached the tack shop owner about refurbishing an old saddle and learned it would cost more than he could afford, Cummings secretly had the work done as a birthday gift.

For every story of Cummings' generosity, however, there are examples of her being tight-fisted, which didn't seem to bother Villegas nearly as much as it did his friends. When his father died in Argentina, he sold his horses and truck to Cummings to finance his trip home to the funeral. To those who questioned this move—wondering why such a wealthy woman would not purchase her lover an airline ticket—he only shrugged and pointed out that freedom from financial worries of ownership would allow him to better focus on polo.

Despite the fact she told Great Meadows officials her plans to soon build a polo field for the club on her property, stories of Cummings' miserly ways quickly became the subject of luncheon gossip. To wit, Turon, frustrated over the problems he had reaching Villegas by phone, gave him an answering machine, which Villegas proudly showed to Cummings one evening. She flatly refused to allow him to install it, noting that the machine would obligate them to return costly long-distance calls. On another occasion, Villegas drove through the stone gateway of the estate to find an elderly maid who worked part time for Cummings wearily sweeping away leaves from the long, winding driveway. He immediately drove into Warrenton and purchased a gas-powered leaf blower. Cummings was reportedly livid over the $108 expenditure when her maid's broom was doing the work quite nicely.

Minor disagreements aside, the couple seemed very much in love. With Villegas at her side, Cummings seemed more relaxed among those who gathered for the Friday night matches. Although hardly gregarious, she was occasionally even seen to smile. A few times, she and Villegas hosted *asados* at Ashland Farm.

Last winter, when players and several of the local patrons took leave of

Virginia for the Florida season, Villegas decided to stay behind. Instead of riding for Ylvisaker as he'd done in years past, Villegas took a job working in an apple orchard in nearby Rappahannock County.

*　*　*

It seems no one can pinpoint the first serious signs that the relationship might have grown sour. Some, in fact, say it hadn't. Others offer vague recollections of instances when they sensed Cummings had grown more demanding and possessive of her lover. Then there are those who point to the fact Villegas seemed to be playing around in the final weeks of his life, no longer spending every night at Ashland Farm. Talk with one person, and he'll tell you Villegas desperately wanted out. Another will say the last time he spoke with Villegas, he was still talking of marrying Cummings.

All that's certain is that on Saturday, September 6, the day before Villegas died, he and Cummings were arm in arm at a charity match in Pittsburgh. Friend Joe Muldoon, Jr., head of the Potomac Polo Club, was also there and remembers seeing nothing that would suggest trouble in the relationship. In fact, he invited Villegas and Cummings to stay at his farm that evening since they were planning to return the following day for a long-anticipated exhibition featuring a top Argentine team against one from the United States. Villegas declined, noting the animals back at Ashland Farm needed his care. He promised Muldoon he would see him Sunday.

"I know it was something he was really looking forward to," Muldoon remembers. "The Argentine ambassador was going to attend and it would have been a great honor for Roberto to play before him."

Instead, at 8:51 the following morning, the emergency dispatcher at the Fauquier County Sheriff's office answered Susan Cummings' call and listened as she told of a horror that had just played out in her home. "I need to report a shot man, and he's dead," she said in a soft voice. Then she carefully spelled out his name: "R-o-b-e-r-t-o V-i-l-l-e-g-a-s. He tried to kill me."

The dispatcher asked Cummings if she had shot Villegas.

"I had a gun, yes," she replied. "I need to talk to my lawyer."

The dispatcher kept Cummings on the line until an investigator arrived, then instructed her to meet him on the front porch of her estate. After asking where the shooting victim was, the deputy walked past her. In the hallway leading to the kitchen, he saw a handgun and four spent shells scattered on the floor. A few feet away, Roberto Villegas lay dead.

As Cummings was taken into custody and charged with first-degree murder, friends of Villegas set about planning his funeral. The service, arranged by Varge and several members of the Greater Meadow Polo Club, was offered to a standing-room-only audience at St. Stephen's Catholic Church in Middleburg. Ylvisaker gave the eulogy ("He loved the sport of polo and everyone loved him."). Earlier in the day, friends from as far away as Florida and Illinois stopped in at the local funeral home for the traditional viewing of the body.

At Varge's request, Villegas was dressed in a polo uniform, a turtleneck hiding his death wound. At his side was the red-and-white helmet that had long been his trademark; positioned at the foot of his flower-draped coffin were crossed polo mallets and a ball signed by his teammates. The following day, his body was flown to his homeland for burial.

* * *

What happened in Ashland Farm's kitchen that Sunday morning has been a chief topic of conversation in northern Virginia's polo community for months. Cummings' high profile attorney, Blair Howard, an avid horseman who gained national fame when he successfully defended Lorena Bobbitt, described his newest client as having been so threatened by the hot-headed Villegas that she killed him in self-defense.

Talking to reporters in front of the Warrenton courthouse following a preliminary hearing, Howard insisted that, for weeks, Cummings had been trying to break off the relationship. He noted she'd gone to the Fauquier County Sheriff's office just two weeks before the shooting to complain that Villegas had repeatedly abused and threatened her. Cummings, in fact, had scheduled a second meeting to seek a restraining order from a local magistrate. "She was clearly frightened for her life," Howard said.

In her two-page complaint, she charged that Villegas had "in the last six months…begun to show signs of aggression toward me with threats to kill me. His words are: 'I will put a bullet through your head, and I will hang you upside-down to let the blood pour on your bed.'" On other occasions, she reported, Villegas talked about drowning her if she refused to marry him and bear him two children. "Roberto Cerillio Villegas… is struck with a mental condition, one that can be very dangerous for the people surrounding him at a critical moment," she wrote. Attorney Howard insists the threat of just such danger prompted his client to fire four shots from a 9 mm Walther semiautomatic into Villegas' neck and chest.

Cummings' lawyer offered a dramatic recreation of the events of September 7 at the pre-trial hearing: Villegas had again threatened Cummings, this time with a bone-handled knife he'd been awarded at a Florida polo tournament. As he attacked her, enraged by Cummings' determination to end their relationship, she fired four shots before bringing down the man to whom Howard referred as "the raging bull." The autopsy report, he suggested, indicated the fourth and last shot finally ended Villegas' mad assault, which had left his client with bloody scratches on her left arm and cheek.

"We're talking about something that happened in her house," Howard told the court. "In defense of her life, in her own home on a Sunday morning, she had every right to take this man's life. That's the law."

Assistant Commonwealth Attorney Kevin Casey, who will prosecute Cummings when the case goes to trial later this year, offers a different scenario. Based on interviews his investigators conducted with those close to the couple, Villegas, not Cummings, was attempting to break off the two-year relationship.

Photographs taken at the crime scene will, he insists, clearly show that Villegas was not attacking Cummings. Rather, he was seated at the small kitchen table, his back to a nearby wall. Indeed, in a gruesome photo, the victim's legs are clearly visible beneath the table. "There is blood on the back of the chair," the prosecutor says. "And there was no blood on the legs of the jeans Villegas was wearing. It seems only logical that, if he had been standing when he was shot four times, blood would have been all over him."

It was not, Casey says, the fourth shot that killed Villegas. Indeed, the medical examiner's report did not single out which of the shots was fatal. Casey will argue that it was the first bullet fired, "the one that tore through the victim's neck, tore out his carotid artery, struck his spine, and burrowed ten inches down his back," that caused Villegas' death. The three subsequent shots, the prosecutor suggests, were fired by a woman jealous of his recent flirtations and enraged by the fact that he had grown weary of her possessive, miserly ways.

But what of the knife that lay on the floor beneath Villegas' arm, the accusations in Cummings' statement to the sheriff's department, and the scratches on her arm and face? Casey has clearly done his homework by learning that virtually all Argentine polo players carry knives in scabbards tucked into their waistbands. "It's a cultural thing," he explains. "The knife is a tool, not a weapon. Roberto Villegas used his when he was doing outdoor cooking, even when he was eating." It would have been unusual, then, for there not to have been a knife at the crime scene.

If Susan Cummings' life had, in fact, been repeatedly threatened and she was as frightened as her statement indicated, why didn't she take the advice of the sheriff's deputy with whom she spoke and immediately get a restraining order against Villegas and post a "No Trespassing" sign at the entrance to her estate? Why wait two weeks to return to town and further discuss the matter? Why continue to see the man who had threatened her?

According to the prosecution, the reason is clear: Cummings' initial claims to authorities were nothing more than thoughtful preparation for the premeditated act she carried out that Sunday morning. The wounds on her arm and face, Casey insists, were superficial at worst. "Anyone who spends a great deal of time outdoors and around animals is going to get a few scratches." The crime scene photos show the knife Villegas allegedly wielded was not found clutched in his right hand, as suggested in earlier news reports. Rather, it lay on the floor beneath his body, pressed against his armpit.

Clearly, those who feel their Argentine friend was the victim of a cold-blooded murder favor the prosecutor's "jealous-and-outraged-Susan-did-it" version. "Roberto was the most even-tempered, happy person I've ever been around," says Varge, "nothing like the person Susan's lawyer is describing. When they played together in matches, it was quite obvious that Roberto was very careful to protect Susan. He was very much a gentleman." Kelly Quinn, an ex-girlfriend of Villegas, insists that never during the four years they dated and worked together did she see any of the abusive or domineering characteristics that Cummings alleges. In fact, Quinn says the only time she could recall Villegas ever losing his temper was during a polo match when an opposing player bumped Villegas' horse, seriously injuring it.

To Bill Ylvisaker, Cummings seemed domineering and distrustful. "She seemed a nice enough person, but very possessive," he says. "Every time I saw them together, she was never more than a couple of feet away from him. I think there came a time in their relationship when he wanted a little more freedom than he had." Villegas' longtime friend Rodrigo Salinas puts it more pointedly: "She had all the power in the relationship. She had the money."

* * *

While some of Villegas' friends insist he continued to talk of marrying Cummings in the days preceding his death, even telling of their plans to move to Montana and establish a polo farm there, others note he admitted growing weary of the relationship and wanted it to end. Still, the close-knit polo set generally holds that it was Villegas who was attempting to free himself from a relationship that had become, in his words, suffocating. In the weeks before his death, he began spending nights in a room he rented on Bear Wallow Road in nearby Warrenton, leaving Cummings alone at her picturesque estate. At the same time, there are those who speculate that Cummings sent him away. Yet most who knew him admit they had been surprised when they began to see Villegas occasionally in the company of other women at some of the Warrenton nightspots frequented by his fellow Argies.

Another theory suggests the deterioration of the couple's romance may, in fact, have had little to do with Villegas' death. Several people who knew them insist the greatest source of disagreement between Cummings and Villegas was their differing attitudes toward Ashland Farm's thoroughbreds. Cummings, always the caregiver, viewed horses as expensive, pampered pets. Villegas thought them simply work animals. The idea of them being ridden in competition a second straight day, as Villegas planned that fatal Sunday, almost certainly met with Cummings' disfavor.

If such a theory is valid, Roberto Villegas may not have been the victim of a lovers' quarrel but, instead, his death was the result of his unacceptable attitude toward Cummings' beloved animals. It remains a tragic story with far more questions than answers.

For now, the truth remains hidden at Ashland Farm, where Susan Cummings has sequestered herself with only her sister and her animals as companions, awaiting her day in court. Her 71-year-old father, seriously ill in Switzerland, reportedly knows nothing of her legal difficulties.

On a recent fall evening, a damp briskness filled the air as sunset fast approached—a certain sign that another summer's polo season had ended and moved southward to Florida. A curious traveler slowed down on Holtzclaw Road, passing the entrance to Ashland Farm. In the distance, a solitary figure meandered toward the majestic stone house. Dressed in jeans, boots, and an oversized sweater, her shoulder length hair framing her faraway face, the woman carried two just-emptied feed buckets. A large black and white cat trailed at her heels. Even from a distance, the scene spoke of great sadness, loneliness that no fortune could sweep away.

◆ *Polo* magazine, January 1998

POSTSCRIPT:

In May of 1998, a jury found 35-year-old Susan Cummings guilty of voluntary manslaughter yet sentenced her to only sixty days in jail. A year earlier, in the same courthouse, a man who had shot and killed a neighboring farmer's cow was given a nine-month sentence. Following Cummings' sentencing, county prosecutor J. George Ashwell told reporters, "For the longest time, we've had a reputation of being pretty damn tough on criminal activity. This verdict has pretty much cast a shadow on that."

Death Angel

After review of your taped senior sermon, I am convinced that your ministry is destined to focus on the dying; lending comfort to those faced with death and those losing loved ones...
  - Written evaluation of seminary student Carroll Pickett in 1956

For hours, the young man paced his cramped quarters, alternately talking in nervous, rapid-fire bursts and falling into long stretches of silence. Occasionally, he took a small bite from the cheeseburger he'd ordered, but, in truth, he had no real appetite. Finally, in an attempt to silence the maddening clock ticking in his mind, he sat on his bunk and focused his attention on the country music wafting from a small radio across the way.

The man—a convicted murderer counting the hours before midnight, at which time he was scheduled to die by lethal injection—was soon on his feet again, approaching the barrier of steel bars and wire mesh separating him from his lone companion. Would it be possible, he asked the prison chaplain, to phone in a request?

Such were the favors, the simple acts of kindness, that the Rev. Carroll "Bud" Pickett was there to perform. In short order, he found the number of the radio station, placed a call, and asked that a song be played. Not wanting to invite an announcement from the DJ that he had a caller from death row on the line, Pickett opted not to explain the reason for his request. He did, however, indicate the importance of its airing before midnight.

Then the two men, strangers to each other only hours earlier, waited. When the song still hadn't been played by 11:45 p.m., the chaplain phoned the station again, emphasizing the urgency. Finally, just minutes before the prisoner was scheduled to make the fifteen-foot walk to the room where he would die, the disc jockey announced the song was coming up next. The chaplain quickly sought out the warden and pleaded that the moving of the inmate into the death chamber be postponed just three minutes.

The convicted murderer's death was briefly delayed while he sat in the 5-by-9 cell, eyes closed, slowly swaying to the gentle rhythm of the Kris Kristofferson song he wanted to hear. In the chill and stillness of the moment, "Help Me Make It Through the Night" called out like an unanswered prayer.

For fifteen years, it was Pickett's job to help strangers—men with evil histories of unspeakable violence and lost hope—through the final hours of their lives. He talked with them, sang with them, and granted their wishes, however trivial, if within reason. They prayed together and read from the Bible. Often, they spoke of the grim circumstances that led to their meeting.

They were men convicted of capital crimes, waiting to receive the ultimate punishment imposed by the State of Texas. He was the death house chaplain, there to serve as the prisoners' final confidant, the last friendly face they would ever see.

On one occasion, an inmate's tearful description of the unspeakable, torturous crime he had committed was so graphic that a nearby prison guard became sick to his stomach. On another, a condemned man spread rumors to other death row inmates that the minister had conducted quick funeral services for executed prisoners without families or loved ones, then watched, laughing, as their bodies were unceremoniously tossed into a creek that runs behind the prison. And that he had once loudly cursed the legal authorities who had seen fit to stay an execution at the last minute. Anti-death penalty *cause célèbre* Gary Graham, the murderer-robber who had earlier seen his execution stayed, spat in his face.

Yet Pickett stood his ground, listening, not judging; befriending, not berating.

Sometimes, those to whom he was assigned sat and stare blankly—frozen statues saying nothing, drawing whatever comfort comes from the physical presence of another human being in the slow-ticking last minutes of their death watch. Others paced nervously, talking constantly.

"No one," the 66-year-old clergyman says as he reflects on his unique career, "regardless of what he might have done in his life, should die alone."

Although he could never tell the inmates so, the gentle, soft-spoken man with strong feelings about the Presbyterian doctrines he has followed and preached throughout his adult life, never embraced the legal process of which he was a part. Yet, as the death row chaplain for the Texas Department of Corrections (now called the Texas Department of Criminal Justice), the minister assigned to accompany murderers and rapists whose time for execution had come, Pickett repeatedly participated in the process—a process in which he, in fact, played a key role in designing. A manual Pickett wrote, *The Team Approach to Execution in the State of Texas*, eventually provided the guidelines for prisons throughout the nation.

He assumed his role at a time when death sentences were carried out at one minute past midnight instead of six in the afternoon, before the national outcry against the death penalty had grown into today's boiling social and political issue, before haunting questions about the possibility that innocent people were being put to death filled the front pages, before a Huntsville execution became a streamlined routine. Yet, even then, it troubled Pickett, conflicted with his life-long spiritual convictions. "My interpretation of the scripture 'Thou shall not kill,'" he suggests, "has always applied to all."

* * *

"To me," he says, "execution has never been anything more than an exercise in revenge. By definition, it is premeditated murder. There is no proof that the death penalty has served as a deterrent to crime, no figures that indicate that it is really that much more cost effective. And it really offers no closure for the victim's loved ones. All it does is create another set of victims."

Yet he was there, standing silently at the foot of the gurney, a hand gently touching the condemned man's ankle, when the state of Texas reinstituted capital punishment in 1982, putting Fort Worth murderer Charley Brooks to death by lethal injection. And even then his work was not done. It was Pickett's responsibility to remain with the body until employees of a local mortuary arrived to retrieve it. He then drove to a nearby motel to meet with Brooks' family.

He experienced the routine 95 times before his retirement in 1995.

"My responsibility," he says, "was always to make the prisoner as comfortable as possible in those last hours, to answer whatever questions he had about the procedure he was facing, to arrange last visits and phone calls. I became his access to the outside world in those final hours."

If the inmate wanted a newspaper or magazine, Pickett went in search of it. He helped order last meals, write letters, and draft wills; he listened as the man on the other side of the bars rehearsed whatever final statement he planned to make from the death chamber. If the inmate had a favorite scripture, Pickett read it. When James David Autry became upset over televised news reports that he was "nervous" about his impending death, Pickett sought reporters to assure them the inmate was, in fact, calmly awaiting his fate. Though a long-standing "no smoking" rule existed in the death house, Pickett often ignored it, providing an occasional cigarette. "I had one guy tell me, 'I know I can't smoke it, but I'd like to die with a cigar in my pocket,'" Pickett remembers. "I went over to a drug store, bought him a cigar, and as we were getting ready to make the walk into the death chamber, I slipped it into his shirt pocket. It seemed like a small thing to do if it somehow made him feel better."

When an inmate confided he was a member of the Church of Wicca and wished to have an ordained witch give him last rites, Rev. Pickett, who performed his role in a nondenominational capacity, got on the phone. "I finally found a woman living in Pearland [near Houston] and explained the situation. She drove to Huntsville in a driving rain and did a wonderful job."

During those final hours after all appeals had been exhausted, Pickett says, often a stark degree of honesty would haunt him for days afterwards. Details of murders committed, confessions to additional crimes for which they had never been convicted, tales of troubled lives that set their course to death row. "They were talking from somewhere deep inside, from years of carrying around the knowledge of crime and sin and immorality. They are heavy burdens most of us can't begin to imagine."

Hearing those burdens described, performing the all-but-impossible task of offering comfort, then watching men die was not a job Pickett sought. Until 1974, in fact, he had never been inside the prison for which the city in which he lives was universally known.

During one of the most infamous outbreaks of violence in Texas penal history, then prison director W. J. Estelle, a member of Pickett's congregation, approached him with a request to come to the downtown Walls Unit. Estelle asked Pickett to counsel family members of the sixteen hostages taken during the 11-day siege and attempted breakout by prisoners Fred Gomez Carrasco, Ignacio Cuevas, and Rudolfo Dominguez.

Before the standoff ended, two prison librarians—Elizabeth Beseda and Julia Standley, both members of Pickett's church—had been killed. In fact, Pickett had been helping Standley plan for her daughter's wedding only days before she was taken hostage. Ultimately, responsibility would fall to the minister to inform both families of the deaths.

"Once that was over," he says, "I swore I would never set foot inside a prison again." For six years, he kept that vow. That is, until the spring of 1980, when Estelle approached him again, this time about joining the prison's staff of chaplains. Pickett's primary responsibility, he was told, would be to minister to terminally ill patients in the prison hospital and psychiatric ward and occasionally conduct funerals for those without families to claim the bodies.

In 1982, Pickett's job description changed drastically. The warden called a staff meeting to announce that executions would soon be resumed. Pickett vividly remembers the meeting. "Nobody in the room had any idea what it was going to be like, even what the procedure was. We all went down to the old death row to see what it looked like. The thing that first struck me was the fact that there were only eight cells. When it had been designed there was no thought that there would ever be more than eight men on death row at any given time."

When the staff visited what would come to be known as the "death house," the population of death row had grown to 100. Now, more than 400 inmates reside at the nearby Terrell Unit, which houses all those awaiting execution.

The prison's infamous "Old Sparky," the electric chair used in bygone days, was stored in a room at the end of the narrow building, replaced by a gurney on which the condemned inmate takes his final breath after three separate chemicals—one a general anesthetic, one that halts the function of the respiratory muscles, and a third that stops the heart—are injected into his bloodstream.

"Knowing that we would all soon be involved in an execution," Pickett says, "was nerve-racking. Sitting around, planning how to put someone to death was an unsettling exercise. And even after we'd settled on all the details—when the prisoner would be brought to the death house, what he would be allowed to do in the final hours, how we'd get him from the cell to the death chamber, and how the actual execution would be carried out— none of us were really comfortable. We practiced over and over, using a guard acting the part of the inmate. Without telling others involved, we'd even instruct him to put up a fight so it could be determined how to deal with it. And even at that none of us had any idea how it would go."

To everyone's relief, that first execution went smoothly. "One of the things I asked the warden to tell Charley Brooks as we waited that day was that none of us had ever done this before," Pickett recalls. "It just seemed that he deserved to know that."

In time, Pickett became able to provide every minute detail to those prisoners who wished to know about the execution procedure. With the exception of rare, minor problems—like the time it took more than a half hour to locate a vein that hadn't collapsed from a prisoner's lifetime of drug abuse, or when the intravenous needle momentarily slipped from a prisoner's arm as the fatal drugs were being administered—the executions, all modeled after the one carried out in '82, were conducted without serious malfunction.

Nevertheless, Pickett had his reservations about the dark exercise and what it had accomplished.

Eighteen years after presiding at the funeral services of church members Beseda and Standley, the minister found himself face-to-face with Ignacio Cuevas, who was finally scheduled to be executed for their murders during the '74 standoff.

"It was an awkward situation," he remembers, "since my responsibilities were to the families of the victims as well as those of the person being put to death." Although relatives of the two murdered women knew about Pickett's long-ago involvement in the siege and its aftermath, neither Cuevas nor members of his family ever did. "I simply felt it would be more difficult for them to accept me and what I was attempting to do for them if they'd been aware I'd had a personal relationship with those Cuevas had been convicted of murdering."

In the final hours before his execution, Cuevas admitted to the chaplain that Ignacio Cuevas was not even his real name; he had taken it from a man he'd killed years earlier.

"One of the things I had to do," Pickett recalls, "was find out what the family wanted to do with the body after the execution. Cuevas's son had come from Pecos and told me he had already built a casket and dug a grave for his father. He said he'd bought a new pickup to take his daddy home in."

Pickett ponders that long-ago night and says it offers a strong argument that there is never real solace to be found in the wake of unspeakable evil. "It has been 26 years since I buried Drew Standley's mother," he says, "and there is still no closure. For her or for the Cuevas family."

One of the traditions attached to the administration of the death sentence that troubled him most, Pickett says, was that of family members' being allowed to witness the execution. "I've always felt it would be easier on everyone if they could find it in themselves not to be there and watch.

"I would meet with them beforehand and do the best I could to explain what they would see, but it rarely prepared them. There is a great difference in watching an elderly loved one die of cancer and seeing a healthy one who, for lack of a better term, is not of dying age, being put to death. Seeing someone you care for strapped down, scared, totally helpless, knowing he is about to be killed, is a traumatic experience beyond almost any other I can imagine."

From his vantage point in the death chamber, Pickett saw witnesses faint, and he watched as others became hysterical and violently ill. "I don't like to think of the number of times I've been told by a family member afterward that I hadn't prepared them for what they actually experienced," he says. "The truth of the matter is, no matter how hard you try, there is just no way to do it."

*　*　*

In keeping with his duties, Pickett never voiced his personal feelings about his assigned task, never discouraged any visit by those who wished to be on hand in the final moments of an inmate's life. As a boy in a rural community on the outskirts of Victoria, he dreamt of the day he would become an algebra teacher and tennis coach; as a man, the minister spent his time as a prison chaplain walking a fine line. In 1977, the Presbyterian church took a firm position against the death penalty, yet it gave Pickett permission to conduct what it classified as "special ministry." The role he agreed to play never got easier.

Living alone at the time he began serving as companion and minister to inmates facing their death, he returned home to long nights of angst and sleeplessness after each execution. "The things I'd talked with these men about," he says, "was privileged, so I couldn't speak to anyone about what they had said. But I had to get it out of my system somehow." Thus he began a routine of speaking his post-execution thoughts into a tape recorder.

Filed away, shared with no one, Pickett has an oral history of the career many of his friends said was certain to drive him crazy.

Although he has never played the tapes, he remembers. One night he sat and listened as a rapist-murderer told of staking his victim to an ant bed, leaving a young woman to endure a death beyond imagination. The Amarillo man who graphically described how he raped an elderly nun. The father who poisoned Halloween candy to cause the death of his own son. The man who killed as many people in prison as he had while a member of free society. Another who admitted the abuse of over 200 children. A young man, frustrated with the disappointments of life, who methodically murdered his entire family. They came to him bearing distressing epithets like "The Good Samaritan Killer," "The Candy Man," and "The Soldier of Fortune Murderer." It became a nightmarish litany.

Many friends and fellow ministers cited such tales as they assured him he wouldn't last at the job. "I was told that after going through the procedure a couple of times, I'd be absolutely nuts," he says. On two occasions, in fact, when circumstances made it impossible for him to attend scheduled executions, the preachers who substituted for him vowed they would never do it again.

In time he sought counsel of his own. "On a couple of occasions," he admits, "I had a difficult time putting things out of my mind and went to a fellow minister for help." One such visit, he remembers, followed the execution of a terrified 24-year-old killer to whom he had carefully described the death house routine. "As I did with everyone, I had assured him that once the drugs were administered it would be only seven to 12 seconds before he died.

"But that night, as I touched his ankle, feeling his pulse, I realized that it had taken longer than usual. When twelve seconds passed and his heart was still beating I felt a tremendous sense that I'd let him down. It weighed on me that he'd gone to his death feeling that I'd lied to him. It took me a long time to shake that. To this day I can see those big brown eyes looking up at me."

* * *

The death house procedure, still in use, was suggested by Rev. Pickett almost two decades ago and has since been passed along to prisons in 38 states. It was essential, he insisted from the start, for the chaplain to gain the condemned inmate's confidence, thus he was given wide latitude in decision-making. In essence, in a prisoner's final hours, the chaplain controlled everything from the moment the inmate was delivered, strip-searched, and placed in a holding cell, until the time the guards arrived to escort him down the narrow hallway and into the sterile cinder-block room where death awaited.

Pickett, who made it a rule never to visit inmates on death row, always waited at the door of the death house cell until they arrived. Though he read the convict's file to learn personal information, he never dwelled on details of the crime or crimes. "The person would not have been there," he says, "had he not done something terrible." That was enough to know for Pickett.

"My purpose was to help him through it in any way I could, to keep him as calm as possible while he waited to die." The clergyman is obviously proud of the fact that never during his tenure did a prisoner physically attack him or the two guards assigned to stand silently at the far end of the death house hallway.

Sitting in a chair outside the cell, Pickett would detail the ensuing sequence of events and ask whom the prisoner might like to have visit him. If no family members were present, long-distance phone calls (restricted to the continental United States), routed through the warden's office, were permitted. Many asked for prayers or that the chaplain read scriptures from the Bible. A few showed no interest in Pickett's services.

He arranged the sequence of emotional visits with wives and parents, brothers and sisters. Then, as time for the execution neared, he helped the prisoner write letters, which he promised to personally mail, and ordered the man's final meal. "There's a myth that they can order anything, but the truth is they are allowed only what the prison kitchen has available. And while most do ask for a rather lavish meal, most only pick at it once it arrives."

The chaplain, in fact, routinely warned them that the drugs that would soon be pumped into their bloodstreams seemed to work more slowly on full stomachs.

Andy Barefoot, convicted of the murder of a sheriff's deputy in

Killeen, asked only for a bowl of sand and a glass of vinegar. "I asked him why," recalls Pickett, "and he said, 'Because that's what Jesus had. It's in the Bible.' The meal was denied. He settled for my reading from Matthew, Mark, Luke, and John for three hours."

And if an inmate planned to make a final statement from the death chamber, Pickett encouraged him to rehearse it. "I tried to explain that whatever they had to say were the words the world would remember them by, so they had to give it some thought." Also, it was in those final hours the condemned spoke most candidly, talking of their crimes, whatever degree of remorse they felt, their questions about faith and the hereafter, or, simply, their anger at "the system" they felt had treated them unfairly.

"While it is impossible not to feel scared," Pickett says, "there is a peaceful atmosphere in the solitude of the last cell they'll ever be placed into. On death row, there is a loud and vulgar noise that is constant. In the death house there is a quiet they have not experienced in years. There, they know, no one is going to harass them or invade their last hours of privacy. I've actually seen relief on the faces of many when they finally arrive there. In many instances, I've had inmates tell me that the few hours spent in the death house cell was the first time they had been treated as a person since coming to prison."

Finally, fifteen minutes before the scheduled time of execution, Pickett would say, "It's time to go," and guards would enter the cell to escort the prisoner through the hallway and into the powder blue-walled death chamber. Pickett walked at the prisoner's side then stood silently at the foot of the gurney as the inmate was strapped in place.

When all was set, after the prisoner spoke his final words into a microphone extended above the gurney—sometimes a whisper, sometimes as if boomed from a pulpit—the warden would give the signal (removing his glasses), and the lethal injections began. It ended in seconds.

But not for Pickett. After remaining with the body until the funeral home ambulance had come, he would visit distraught family members, sometimes late into the night. And then his own reflective vigil often lasted until daybreak.

* * *

Adhering to procedure wasn't always easy. While his focus in those final hours was to keep the inmate as calm as possible, often those in law enforcement demanded one final chance to obtain a confession or details of the crime for which the prisoner had been convicted. One sheriff even suggested that Pickett disregard the confidentiality vow he'd taken as a minister and wear a wire so that any admission to other crimes of which a particular inmate was suspected might be recorded. Ultimately, Pickett went to the warden with a request that then-Texas attorney general Jim Maddox be kept away from the death house on execution day. "He always wanted to talk to the prisoner, to ask for details of the crime," Pickett remembers. Maddox, he says, only made an already bad situation worse with his demanding demeanor and monopoly of the condemned man's final hours.

"One of the most important parts of my job," Pickett recalls, "became keeping people out of the prisoner's cell until a quarter to twelve when the guards came for him."

Most of those who made the short trip to the death house already knew they would soon meet Pickett. Inmates whose executions had been stayed at the last minute had returned to describe the events and the demeanor of the chaplain to fellow death row inmates. "For that reason—knowing that word of anything I said and did was going to get back to death row—I made it an iron-clad rule never to promise anything I couldn't deliver."

Despite such caution, troubling stories made their way back to death row. There was the time, Pickett recalls, when a condemned prisoner balked at being strapped to the death chamber gurney. The inmate sat up and began fighting the guards who were trying to strap him down, at which point the chaplain—a minister who was standing in for Pickett, who was out of town on a family emergency—gently placed his hand on the man's chest in an attempt to calm him. As the man lay back, terrified, he asked the chaplain to maintain physical contact. And so he did, keeping his hand on the man's chest throughout the procedure.

The following day, a newspaper headline read, "Chaplain Holds Inmate Down While He Dies." Word spread quickly through death row.

"While I was asked by almost every prisoner I met, I never shared my thoughts on the death penalty. My response was always that how I felt had nothing to do with why I was there or what was about to happen.

"My feeling about capital punishment had absolutely nothing to do with the person I was there to help. I'd tell them that I wasn't the judge or jury, that I didn't make the law. Nor was I there to enforce the law. That was not my business. I wanted them to know that it made no difference how I felt about capital punishment or the court system or death by lethal injection because I had absolutely no control over those things."

And so, none of the 95 men the chaplain walked to their deaths ever knew that he embraced the definition of their fate fashioned by *Nightline* host Ted Koppel. "He came down and did one of his shows on an execution," Pickett remembers, "and at some point referred to what we were doing as 'sterilized killing.' It's the best description I've ever heard."

Yet for years, Pickett made the best of a situation with which he spiritually struggled. "I came away from the experience," he admits, "with far more questions than answers."

The executions of men whose crimes had been committed years earlier, when they were only teenagers, troubled him most, he says. "I would find myself thinking back to my own teenage years and saying to myself, 'There but for the grace of God...' I've talked with men who were as gentle as anyone I've ever met, people who knew they had done a horrible wrong and were genuinely remorseful, people I'd have been comfortable with if they visited in my home. Yet for one terrible mistake..." With that his voice trails. The law as written, he concedes, offers no possibility of redemption for such men, no differentiation between them and the hardened career criminal.

And there are those he viewed as too intellectually challenged to grasp the severity of their situation. "For [then Governor George] Bush to say that the State of Texas has never executed a mentally retarded person is just not true," he says. "I've been there; I've talked to them."

During the course of his work for the prison, did he meet and counsel any prisoner whom he felt had been wrongly convicted? "Yes, I was convinced that some of them did not commit the crimes for which they died." To be more specific, he says, would uselessly reopen old wounds suffered by family members.

In retirement, Pickett distanced himself from the prison and the death house. These days he sleeps better, smiles more often, and enjoys life with his wife, Jane, whom he married ten years ago. But he has the memories and the answer-less questions about a legal system demanding a life for a life. And one promise he continues to keep to the man who first persuaded him into the job.

"When [former prison director] Estelle retired and moved to California," he says, "he asked that I do something for him."

In honor of that favor, on the anniversary of the 1974 siege, Rev. Carroll Pickett dutifully visits the local cemetery to commemorate the deaths of prison librarians Elizabeth Beseda and Julia Standley.

There, at Estelle's request, he places a single red rose on each woman's grave.

◆*Dallas Observer*, September 2000

POSTSCRIPT:

In 2002, Pickett's book, *Within These Walls*, which I coauthored, received the Writers League of Texas' Violet Crown Award as the year's best book of non-fiction. Today, Pickett travels extensively, speaking out against the death penalty.

Reminiscing With Racehorse

Show me the phone, lend me a dime
I ain 't rollin' over, I ain't doing no time
Ain't coppin' no plea, I'm hip to your game
I ain't talking to no one 'cept Racehorse Haynes
▪from the song "Racehorse Haynes" by Tom Russel & Andrew Hardin

When attempting to examine the legendary life of Richard "Racehorse" Haynes, a man generally considered one of the premier criminal defense lawyers in modem judicial history, it seems prudent to first clear away some of the old wives' tales and outlandish myths, to offer up, as they say, the truth and nothing but the truth.

So, no, despite the fact there are alumni who will swear they were on campus that day and witnessed the event, Haynes did not jump from a plane and parachute into the University of Houston fountain as a publicity stunt during his successful campaign to become student body president. And, no, he didn't really nail his own hand to the jury box railing while defending members of a biker gang alleged to have crucified one of their female companions. Still, one need not look hard to find people who insist they were in the courtroom and saw it with their own eyes.

We'll deal later with the time he supposedly stood before twelve stunned jurors and drank deadly insect poison and another when he repeatedly shocked himself with a cattle prod in defense of a man charged with keeping an unsuspecting drifter locked away at his Texas ranch-turned-slave camp.

Seated in his Houston office that looks more like a museum than a workplace, walls and shelves cluttered with plaques, books, framed photos, and mementoes of all manner of professional achievement, Haynes, now 76, puffs on his ever-present pipe, smiles, and offers up an innocent shrug. Hey, there is some measure of reality to each of the stories, he explains. If he didn't actually do everything you've heard, he did, at least, seriously consider such theatrics before abandoning the ideas in the name of common sense and physical well-being.

And he'd like it on official record that he's not the originator of such embellishments. Oh, maybe sometimes, after hearing the stories retold for the umpteenth time or reading them again in a newspaper or magazine account of his career, he doesn't always dash to the phone to set things straight. But, hey, what's the harm?

Even the true origin of his nickname has been lost in fuzzy folklore. True, it was given Haynes by a junior high football coach when he was growing up in the blue collar Sunset Heights section of Houston. But it had far less to do with the youngster's speed afoot than the fact he seemed interested in carrying the ball only from sideline to sideline rather than advance it upfield. "You a football player or a damn racehorse?" the coach is said to have bellowed.

Haynes, as anyone with the mildest interest in modern Texas history knows, became the latter. Today, when asked for his autograph by trial-goers or admirers he encounters on the banquet circuit, he adds a quick cartoon drawing of a horse's head to the signature. Bestselling books— Tommy Thompson's award-winning *Blood and Money*, Steve Salerno's *Deadly Blessing*, Mike Cochran's *Texas vs. Davis*, Gary Cartwright's *Blood Will Tell*, etc.—have recounted high profile cases he's worked; so have numerous made-for-television movies. He's been involved in everything from the historic Watergate investigation to the aftermath of the shutdown of LaGrange's infamous Chicken Ranch that was immortalized on Broadway as *The Best Little Whorehouse in Texas*. Every organization from the International Society of Barristers to the American Academy of Achievement has honored him. *Time* magazine called him one of the six best trial lawyers in the country.

Such is the manner in which larger-than-life legends are seeded and grown. Haynes' legend has provided the flamboyant, 5'9", ex-welterweight boxer, South Pacific war hero, motorcyclist, sailor, and millionaire several times over with a reputation that has grown to nine feet tall and weighs in at a junkyard-dog-mean 500 pounds. Like the songs and stories say, if you're in deep trouble—and have deep pockets—you contact Racehorse Haynes. It has been the clarion call of desperate people for over forty years.

Only days earlier, he had returned from Virginia Beach, where he successfully defended a young man accused of stalking and solicitation of capital murder. Which, of course, begs the question why, at his age and with legacy and finances in good order, he continues to put himself through the grueling demands of being a trial lawyer .

"I like the feeling I got when that verdict was announced," he explains. "In preparing for the trial, I'd met that boy's mother and father, his brother, his aunt…all really nice people, all devastated by the situation they found themselves in. By doing what I could to see that my client didn't spend half his remaining life in prison, I felt I was able to make that family whole again. When that happens, it is just as rewarding and as much fun as it was when I started out."

Keeping people out of jail or prison is what Haynes does. And the style and flair he displays in doing so has been met with great admiration from some, condemnation from others. "For 48 years," he admits, "I've been asked the same question every defense attorney hears: How can you look yourself in the mirror after representing so many people you know to have done terrible things? That just tells me those asking have assumed a great deal and simply can't tolerate the concept of fair representation of someone who just might not be guilty. As I've told law students and young lawyers for years, I'm not the judge; it's not the attorney's prerogative to determine guilt or innocence. I don't get people off. The jury acquits them."

Yes, but what about those times when he knows for certain his client is stone cold guilty, that he or she committed a crime that screams out for justice? "Then I do my best to see that real justice is done. In the first place, I never try to compel a client to confess to me. All I ever want to hear from them is what they think the prosecutor is going try to prove to a jury. We plan our case from there, always assuming that the state is going to ask for the highest degree of punishment possible. If it looks like my client is, in fact, guilty, the goal is to see that he gets something less, something more fair and reasonable. If he is innocent, we go hell-bent after an acquittal."

This, remember, is the guy who once outlined a hypothetical defense thusly: "Let's say your neighbor sues you, claiming your dog bit him at such-and-such time and place. You've got three defenses. Number one, my client's dog doesn't bite; number two, my client and his dog were somewhere else on the day the alleged bite occurred; or, number three, my client doesn't have a dog."

Even Haynes' rare defeats have, in a manner of speaking, been triumphs. During his career, he has defended 38 clients who faced the death penalty on capital murder charges. "Nobody's been sentenced to die yet," he says. Then, as he tamps his pipe, he makes a telling admission: "But I still live in sheer terror of getting a death penalty case and failing. Every defense attorney does."

Throughout his near half-century career, Haynes has rarely experienced failure. Still, he won't disclose his win-loss record. "Trials aren't sporting events," he argues. Yet all one need do is recollect some of the most highly publicized cases in Texas criminal history as proof of his success:

In 1969, Dr. John Hill, a celebrated Houston plastic surgeon, was charged with killing his socialite wife, Joan, by injecting a deadly bacteria into a dessert he served her. The case was a tabloid writer's dream: ruthless ambition, high society, beautiful people, a vengeful father, hapless assassins, and, most importantly, River Oaks wealth.

It was the kind of challenging case most litigators dream of. And, as Haynes launched his defense of Dr. Hill, word quickly spread that there was a good chance the doctor might actually beat the rap. Why? Because Haynes had confided to several friends that he was convinced of his client's innocence. Unfortunately, the world would never know. In his first court appearance, the judge declared a mistrial—a temporary victory for Haynes and his client. But before the doctor could be retried, he himself was the victim of a contract murder.

Still, the nationwide publicity generated by the case greatly advanced the celebrity of the engaging attorney with the strange nickname, slow drawl, and trademark pinstripe suits and ostrich-skin cowboys boots.

Then, in 1976, eyewitnesses swore they had seen Fort Worth multimillionaire T. Cullen Davis enter his mansion on an August night shortly before his estranged wife, Priscilla, was found seriously wounded, her 12-year-old daughter, Andrea, and boyfriend Stan Farr dead. The wealthiest man ever tried for murder, Davis reportedly paid Haynes a quarter million dollars to defend him in a trial that lasted six months, making it the lengthiest and most expensive murder trial in Texas judicial history. Davis got his money's worth, ultimately acquitted to the surprise of many who had closely followed the soap opera-like case.

And then, just when it seemed Haynes' work was done, Davis was suddenly back in custody, charged with hiring a hit man to kill not only his divorce attorney, but a dozen others on his enemies list. This time, there were even FBI surveillance audio and video tapes that seemed to make Davis' guilt slam-dunk clear. Thus Haynes was called on to defend his wealthy client twice more—once in a Houston courtroom, where the proceedings ended in a hung jury, and later in Fort Worth, where he finally managed to again convince a jury of his client's innocence. Cullen Davis left the courthouse a free man. Though he won't confirm it, the four-year legal ordeal reportedly earned Haynes $3 million.

Head-shaking members of the legal community began referring to the high dollar Haynes as a miracle-worker. Others, less charitable, acknowledge him as a legal gunslinger. Several years ago, one judge split the difference, calling Haynes a "charming little jerk."

Retired Associated Press reporter Mike Cochran, who covered each of the Davis trials and later wrote the definitive book on the saga, calls Haynes "as good a courtroom lawyer as I've ever seen." No small praise from a man who has seen the likes of legal icon Melvin Belli in action as he defended

Lee Harvey Oswald's killer, Jack Ruby.

"Racehorse has this charisma and showmanship that just takes over the courtroom the minute he walks in. The guy is spellbinding. And he's tough as a floor safe."

Veteran Fort Worth defense attorney Jack Strickland, who prosecuted the Davis solicitation of capital murder case, is not so generous. Still, he admits a begrudging respect for his old adversary. "I think Haynes is an exceptional lawyer," he says, "but that's not to say I agreed with the tactics he used in the Davis case, trashing the victim [Priscilla Davis] the way he did. There's no question we really went at each other, and there were definitely hard feelings when the case was over."

Time, however, has thawed the relationship. "We've seen each other on social occasions a few times," says Strickland, "and even served as co-counsel on a drug case a few years ago.

"Richard is bright, as fast on his feet as anyone I've ever seen, and has a phenomenal memory. And he's always prepared. Having said that, he's also a man who can stand in front of a jury and say the most outrageous things imaginable. And somehow manage to keep a straight face while doing so."

The historic Davis case, Strickland says, brought out the worst in a lot of people. "On both sides," he admits. At one point, the former assistant D.A. even publicly suggested that Haynes and his team of attorneys had crossed the line from advocates and become accomplices to the crime with which their client was charged.

Interestingly, the personal wars, the courtroom tactics, or even the brilliant examination of witnesses no longer come to mind as Haynes reflects on the milestone events of the Davis trial. Rather, it is an angry and tearful late night call that came from his wife, Naomi (to whom he's been married for 53 years and delights in referring as "the widow Haynes").

"She'd just had the flower beds landscaped," he recalls, "and my two Rhodesian ridgebacks had gotten in them and torn them all to hell. I said something like, 'Darlin', I'm up here [in Amarillo] trying the Super Bowl of capital murder cases, and you're calling me about the dogs tearing up the flower beds? I don't have time right now to worry about that. If it'll make you feel any better, just get a pistol and shoot the sons-a-bitches.'

"Well, all that did was cause her to cry harder and get even madder. She said, 'That's just like you. I'm here alone, I need somebody to talk to, and you're only interested in your stupid trial.' I could tell she was really steamed. So, I said, 'You're absolutely right. I apologize. I'm dead wrong. Put the dogs on the phone, and I'll talk to them.'"

In the early '80s, former Dairy Queen waitress Vickie Daniel was charged with killing her husband, Price Daniel, Jr. The fact the victim was not only the former Speaker of the Texas House, but also the son of Price Daniel, Sr., one of the most popular governors in the state's history, fueled a gossip fire storm in the little East Texas community of Liberty. And Racehorse was summoned. Even before the murder trial, he would have to defend Vickie in a lengthy and raunchy battle against her rich and powerful in-laws for custody of her children. When he finally laid out his case, Haynes rose to present his closing argument in the historic old Liberty County courthouse, and a triumphant marching song suddenly began to filter through the open windows.

"The high school band was practicing nearby," Haynes recalls, "and it was nothing more than happenstance that it struck up the 'William Tell Overture' just as I got ready to address the jury. The prosecutor jumped out of his chair and objected, saying I had orchestrated the whole thing. I explained to the judge that I didn't—but if I hadn't been dumber than a bucket of hair, I'd have certainly given it some thought."

Vickie Daniel got custody of her kids, was later acquitted of the murder, and *Law & Order's* Fred Thompson played the role of Racehorse in the movie that soon followed, getting Haynes' good ol' boy mannerisms down far better than *NYPD Blues'* Dennis Franz had when he played the defense attorney in the film based on the Davis case.

The Daniel case, legal experts suggest, broke new ground in the defense of battered spouses. Once a near automatic murder conviction, a guilty verdict under such circumstances is now far more difficult to achieve. "There's no question about that," says longtime Dallas civil attorney and jurisprudence historian John Collins.

"What he's done throughout his career," says Collins, who worked with Haynes on a bribery case back in the early days of their careers, "is prove time and time again that the keys to success are thoroughness in preparation and being articulate in the courtroom. He is a prime example of all the positive things the advocacy system of justice is supposed to be."

Entering the courtroom without a bulging briefcase, a stack of law books, or even notes on a legal pad has long been one of Haynes' disarming tactics, Collins points out. "But, as history shows, he comes to work with a keen awareness of the smallest weakness there might be in the government's case, completely prepared to give the prosecution a run for it's money."

Such has been the routine of the man who likes to say, "I've represented a great many men and women in what I call 'the Smith & Wesson divorce.' Someone pulls the trigger, and the marriage is over."

* * *

Even before the headlines, before the fees that now start in the

$500-per-hour range, before a last name became unnecessary, and before courtroom stardom, Haynes had long been serving up proof that he was on the way to becoming Texas' new litigation giant, the heir apparent to the title so long held by his mentor and first boss, Percy Foreman. During a ten-year period that began in the late '50s, Racehorse represented 163 clients charged with DWI—and never lost. "That," he immodestly boasts, "is still a record."

The closest he ever came to losing, in fact, was in a Dallas courtroom as he defended a young SMU student who had been arrested while driving home following a fraternity party. "My own vanity got in the way," Haynes admits.

Having had a front tooth knocked out during a motorcycle racing accident just days before the week-long trial was set to get underway, Haynes was self-conscious about the temporary replacement a dentist had put in place. As a result, he was far more reserved in his defense than usual. "I didn't say anything unless I had to," he recalls, "and, by the time the trial was drawing to a close, I knew that I hadn't connected with the jury."

When time came for closing arguments, Haynes knew desperate measures were in order. "I walked up to the jury box, explained about the tooth and asked if they minded if I took it out so I would feel more comfortable talking." With that he removed the temporary tooth, set it on the railing, flashed a gaping smile, then gave an impassioned argument on behalf of his client.

It took the jury twelve minutes to return with a not-guilty verdict.

Then there was the aforementioned Outlaws gang crucifixion case in Titusville, Florida. It's the one, many say, that served as the true genesis of the Racehorse Haynes legend. With clients with nicknames like Fat Frank, Crazy John, Super Squirrel, and Mangy, at least one of whom had a dead rat pinned to his jacket while a couple others had a habit of French-kissing whenever they saw cameraman, Haynes saw the case as a definite challenge. The charges weren't pretty. After learning one of the gang's female groupies had violated a rule that stated all profits earned from what Racehorse delicately refers to as "the world's oldest profession" were to go into the gang's treasury, they allegedly punished her by nailing her to a tree.

"Actually, it sounds a little worse than it really was," Haynes insists. "They just nailed her hands to the tree. She wasn't killed; wasn't even hurt real bad. But the whole state of Florida was up in arms. Truth is, it probably wouldn't have been that big a deal if the victim's daddy hadn't been a rather prominent citizen who was calling in all kinds of law enforcement favors in an effort to get the whole gang strung up."

Haynes put the father's "unreasonable persecution" of the gang on trial and offered pretty compelling evidence that the victim had actually *volunteered* for her punishment. At one point during the trial, however, he began to feel his case needed a dramatic boost and went in search of a medical expert. What Racehorse wanted to know was how painful having a nail driven into one's hand might actually be.

When the doctor explained that there were places on the hand, particularly the webbing between the fingers, where there was very little feeling, Haynes, the story goes, became almost giddy, fantasizing about a scene in which, just before delivering his closing argument, he would have the doctor inject his hand with a local anesthetic and mark a spot where no serious damage could be done. Then, as he passionately argued that little serious damage had been done to the victim, he would grab a hammer from his briefcase, place a hand on the jury box rail, and drive the nail into it.

"To be perfectly honest about it," he now says, "that wasn't my first idea." His wife had accompanied him to Florida. "I first asked her if she wanted to be famous," Haynes remembers, "then explained how she could come up and stand by the jury box and I would hammer the nail into her hand. As I recall, Naomi said something like, 'Not only no, but hell no,' and stormed out of the room."

Suffice it to say, the longtime Mrs. Richard Haynes is a lady of great patience and understanding.

Ultimately, Haynes judged his case strong enough and reluctantly dismissed the theatrical notion. Fat Frank, Mangy, and the gang were acquitted. And the victim? "My understanding," says Haynes, "is that she became quite the celebrity in the bars down in Florida, telling her story and showing off her stigmata."

It's getting late, but now the gifted storyteller is on a roll. There was the client accused of killing his girlfriend by having her ingest a potent insecticide he'd allegedly dissolved in her drink. Haynes contacted the manufacturer of the poison and learned (a) despite any amount of shaking or stirring, it would not dissolve in liquid, and (b) it would be impossible to swallow, since it would immediately stick to the roof of the mouth. "So, I began thinking I might demonstrate that to the jury," he admits. Ultimately, however, there was no need because he succeeded in having the case dismissed.

He did, however, do that show-and-tell with the electric cattle prod in a Kerrville courtroom in an effort to prove to a jury that the means by which his client had allegedly killed a drifter being held on his "slave ranch" wasn't as lethal as the prosecution would have them believe. "It was pretty damn painful, though," Haynes admits. But, he reflects, worth it. The accused rancher received five years probation.

And there's the story about his defense of angered Fayette County Sheriff T.J. Flournoy, who assaulted Houston TV reporter Marvin Zindler after he'd exposed the existence of LaGrange's famed Chicken Ranch brothel. ("Aw, we settled that one, and Marvin, an old golfing buddy of mine, agreed to donate his money to charity.") And the one about his client Robert Allen, formerly head of President Richard Nixon's Texas campaign organization, who served as a conduit for funds routed through Mexico to eventually pay the Watergate burglars. ("My guy didn't really do anything illegal. He thought he was just handling campaign funds.")

A Dallas case won back in the mid-'80s, he acknowledges, would be a much more difficult task in today's climate. The man he was defending was a Briton named Ian Smalley. A cattle rancher and international arms dealer, he was charged with attempting to smuggle 100 military tanks to Iran and over 8,000 anti-tank missiles to Iraq to help the countries ward off possible attacks from neighboring Russia. If convicted of violating the U.S. Neutrality Act, Smalley could have faced up to 70 years in prison.

Haynes argued his client had been duped into believing the shipments were secretly authorized by the federal government. "The whole case turned on a tape of a conversation he'd had in which, according to the transcripts, he said he was 'going to the airport to meet the Russians.' I listened to that tape until I had a headache, and for the longest time I kept hearing the same thing that I was reading on the typed transcript," the attorney remembers. Finally, however, he became comfortable with his client's thick accent and heard what had actually been said: "I'm going...to beat the rush hour."

On his lengthy resume, then, are alleged corporate thieves and capital murderers, prostitutes, drunks, deviants, and doers of all manner of dastardly deeds. "I've made some interesting friends over the years," he says.

* * *

The Sunset Heights streets of Haynes' boyhood were not so much mean as they were tough and demanding. The people who called the north Houston neighborhood home—including the parents of heart surgeon Dr. Denton Cooley and network anchor Dan Rather—fought a constant battle against two-dollar tribulations and second lien woes. So hard were times for his construction worker father in the '30s that, for a while, young Haynes lived in San Antonio with his grandmother. It was, he reflects, a blessing in disguise.

From age two to 10, he was cared for by a petite, energetic lady who rolled her own cigarettes, read to him from Shakespeare and the Bible, and taught him to write and do arithmetic. By the time Richard Michael Haynes was ready to attend school, he was able, without help, to fill out the paperwork required to skip the first and second grades.

Viewing him as something of a prodigy, the local paper published his picture. "Years later," he says, "Granny would tell me the home schooling she gave me was the worst possible thing she could have done. She said, 'It got your picture in the paper for the first time, and you've been in love with that idea ever since.'"

Far from publicity shy, Haynes had little room for argument. "Still," he says, "in everyone's life there is a great teacher, a great influence. My grandmother was mine."

When the Haynes family finances finally took a turn for the better, Richard was called home to the little white frame-house on 26th Street. By the time he was ready to graduate from Reagan High School, he had earned a reputation as one of the city's premier amateur boxers and an excellent student whose teachers were encouraging him to consider studying for the medical profession. If, however, Haynes was going to afford higher learning, it would only be with the help of a G.I. Bill. Thus, barely seventeen, he joined the Marines and spent 1944 through '46 in the South Pacific.

And for his heroic actions during the assault on Iwo Jima, pulling two wounded and drowning Marines from the cold February waters, he earned the Navy and Marine Corps medal. "What I'm most proud of," he says, as the familiar impish grin crosses his face, "is the citation that read something like 'with unselfish concern for his own safety.'" Then he comes to the punch line: "That's the only time in my life I've ever been called 'unselfish.'"

A man of famed dark humor and good-ol'-boy self-deprecation, Haynes admits there was precious little humor to be drawn from his World War II days. "You grow up pretty fast sitting in a fox hole," he says. He quickly learned the battlefield offers no safe haven. "We had this fella we all called Pops because he was about ten years older than most of us. He was married, had a couple of kids back home, and had already seen more than his share of combat. So, on the day we assaulted Iwo, the commander told him to remain aboard the troop ship out in the bay and work the radio.

"We later learned that Pops had been walking out of the ship's mess hall when a stray Japanese shell killed him."

From that day, Haynes says, he's remained keenly aware of the frailty of life. He reaches across the mounds of paperwork piled on his desk and picks up a small vile filled with volcanic ash and sand from the Iwo Jima beach. "I keep this," he says, "to remind me of people like Pops and how lucky I was to get back home in one piece."

Says Huntsville's Jack Kerr, former Sam Houston State University professor, product of the Heights, and friend of Haynes for over fifty years, "The unique thing about Richard is his genuine concern for and understanding of people. He's been that way since we were kids. Becoming wealthy and famous hasn't changed that a bit."

Every Wednesday, Kerr says, Haynes and old buddies from the Heights gather for lunch. "On those days, with all the reminiscing and storytelling that goes on, you wouldn't even know he's a lawyer."

* * *

When he enrolled at the University of Houston in the fall of '46, paying his way with a government loan and partial athletic scholarship from the basketball and track coaches, it was with the long-range plan to become a doctor. "That," he says, "didn't last long. I got me a part-time job at the medical center and immediately saw the frustration that the work offered. There were so many patients that no one could seem to help. There was no way to stop them from dying or, in some cases, even ease their pain. I knew I wouldn't be able to handle that."

So, he exchanged his weekend medical center job for one pumping gas, decided to pursue a degree in accounting, and set about making a name for himself on campus. The latter he did with a vengeance. It was a time when the nation lived in fear of the Communist threat and schools across the country were requiring that students sign documents stating they had no allegiance to the Communist Party. Though still years away from his days as a lawyer, then student body president Haynes not only refused but led rallies against the idea. "I was damned sure no Communist," he recalls, "but the idea of making it official by signing a piece of paper seemed absolutely ludicrous. So, yeah, I raised cane."

He's been doing so ever since. It just took him a while to find a proper stage for his showmanship. Upon graduation, he lasted less than a month with the accounting firm that hired him, quitting, he says, before he was fired. "I began to think that maybe a military career was the way to go," he says. For the next two years, he served as a paratrooper and hand-to-hand combat instructor with the 11th Airborne Division.

"It was my wife who made me a lawyer," he says. "She wasn't particularly thrilled with the idea of me jumping out of airplanes for a living and suggested that, 'as a backup,' I might want to think about going to law school."

Haynes didn't need a great deal of encouragement. During his undergraduate, days he'd often skipped class to visit the Harris County courthouse and watch the legendary Percy Foreman argue cases. "He was absolutely brilliant," Haynes remembers. And then he's grinning again. "Quite honestly, another thing that influenced my decision was all those Mickey Rooney 'Andy Hardy' movies. In them, Andy's father was this wise and caring judge who seemed to always have the right answer to every problem imaginable."

Thanks, then, to Naomi Haynes, Percy Foreman, and the fictional Judge Hardy, the Racehorse again changed his course. And in a roundabout way, Haynes' dog, Baron, also did his part.

Which invites yet another story:

"I'd just finished classes one afternoon," Haynes remembers, "and got this frantic call from my mother. She'd been keeping my dog for me, and he'd gotten out of the backyard and had been picked up by the dog catcher." Haynes immediately drove to the local pound to await Baron's arrival. "In those days, all you had to do was prove you were the owner and pay a $5 fee to get your dog back."

It was early evening before the dog catcher arrived with a truckload of yelping and frightened strays. Anxiously, Haynes pointed out his dog to the man in charge of the pound and extended a five dollar bill. "He said, 'Nope, you'll have to wait until tomorrow.' We argued for some time until it was clear he was not going to let my dog go home with me. So, I just reached over, flipped the latch, and told Baron to come with me."

As Haynes and his boxer were walking away, the pound administrator pulled a pistol and fired two shots into the air. "That's when I lost it," Haynes remembers. "I turned and said, 'You ignorant S.O.B., are you going to shoot me in the back for taking my own dog? I love him, but I damn sure don't want to die for him. I'll just sit outside the pound tonight and get him in the morning.'"

That's when the man slapped Haynes. And Baron jumped into the fray, attacking the man who had struck his master. "He started hitting my dog with his pistol, so I took it away from him and tossed it into some nearby weeds."

Baron wound up back in the pound for the night. Haynes went to jail. The following day, the boy-and-his-dog story not only made the local papers, but was also picked up by the wire services. In short order, Haynes was released, Baron was allowed to go home, and the pound administrator was fired.

Only years later, long after being hired to work part-time in Percy Foreman's law firm, did Haynes learn that the story of his pet's rescue had a great deal to do with his getting the job. Foreman, in fact, explained that people's affection for dogs would ultimately provide the new attorney with a valuable courtroom tool. "If," Haynes' mentor explained, "you can show that the victim ever abused a dog, you can pretty well bet that your client won't be convicted."

There would, however, be lessons a young Haynes had to learn the hard way. After defending an elderly client accused of embezzling a sizable amount of money from a bank, he was feeling good about the defense he'd put on and, in fact, told his client that he felt pretty confident the jury would come back with a not-guilty verdict. "If they do," Haynes said, "I want you to be sure to thank the judge and the jury."

Indeed, the man was acquitted—and dutifully followed his lawyer's instructions. "Judge," he said, "I want to thank you." Then, turning to face the jury, he said, "And members of the jury, I not only want to thank you… but I promise you I'll never do it again."

"I should have known better," Haynes reflects. "Once before I'd suggested that an acquitted client thank a judge whose mother had been my Sunday School teacher when I was a kid, and his response had been, 'Don't thank me you little turd. I know you're guilty.'"

Such events, however, did little to tone down the flamboyance that had already become Haynes' trademark. His first victory had come in the form of a $5,500 fee for the settlement of a client's personal injury claim. "I went straight to the bank, cashed the check, and asked for fifty-five $100 bills," he recalls. With one, he purchased a bottle of scotch and a bottle of bourbon then phoned several law school buddies and invited them to a celebration in his tiny office. The guests arrived to find the other fifty-four bills scattered on the floor, chairs, and desk. The show-off Haynes offered a mock apology for not having had time to clean the place up.

It was not insurance claims or defending those accused of drunk driving, which began to earn him sizable fees, that stirred Haynes' passion. For that matter, even the verdicts in the high profile murder cases have not provided the personal satisfaction he received from a long ago pro bono defense of a black man accused of stealing some materials from a construction site.

"There was no question in my mind that the man was innocent," he says, "and I worked my butt off to convince the jury of that." Having successfully done so, Haynes was invited to a post-trial celebration at his clients' home. "It was this little ol' shotgun house way down in the ghetto," the lawyer recalls. "His wife and grandmother had cooked this wonderful meal, and the kids had made all these little signs that said things like, 'God bless you, Mr. Lawyer.' There was barbecue and soda pop, singing and dancing, and more than a few happy tears."

He still insists, it's the nicest party he's ever attended. "I went home that night feeling that I'd done something pretty damn good," he adds.

It was that case and its warming aftermath that convinced Haynes to devote 10% of his time to pro bono representations. "It's my tithe," he explains.

* * *

Though his schedule doesn't indicate it, Racehorse Haynes insists he's finally slowing down. He still enjoys getting out in his power boat, but he recently sold the 64-foot sailboat he'd piloted all over the Gulf of Mexico for over twenty years ("I named it *Integrity*," he says, "because for years people said I didn't have any."), and he doesn't ride his Harley as often ("Too many idiots on the highway today, talking on cell phones while going 90 miles an hour."). His firm is smaller now, with only three fellow lawyers and four clerks and paralegals. He avoids the 80-hour work weeks that were once commonplace, and he's become more selective in choosing cases. "For instance," he explains, "I've made up my mind to stay away from the corporate criminal cases that often take years and a ton of paperwork to resolve. I don't want to start anything I can't finish.

"But, Good Lord willing, I'd like to keep doing what I'm doing for four more years." Age 80, he says, seems like a good stopping place.

Then what? There are, after all, just so many banquets and roasts at which one can be honored, so many lazy days on the water to enjoy, concerts to attend, books to read, or memoirs to write.

"I have a couple of fantasy scenarios that come to mind now and then," he admits. "In one, it's the last case of my career, and I'm defending a client who everyone in the courtroom thinks is guilty as sin. But I do such a fantastic job of cross-examining one of the people testifying against him that the witness suddenly throws his hands into the air and blurts out a confession that he is the one who really committed the crime."

And the other?

Haynes grins again, leans back, and strikes another match to his pipe. "I'm standing in front of a jury, see, giving one hell of a closing argument, when I have this heart attack and fall to the floor. Barely able to speak, I whisper a request that the judge allow the jurors to leave the box and gather around me so I might complete my argument before I die. "

◆ *Dallas Observer*, October, 2003

CSI: Texas

On an early Sunday morning, now a decade past, an urgent call came from the Johnson County Sheriff's office, forcing Max Courtney's absence from his regular place in the Fort Worth Presbyterian Church choir. Instead, the veteran crime scene investigator and forensic scientist hurriedly traveled south toward one of the most gruesome and demanding assignments to which he'd ever been summoned.

In an apartment in the rural community of Grandview, two young women—19-year-old Jennifer Weston and 18-year-old Sandi Marbut—lay dead in ink black pools of blood. One had been stabbed 69 times, the other 39.

Over the course of several long, blurry days, Courtney, exercising the expertise he developed during his 33-year career, methodically pieced together the nightmarish details of the murders. Relying first on bloodstains, prints, and the physical appearance of the apartment, then on the elaborate range of equipment in his laboratory, he developed a horrifying story he would eventually relay to a jury in the historic old Johnson County courthouse in Cleburne.

The killer, he determined, had first overpowered and murdered Marbut in the downstairs area of the apartment. Roommate Weston, apparently wakened by the assault, had come downstairs and was attacked by the intruder. She somehow managed to briefly get away and was running back toward her bedroom when her assailant caught up to her at the top of the stairs. There he stabbed and killed her.

He then stepped over her lifeless body and walked into a nearby bathroom, where he washed blood from his hands, leaving stains on the floor and in the sink. Next, he went into Weston's bedroom, searching her closet and going through the contents of her purse. After stepping over her body again, he returned to the downstairs area of the apartment. Finally, he opened the front door to be sure no one was out front, locked it from inside, and fled. According to the coroner, approximately eighteen hours passed between the time of the murders and the discovery of the young women's bodies.

Initially, it sounds very much like the opening scene of a highly-rated television drama or the first few pages of a paperback murder mystery. Today, crime scene investigators are emerging as law enforcement's new celebrities, scientists seeking crime solving clues with a *Star Trek* array of gadgetry. Almost magically, they turn a minuscule piece of evidence—a single strand of hair, a drop of blood invisible to the naked eye, shards of a bullet, a fiber, a fingerprint, or a tooth mark—into names and faces of serial killers, rapists, arsonists, drug dealers, and other ill-meaning stalkers of the night.

The national fascination with a profession once viewed as dark and ghoulish, most pop culture historians agree, began in the bloody glove, Bruno Magli footprint, Bronco chase days of the celebrated O.J. Simpson trial in the mid-'90s.

For real life crime scene investigator Courtney, however, it has been a lifelong passion. The Grandview case is but one of hundreds he can recall.

The intruder who entered that apartment, Courtney became certain, had worn boots. Using the chemical luminol, he and an assistant discovered a well-defined, unusually patterned print on the floor of the apartment. Of all the evidence gathered from the crime scene, it would be that single bloody boot print that ultimately led to a 1994 conviction of 20-year-old New Mexico native Bobby Ray Hopkins. That and what the self-effacing Courtney describes as an investigator's most valued tools: a generous amount of patience, good fortune, and help from others.

When he showed a photograph of the boot print to Grandview police chief Doug Allen, the officer's eyes widened. "My god," he said, "we've got that boot over at the sheriff's office."

It happened that Cleburne-based Texas Ranger George Turner was returning home on a Saturday evening when the bodies were found, and he stopped at the scene. As local authorities worked inside the apartment, Turner instinctively mingled among the growing crowd outside and heard talk that Hopkins had recently argued with one of the young women. Locating him at a residence on the opposite side of town, Turner immediately noticed what appeared to be bloodstains on one of the man's boots. He drove him to the sheriff's office for questioning, and, despite not having enough evidence to jail him, the Ranger suggested that local authorities keep Hopkins' boots so that blood tests might be done.

Ultimately, Courtney's Fort Worth laboratory detected three types of blood on the boots: that of Hopkins and his two victims

It is but one of numerous stories that mark the celebrated career of the man many list among the country's premier crime scene investigators. One need only look to local crime history to find that Courtney, always working in the background, played a vital role in the solution of numerous high-profile crimes. There was the murder of Fort Worth socialite Karen Koslow, after which local authorities had initially suspected her husband. Summoned to the crime scene just hours after the body was found, Courtney and his staff soon offered the opinion that the crime had, in fact, been committed by intruders known to the family. In time, it was proven two youths hired by the Koslow's teenage daughter, Kristi, committed the murder.

In the aftermath of the nationally publicized murder of Mansfield teenager Adrianne Jones by Naval Academy Midshipman Diane Zamora and Air Force Academy cadet David Graham, Courtney located and identified small but critical bloodstains in the car where the fatal assault began.

Courtney also conducted the investigation inside the North Richland Hills home of true crime writer Barbara Davis after a 1999 police drug raid ended in the highly controversial shooting death of her 25-year-old son, Troy.

Yet for years, Courtney's highly specialized craft was virtually unknown to the general public. That, however, was before the entertainment world got wind of the drama and dedication associated with the art of forensic investigation and bumped its practitioners above world-weary detectives and two-fisted private eyes onto the prime time marquee.

*　*　*

Channel surf on any evening, and you'll find them in fiction and fact, from the popular network dramas *CSI* and *Crossing Jordan* to cable channel documentaries like *Forensic Files*. Check the best seller list and there's novelist Patricia Cornwell's medical examiner protagonist Dr. Kay Scarpetta solving yet another crime that baffled even the most experienced police detectives.

Forensic investigation and those involved in its often grizzly practice have so fascinated today's society that the American Academy of Forensic Scientists is being flooded with queries from those interested in entering the profession. "There is no question that television has romanticized forensics," Phoenix's Susan Narveson, president of the American Society of Crime Lab Directors, recently told *Time*. Currently, there is a waiting list for the 60-student University of Texas-Arlington class on the subject taught each semester by Tarrant County pathologist Patricia Eddings.

In fact, on university campuses nationwide, a growing number of students are leaning toward the crime-fighting science. At the University of Central Florida, just a stone's throw from where scenes for *CSI: Miami* are filmed, 650 students are currently enrolled in the school's forensic science program.

Dr. Barry Fookes, who oversees the forensics department at Central Florida, estimates that as many as 7,000 undergraduate and post-graduate students are now enrolled in forensic science studies nationwide, double the number of five years ago. "Recently," he says, "I've had calls from the University of Texas at El Paso and the University of Windsor in Ontario, Canada, expressing interest in beginning forensic programs." Already, Texas Wesleyan University in Fort Worth has added forensic science to its curriculum.

"There's no question," Fookes says, "that there has been a new interest generated by the successful television programs. Which is fine. On the other hand, we make our students aware that what they'll be dealing with here is a hard-nosed science, not glamorous fantasy.

"At the same time, I want them to know it is a fascinating pursuit. I tell them that it is a little like going to the library, finding a good murder mystery and reading only the last page. What their job as a forensic scientist becomes is to determine what the plot was."

While it was once primarily Florida residents working toward Bachelor degrees in forensic science or a Masters in DNA analysis at Central Florida, students are now arriving in large numbers from out-of-state, Dr. Fookes notes. "Eighty-five percent of our graduates are currently working in the forensic profession," he adds.

One, he points out, is Emily Dawson, a drug analyst who did her internship in Max Courtney's Texas lab.

Now working for the National Forensic Science Technical Center in Largo, Florida, Dawson applied to Courtney's lab in 2000 because of its reputation. "I learned a great deal while I was there," she says. "The most remarkable thing about Max is the fact he is so well versed in virtually all of the forensic disciplines.

"When I first decided this was a career I wanted to pursue," she adds, "the field wasn't really that big. Here in Florida, at least, it has really grown." In part, she acknowledges, because of the glamour treatment it's recently received.

The Orlando Sentinel recently reported that a half dozen high schools in Orange County, Florida, have added forensic study to their curriculums. At West Orange High in Winter Garden, 65 students now attend two forensic science classes, and a third will soon be added to meet the growing interest.

Closer to home, at Arlington's The Oakridge School, science instructor Lori Lane has included forensic science for the 65 students enrolled in her middle school biology classes for the past six years. And last year, she began a popular crime scene course in the prep school's summer enrichment program.

"The kids love it," Lane says. "And, she adds, the recent successes of the aforementioned TV shows has created a new level of enthusiasm and a steady stream of questions from her students. "I've made it clear to them that crimes aren't generally solved so quickly and by so few people," she says. "What I've tried to give them is a real world look at what forensic investigation is about. We deal with everything from latent fingerprint analysis to grid-searching a crime scene to identify the race and sex of skeletal remains.

"What I'm trying to do is help to improve their skills at critical thinking and problem solving."

An intern under Eddings at the Tarrant County M.E.' s office for two years, Lane found the work fascinating but the openings for certified, full-time positions scarce. "Another thing I point out is that it is a difficult field to break into," she says.

Still, applications for internships offered by the Fort Worth-based Forensic Consultant Services have increased dramatically, now arriving from as far away as Iowa and South Carolina. "The first thing I tell them," says owner and lab director Courtney, "is that it isn't like what they've seen on TV."

Truthfully, he admits, he's never watched any of the popular shows. But he's heard stories about them. In real life, he insists, the work he and his team of experienced scientists do is more tedium than thrill, more frustration than fancy.

* * *

Nothing on the exterior of the long-abandoned old brick mortuary located in Fort Worth's Hospital District signals a welcome to visitors or suggests the manner of work that goes on inside. Only the steady stream of law enforcement officers who appear at the always-locked front door, bringing with them bags of evidence for analysis or picking up reports needed to make their cases, provides a sign that it's the headquarters of the only privately owned forensic laboratory in the state.

Inside, Courtney, 57, puffs on his ever-present pipe, filling his cluttered office with the sweet smell of Sir Walter Raleigh as he begins another day of gathering and interpreting evidence that will ultimately help determine the guilt or innocence of those accused of crimes ranging from murder to drunk driving—without cameras rolling or scripts to follow. Only on those days when he is scheduled to appear in court as an expert witness does he bother with a suit and tie. Most often, he's comfortable dressed in jeans and a sport shirt.

He and his staff work amidst an assortment of microscopes and computers, ballistic testing equipment, scales, high-tech cameras, and bulging filing cabinets in search of information that will speed the legal process in jurisdictions throughout North Texas. Currently, Forensic Consultant Services does lab work, aids in crime scene investigations, and conducts teaching seminars for dozens of neighboring departments (Arlington, Grand Prairie, Burleson, Mansfield, Cleburne, Hurst, North Richland Hills, etc.). As its reputation has grown, calls have come from as far away as Florida, Louisana, Kentucky, Arizona, Colorado, and California.

When the Fort Worth Police Department's drug lab was recently shut down for a three-month renovation, the investigation process didn't skip a beat. The department simply contracted FCS to do its testing.

Yet, here, solutions are not neatly reached in a quick, one hour crime-to-capture story line.

Sitting beneath a framed quotation from Edgar Allan Poe's "The Murders in the Rue Morgue"—"It is not our part, as reasoners, to reject it on account of apparent impossibilities. It is only left for us to prove that these apparent 'impossibilities' are, in reality, not such..."—Courtney explains the philosophy that drives his profession. "Our client," he says, "is not the prosecutor or the defense attorney, not the accused or the victim. Our client is science and the truth it provides.

"Guilty is a word invented by lawyers, and I've never seen it as my job to help sway a judge or jury. My mother always told me there were two sides to every story, and as a scientist, I'm duty bound to examine all the evidence brought to my attention and evaluate it as honestly as I can." It has, he says, been the philosophy of FCS since it began in a small building in his backyard in the winter of 1984.

If his findings prove damaging to a scenario an attorney—for either the state or the defense—hopes to present, so be it.

"I've seen him talk himself out of a lot of jobs," says criminalist coworker Frank Shiller. "Max is a no-nonsense, call-it-as-he-sees-it kind of scientist. It is that approach which has, over the years, established his credibility and integrity."

"That he will sometimes appear as a defense witness and sometimes for the prosecution," says noted Fort Worth attorney Jack Strickland, "is a clear indication of his professionalism and reputation. Not only is he respected as a superb forensic expert, but one who is trusted by both sides."

In fact, for the usually easy-going Courtney, the abuse of forensic science—particularly by those to whom he refers as "40-hour wonders"—is one of the few things that prompts him to climb onto the soapbox. "A few years ago," he recalls, "I was in a courtroom and watched a police officer who had taken a few courses in ballistics and crime scene investigation testify that because of the angle of the entry wound to a victim, the fatal shot had to have come from someone who was five feet, nine and one-quarter inches tall." Not surprisingly, the accused had earlier been measured at that exact height. "Now, that's TV-type stuff," Courtney adds, "absolutely ludicrous." His tolerance of fools, false witnesses, and forensic guns-for-hire is nonexistent.

His disdain for shortcuts and speculation, legal mumbo-jumbo and courtroom theatrics has, over the years, become legendary. "People describe me as a criminalist, a forensic expert, a crime lab director," he says, "but in my own mind, I'm simply a scientist. That's my job, and I work hard not to forget it."

* * *

No TV show or mystery novel directed Max Courtney toward his profession. The choice came almost by accident.

Certainly it is a giant leap from his teenage days of high school football stardom and oil field roughnecking in West Texas, far removed from youthful plans to put a college degree in chemistry to use in the oil fields of his heartland.

Once a talented end for legendary schoolboy powerhouse Odessa Permian High, he earned an athletic scholarship to what was then called West Texas State University in the Panhandle community of Canyon. There, however, dreams of continued glories were cut short by a career-ending knee injury just six weeks into his freshman season. In that one painful moment, Courtney went from dedicated jock to full-time scholar, ultimately earning a Bachelor's then a Master's in chemistry. Then it was off to Texas Christian University to begin work on his Ph.D.

"Finally," he says, "I reached a point where I was tired of being in school and decided it was time to start looking for a job." While checking the *Fort Worth Star-Telegram* classified ads in 1970, he learned the Fort Worth Police Department was in the market for a chemist. Leaving academic pursuits to the future, he scheduled an appointment with Rolland Tullis, director of the FWPD crime lab, with no clue what the job he'd applied for entailed.

Over the next decade, Courtney became first-hand familiar with the seemingly endless links between science and criminal investigation. While detectives and uniformed officers worked in the spotlight, Courtney found comfort in the solitude of the laboratory where his growing expertise ranged from the analysis of drugs and blood to hair fibers, fingerprints, and ballistics. Aside from regular visits to crime scenes and occasional appearances on the witness stand, he conducted his work in the background, far removed from the public eye.

Then and now, that's the way he likes it.

Not until the academic muses again called out did Courtney begin contemplating a career move that would not only fill a growing need in the local law enforcement community but also allow him the opportunity to share a decade of accumulated forensic knowledge with others. In 1980, he moved from the police department's crime lab into a classroom at the University of Texas-Arlington where he taught aspiring criminal justice students. And, as time permitted, he served as a forensic consultant to several neighboring police agencies, joining them at crime scenes and lecturing at occasional weekend seminars on various investigative techniques.

"Joe Watson, the police chief in Hurst, was among those constantly complaining about the length of time it took to get evidence processed," Courtney recalls. Like most small agencies with neither budgets or manpower to conduct their own evidence processing, the Hurst Police Department was relegated to the frustrating take-a-number-and-wait process common at the only forensic labs available to them—the Fort Worth PD and the Department of Public Safety lab in Garland. "One day Joe off-handedly suggested that I open my own lab."

Soon, Courtney was assembling a small, experienced staff.

"For the first year," he admits, "we really struggled. I did a little consulting here, some testing there, but it took a while for word to get around that we could be of real benefit to the smaller law enforcement agencies that didn't have the luxury of their own crime labs."

Among the first to sign up Courtney and his FCS was Mansfield police chief Steve Noonkester. "Max had trained me in crime scene investigation when I was with the Fort Worth Police Department," he says, "and I knew that his work was flawless. I was 100% confident in his abilities, and it made a great deal of sense to me to be able to call on him with whatever forensic needs we might have."

Admitting that the last television cop show he watched was the sitcom *Barney Miller*, Noonkester suggests that you'll find no Hollywood glitz attached to the manner in which Courtney arrives at his results. "He has the knowledge, the skills, and the equipment necessary to find the truth. That's all he's interested in. And he goes about his work so methodically that it drives you crazy."

But, Noonkester quickly adds, the relationship has paid off on numerous occasions. And not only on crime scene investigations and drug testing.

In 1994, a Mansfield officer-in-training witnessed an automobile accident and became involved in a high-speed pursuit of the fleeing perpetrator. Ultimately, the driver stopped, jumped from his car, and squared off in a defensive stance that led the young officer to shoot and wound the man. In time, a civil lawsuit was filed against the city and the police department.

"There was no doubt in my mind or that of our city officials that the response of our officer had been justified," Noonkester says, "so we made preparation for a trial." And they hired Courtney to do a detailed recreation of the shooting. "He even went so far as to locate the man's car, which had been junked and the motor removed and sold, and had it re-built. He used every skill and every piece of equipment he had." By the time the case went to trial, Courtney and his staff had prepared a presentation that described the event in second-by-second detail.

The trial, Noonkester recalls, went on for months, yet it took the jury only 16 minutes to return a no-fault verdict. Courtney's examination of the case, he notes, is now used as a teaching tool in forensic classes throughout the nation.

Today, it seems, no case, criminal or civil, is resolved without benefit of some form of scientific evidence and expert testimony. Forensics, once a foreign word to the mainstream, is now an ingrained part of the judicial mix. Which is one of the reasons Courtney and his eclectic staff of fellow scientists now have their hands full.

Among the four full-time criminalists working alongside the lab director/owner are his former Fort Worth PD crime lab boss, Shiller, and Tom Ekis, a one-time Baptist missionary who developed a fascination for forensics, particularly fingerprint examination, while a UTA student of Courtney's. The combined crime lab experience of his staff, Courtney brags, adds up to well over a century. "Everyone we have," he says, "is a generalist, qualified to do everything from crime scene investigation to drug testing, classroom instruction to trace evidence examination."

And while drug analysis fills the majority of the FCS hours—the lab now averages almost 4,000 tests annually—it is those times when Courtney and his staff are called into the field to search homicide scenes for hair and fiber evidence, finger- or footprints or tire tracks, or to read the secrets hidden by blood spray patterns that cause the adrenalin to flow. And add to a collection of war stories that rival the best efforts of today's novelists and screenwriters.

"I probably shouldn't say it," Courtney says, "but there are times, after we've been working on drug cases day after day, when I find myself hoping the phone will ring and we'll be called to the scene of a homicide." It is there, he admits, that the real challenge awaits.

Such calls come at an average of forty times a year.

There was, for instance, the gruesome case of the exotic dancer who had been murdered by her live-in boyfriend who was stationed at Carswell Air Force Base. The airman, in fact, had called in a missing person report. Several days passed until the woman's body, severed into two parts, was found in a box in a rural area between Dallas and Fort Worth.

"On rare occasions," Courtney says, "you run into a situation where it looks as if the criminal has gone out of his way to help you. Not only did we find a complete set of fingerprints on the box—which is rare—but the box had been lined with old newspapers from the airman's home town." Presented with the overwhelming amount of evidence Courtney collected, the airman confessed.

Then there are the times when things aren't as they initially seem: "I was called to a home one night where, from all indications, a pretty forceful beating had resulted in a homicide. The victim lay on the floor with a pretty good gash on his head, and there was a considerable amount of blood all over the room. But there was nothing about the evidence—or lack of it— that made any sense. There was no sign of forced entry, no weapon, and the random pattern of blood was strange. While there were a few things out of place, there was no real sign of a struggle. We found no fingerprints in the house other than those belonging to the victim."

Still, all the tell-tale signs of a murder were present. Until Courtney completed his crime scene investigation and compared notes with the medical examiner who conducted the autopsy. The deceased, it turned out, suffered a seizure, during which he had fallen, causing the laceration to his head. Then, during a convulsive state, he had scattered his own blood throughout the room before dying.

Case closed. Death by natural causes.

The approach to each suspected homicide investigation follows the same carefully rehearsed pattern. When contacted by law enforcement officials, Courtney asks the location of the scene—whether it's indoors or out—and if it's been determined whether death was the result of a gunshot, stabbing, or some still unknown manner. It is such information that will determine whether he needs trajectory lasers (to determine the angle of the bullet entry), luminol (for detecting blood), strobe lights (to illuminate an outdoor crime scene), etc. Additionally, there will be such standard equipment as cameras and fingerprinting kits.

"The proper equipment," he says, "is essential. But to successfully accomplish what needs to be done still depends on people. You can take every forensic bell and whistle that money can buy and let me have someone like [coworker] Frank Shiller, and I'll come out ahead every time.".

Courtney has completed crime scene investigations in as little as two or three hours; some have taken as long as two days.

Upon arrival, he and his staff talk with investigators to learn what they might already know about the crime and request a walk-through of the scene. Then they begin photographing the body and the locale where the crime occurred. "One of the things we have to do as quickly as possible," Courtney explains, "is clear a path to the body, marking or collecting any evidence we might find, so the medical examiner can do his work. Once we've secured any evidence that might be available and outlined the location of the body, we begin our search."

That's the hard part, he says. For instance, if a crime occurred in a house, it's necessary to make a room-to-room search, looking for anything from spent cartridges to blood stains to financial records that might suggest a motive. Then comes the tedious fingerprint and luminol processing. Throughout the investigation, Courtney stays in contact with law enforcement officers assigned to the case.

He recalls one occasion when such communication resulted in the murderer's arrest even before crime scene processing was complete. "While we were working," he remembers, "a call came from a credit card company to the victim's answering machine, asking about a questionable charge that had been attempted. We began looking around, found the card number in some papers, and passed it along to the investigating officers.

"They made a call to the card company and learned that someone had tried to use it in Vicksburg, Mississippi. We were still gathering evidence when the killer was arrested and the murder weapon was found in his car."

Though keenly aware of the anguish that results from criminal behavior, Courtney has learned over the years to detach himself from the violence he investigates. It's a lesson he lives by. Most of the time.

In the early '90s, the decomposing bodies of a Haltom City woman and her five-year-old daughter, beaten to death during the Christmas holidays, were found in a closet that had been nailed shut. In truth, it wasn't a difficult crime to solve; the husband and father left a note admitting to the murders.

"But I know that one really got to Max," says his wife Ginger, who serves as business manager of FCS. "The cases that involve children and young people always do."

* * *

"What Max Courtney tells you," says Texas Ranger Turner, "you can take to the bank. I've yet to meet anyone in law enforcement who doesn't trust him completely. He played a very important role in solving that Grandview case back in '93."

It's a fact not lost on Melody Smith, victim Jennifer Waltson's mother. "There's no way I'll ever be able to repay him for all the work he did on the case," she says. "I remember him coming up to me during the trial and introducing himself, telling me that he knew it was hard for me but that things were going to get better, to be strong.

"Listening to him testify about what had happened to my daughter and Sandi was one of the most difficult things I've ever had to do," she says, "but at the same time I appreciated every word he said because I knew he was telling the jury what it needed to know."

Now, a decade later, it's not the gruesome details of the testimony that stick in Smith's memory. Rather, it's an exchange between Courtney and the attorney defending the man who murdered her daughter. "He [the defense lawyer] was asking Mr. Courtney how many hours he had put in on the case and how much he had been paid by the prosecution.

"The amount of time he'd spent on the case was incredible, hundreds of hours. But he quickly said that he would not be charging the county for the full amount of time. The defense attorney seemed taken aback and asked why.

"Mr. Courtney told him that he didn't think Johnson County could afford such a bill. Then he said, 'A lot of what I've done is simply because those girls and their families deserve it.'"

Which is to say that something more than a fascination with science drives Max Courtney. "I love what I do. I like the idea of coming to work everyday, never knowing what it will bring," he says. "There's a need for what I do, and, frankly, I feel I'm good at it. That said, I'm still learning." And maintaining a keen perspective toward the dark and often sleepless nature of his profession.

"I called him recently," says Smith, "just to let him again know how much I appreciate what he did for my daughter. I know he's busy, and I felt a little guilty for taking his time. But he said he was glad I had called. He told me that it helped to remind him of the reason he does what he does."

It was a response neither scripted nor rehearsed.

◆*Dallas Observer*, March 2002

The Thirteenth Juror

On a day in November, 2003, the nation's trial junkies, having followed the strange and gruesome murder tale of New York multi-millionaire Robert Durst, shook their heads in collective disbelief. Here was a man who freely admitted he'd shot and killed his elderly Galveston neighbor Morris Black then chopped the body of the 71- year-old, ill, retired seaman into pieces, placed them in plastic bags, dumped them into Galveston Bay, and fled. Add to the gory details the fact that, while the victim's torso, legs, and arms eventually surfaced, discovered by a father and son fishing, Black's head was never found.

The dark and disturbing case had all the signs of a prosecutorial slam-dunk.

Heir to a real estate fortune, Durst's behavior even prior to the crime had been bizarre enough to expect his high profile attorney, Houston's Dick DeGuerin, to opt for some kind of insanity defense. Having earlier disappeared from New York, Durst lived in the San Francisco area for several years, then in Dallas for a time, never working, but instead passing himself off as everything from a writer to a botanist to anyone who inquired. After renting the modest Galveston apartment, he shaved his head and eyebrows, looking more homeless than wealthy, and donned a wig, makeup, and frumpy dresses to pose as a mute woman named Dorothy. Since the 1982 disappearance of his young socialite wife, he'd been under strong suspicion of having murdered her and disposing of her body. New York authorities, however, were never able to gather enough evidence for an arrest.

Finally, while on the run following Black's death, Durst was arrested outside a deli in Bath, Pennsylvania. The man worth millions had shoplifted a $5 chicken salad sandwich. No wonder the media began referring to him as a madman.

Yet late last year, during the August-to-November trial, Durst took the stand and quietly insisted he'd acted in self-defense and mutilated and disposed of Black's body in a state of blackout panic. After 32 hours of deliberation, the jury acquitted the 60-year-old defendant of the horror story crime. Not guilty. DeGuerin and his staff had clearly earned the $1.1

million Durst reportedly paid for their services.

But how—with all the gruesome details and Durst's own testimony—could the eight women and four men in the jury box have reached such a stunning verdict?

Sitting in his Lewisville office, 47-year-old jury selection expert Robert Hirschhorn, one of the behind-the-scene members of DeGuerin's team, offers a too-simple explanation: "We lowered the jury's expectations of our client."

In truth, they did much more. Long before the actual trial took place, Hirschhorn orchestrated months of focus groups, surveys, and mock trials in an effort to determine the best possible way to mount Durst's defense. "We knew," Hirschhorn admits, "that we had an uphill battle, not only because of what had occurred following the murder but the well-publicized behavior of our client even before the crime occurred. "

It became obvious early on that it would be necessary to have a jury that could focus its attention on the day when Durst said he and the victim struggled over a .22 pistol during a heated argument. Durst, the defense would have to stress, was being tried only for murder, not cross-dressing, not strange behavior, not even mutilating a body.

And it would also be important to have a jury that could get past any preconceived idea that a person with the financial and educational pedigree of their client had to be a smooth and polished public speaker. "The truth was, Bob Durst had very poor communication skills, could not make eye contact when talking with anyone, would often lose his train of thought in mid-sentence, and," says Hirschhorn, "suffered from Asperger's Syndrome [a neurological condition associated with a high functioning level of autism]."

Add an admitted drinking and drug problem to the mix, and members of the jury would be served a profile of a defendant whose life had been a colossal mess long before he took the stand.

Regarded as one of the premier practitioners of a craft part legal, part psychological, and—by his own admission—more than a little speculative and luck-based, Hirschhorn did in the Durst case what he's been doing in high profile, high dollar criminal and civil cases since 1984. Not only does he assist attorneys in selecting those who will sit in judgment. He conducts focus groups and voir dire workshops, oversees pre-trial polling, puts on mock trials, and organizes "shadow juries" that, in effect, provide lawyers with an indication of how their case is going even as the trial is underway.

Name a celebrated case today, and odds are both the defense and the prosecution will have hired experts to assist in picking the jury. And it is not unusual for one of those to be the bearded, boot-wearing former defense attorney. Just check his resume. Hirschhorn helped select the juries that acquitted U.S. Senator Kay Bailey Hutchinson of ethics violations and found William Kennedy Smith not guilty of date-raping a Jupiter, Florida, woman. When Terry Nichols was tried for his participation in the bombing of the Oklahoma City Federal Building, Hirschhorn helped pick the jury that acquitted him of all murder charges. He successfully championed members of the Waco-based Branch Davidians who were tried for the deaths of ATF raiders on that infamous day at Mt. Carmel. Yet his efforts are not confined to the defense side of the courtroom. He aided the government in selection of the jury that found Arkansas governor Jim Guy Tucker guilty in the Whitewater fraud and conspiracy case. Nor, it should be noted, does he bat 1.000. A jury he helped pick for the defense quickly found accused Houston murderer Clara Harris, charged with repeatedly running over her husband with her car, guilty.

Yet, having aided the defense in over 20 capital murder cases during his two decade career, Hirschhorn, an outspoken opponent of the death penalty, points cautiously to the fact no client he's worked for has received the ultimate punishment. "I live in fear that someone will be sentenced to die on my watch," he admits, "and work very hard to see that it never happens."

It is that degree of dedication and a steadily growing list of successes that have caused his business to flourish to such a degree that he now spends an average of 150 days a year on the road, in courtrooms, in attorneys' offices, and at speaker's lecterns from coast to coast. His four-person firm averages working on 150 cases a year. Hirschhorn himself handles 50 to 60.

And, clearly, he's among those who have made believers of lawyers who once viewed what he does as little more than voodoo psycho-babble guesswork.

"I came up in the old school," admits DeGuerin. A protege of legendary Houston attorney, Percy Foreman, he had his doubts about the true "expertise" of those in Hirschhorn's field. "I remember a client of Foreman's," DeGuerin recalls, "who once asked him if he thought they should hire a jury expert to help in preparing for her trial. Percy just huffed. 'Little lady,' he said, 'I'm the jury selection expert around here.'"

It was, DeGuerin says, an attitude he, too, firmly embraced until he decided to hire Hirschhorn to help in preparation of Senator Hutchison's 1994 trial. "The state had its own expert," DeGuerin remembers, "so I felt we should have one, too. And we absolutely blew them away during jury selection." So much so, the attorney recalls, that it was the reason prosecutors suddenly opted to abandon the case, forcing the judge to order an acquittal. "I was impressed with Robert's insight and techniques,"

DeGuerin says. "He made me a believer."

* * *

Hirschhorn came to his profession via a serendipitous route. A newly-licensed defense lawyer working in a San Antonio firm in the early '80s, he was approached by a client whose case seemed impossible to win. "He was charged with armed robbery," Hirschhorn recalls, "and there were several eyewitnesses to the crime. He'd been arrested less than 100 yards from where the holdup had taken place and was still carrying the gun he'd used. After hearing the facts, I saw absolutely no way to successfully defend the guy. So I reverted to an old lawyer's trick that I felt would get me off the hook."

He quoted the potential client an astronomical fee. "But the guy didn't even blink. He just asked who to make the check out to," Hirschhorn remembers. "As soon as he left the office, I went to my boss and asked him what I should do. He laughed and said for me to pray that the guy's check would bounce. 'If it doesn't,' he told me, 'call Cathy Bennett and hire her to help you.'"

The inexperienced 24-year-old Hirschhorn had to ask who Cathy Bennett was. That despite the fact she'd recently been featured on television's *60 Minutes* after helping select the jury that acquitted maverick car manufacturer John DeLorian, who had been charged in federal court with attempting to broker a $24 million cocaine deal to save his struggling company. Despite viewing a hotel room video of the deal being made, jurors had not been convinced of his guilt, and DeLorian walked from the courtroom a free man.

What Hirschhorn quickly learned was that Bennett, a former Houston-based legal aid with an uncanny knack for reading the responses of both judges and juries, was considered a pioneer in the field of jury selection.

Bottom line: the jury Bennett helped select in the case of the accused robber eventually came back with a not-guilty verdict. "I was absolutely amazed by what she had done," Hirschhorn says. "As soon as the trial ended, I told her I wanted to work for her, to have her teach me how she did what she did. For the next two years I carried her briefcase, watched, and listened. I literally enrolled myself in Cathy Bennett University."

By 1985, he was not only at her side in the courtrooms but had also persuaded her to marry him. Today, despite the fact she died of breast cancer seven years later, the firm Hirschhorn oversees still carries the name Cathy E. Bennett & Associates and adheres to her vision. "One of the reasons I do this," Hirschhorn says, "is to keep her message and her spirit alive."

Even as his late wife's health deteriorated, he recalls, she continued to work alongside her still-learning husband. "I've never known anyone with the energy Cat had," he says while seated in his small office on the second floor of a Lewisville bank. Since the 1991 William Kennedy Smith case was the last they worked together before his wife died, it remains the victory Hirschhorn ranks above all others.

"At that time, we were just trying to make a go of the firm, hoping to make a living," he recalls, "and Roy Black [the famed Palm Beach attorney representing Smith] phoned to say he was interviewing jury consultants.

"Cat hadn't made it known that she had cancer and was taking chemotherapy treatments, but she was actually doing very little work by then. When Black suggested we come to Florida and visit, Cat instead said she'd prefer it if Smith came to Texas—alone—for a few days. For the entire time he was here, she grilled him unmercifully. Then, after he left, she phoned Black and said, 'Your guy's innocent—and I want to help him.'

"It was remarkable that she was able to do what she did," Hirschhorn says. "Despite the fact she was having to spend most of her time in bed or at the hospital having blood transfusions, she missed being in court only one morning in the month it took to select the jury."

And as he and his wife helped to whittle down the list of 450 prospective jurors, Hirschhorn recalls, a strong bond developed between Cathy and their high profile client. "We were staying at the Kennedy compound, meeting Senator [Edward] Kennedy, Sergeant Shriver, John Kennedy, Eunice, and other members of the family," he says, "but Cat was too ill to really enjoy any of it. Yet, when we'd have to go to the hospital for her transfusions, Will would always go with us, just to sit with her. When there was a break in the trial for the Thanksgiving holiday, he flew her to [Washington, D.C.'s] American University to look into an experimental treatment program he thought might help."

Just six months before her death at age 42, the last jury she ever helped to select deliberated for only an hour and 17 minutes before finding William Kennedy Smith not guilty. "I'll forever be grateful," says Hirschhorn, "that she lived long enough to hear that verdict."

* * *

It is unlikely that even the optimistic Cathy Bennett-Hirschhorn could have predicted the growth of the firm that bears her name or the latter day strides taken in trial preparation and jury selection nationwide. When she began in 1972, she knew of only two others in her field. Today, her former husband estimates, as many as 1,500 jury selection experts are available to lawyers and clients with pockets deep enough to pay the price.

Hiring a jury selection expert isn't for the financially faint of heart. Consider the consulting services fees that appear on the Cathy Bennett & Associates website: Jury selection, $7,500 per day; 20-person mock trial, $12,000 for one day, $24,000 for two; focus groups, $12,000-$18,000; survey of a potential jury pool, $15,000-$50,000; shadow jury, $1,500-$3,000 per day; witness preparation, $450 per hour.

Hirschhorn, who is quick to note he doesn't always demand such astronomical fees (last year alone, he spent three months on four cases that didn't even cover expenses), makes no apologies for the prices quoted on his website. "Cat's vision was that it would be the firm's role to help those who needed our kind of expertise. If they were wealthy and could afford it, we charged the full boat. If not, we negotiated something they could deal with. That's the way we still work."

For a time, he admits, it appeared the firm's 2003 earnings would dip considerably. But then came the call to join the team preparing Durst's defense. "That," he says, "filled the chest back up."

Fees aside, there's always plenty of work. When he began consulting, Hirschhorn notes, he might see a fellow consultant on the other side of the courtroom once every twenty or so cases. "Now, it's one out of every two. With stakes as high as they are in today's courtrooms, lawyers—defense and prosecution—are not going to leave anything to chance."

Today, Hirschhorn has no qualms about lending help to the competition, conducting seminars and providing instructional tips on his well-visited website. "There's room for everyone," he says. "The legal community has given so much to me that I want to give something back. And the better everyone is at his or her job, the better the system is going to work."

* * *

What, then, are the tools of a jury selection expert, aside from the nebulous "insight" DeGuerin alludes to? Hirschhorn lifts four fingers. "It's 50% common sense, 30% intuition, 10% knowledge…" And then he smiles. "And 10% damn good luck."

DeGuerin adds a fifth to the list of intangibles: "Robert," he says, "is a very touchy-feely kind of person who is able to quickly gain the confidence of a client." When Hirschhorn first met Senator Hutchison, for instance, he bypassed the formal handshake politicians usually use and embraced her. When Durst all but refused to cooperate in his own defense during trial preparation, Hirschhorn broke the ice. "We were talking one day, and all he would do was stare down at the floor," he recalls. "I told him to stand up, then walked over and hugged him. Tears welled in his eyes, as if it was the first time anyone had ever done anything like that." Thereafter, Durst's attitude improved markedly.

"Part of my job," Hirschhorn admits, "is to love the unlovable, to find the good in a person."

Too, he must make quick judgments of people and their capacity for fairness. "You're not always looking for the person with a lot of academic initials after their name," he says, "but you want them to be smart, to be willing to think, and to be able to somehow relate to the case." Members of the Durst jury, for instance, ranged from a high-ranking Halliburton official who had only a high school education to a woman whose brother-in-law had once been involved in a similarly bizarre situation: he had been out riding around with several friends late one night before passing out. The following morning, he woke to find a dead girl seated next to him in his van and—though he hadn't killed her—panicked and hid the body.

At times, it hasn't been easy to convince those who hire him that he knows what he's doing.

When he agreed to help two of his former San Antonio St. Mary's Law School professors in the prosecution of Arkansas governor Tucker, he faced one of his greatest challenges. Among the jury pool for the closely watched case was a young woman who arrived at the Little Rock federal courthouse dressed in full *Star Trek* regalia, including two plastic phasers, which she had to hand over to security. But after hearing her responses to the lawyers' questions, Hirschhorn said, "I like her."

The attorneys rolled their eyes and suggested an immediate meeting with special prosecutor Ken Starr, who was overseeing the case. "My argument," remembers Hirschhorn, "was that if she was seated on the jury, she would be willing to hear our side of the case. On the other hand, there was a good likelihood she would do something that would get her tossed out, thus saving us a precious peremptory strike." Starr finally agreed, and two days later the young Trekkie was dismissed after violating the judge's order by giving an interview to a local newspaper reporter.

"Robert is far and away the best jury selection consultant in the business," says Ft. Worth criminal defense attorney Jeff Kearney. "There is no second place. Not only does he provide you with great insight into people, but his advice—like urging lawyers not to talk like lawyers when they're addressing a jury—has been invaluable." Kearney, who has been seeking Hirschhorn's help for over a decade, points out that he's never lost a case in which the celebrated expert helped select the jury.

There are, Hirschhorn notes, times when pure luck plays its role. Working for lawyers representing Wal-Mart in a case in which a customer claimed a stack of ironing boards fell on her, causing severe brain damage, he repeatedly argued that the only logical defense was that the plaintiff was simply faking her injury. The lawyers begrudgingly agreed, despite the fact that, throughout the trial the woman sat drooling and making only occasional grunting noises. "Needless to say, the people I was working for were pretty nervous. One them, in fact, told me that if the jury came back with a $100 million verdict, he would personally strangle me."

But, during a lunch recess when the courthouse was all but empty, the allegedly injured woman and her husband stood in the hallway just outside the women's restroom. There, they began to heatedly discuss whether to accept a settlement or wait to hear the jury's verdict. As they argued, neither was aware a member of the jury was in the restroom and could overhear their discussion. "They [the jury] came back with a complete defense verdict," Hirschhorn recalls. "For which I could take very little credit."

* * *

While devoted to what he calls "the best job in the world," Hirschhorn insists he is not the workaholic his schedule suggests. Now remarried— to Angela, a former nurse and friend of his first wife—he points in the direction of a photograph that sits atop a bookshelf in the comer of his office. There, smiling, are the images of his ten-year-old son Troy ("He's named after former Cowboys quarterback Troy Aikman.") and six-year-old daughter Micki ("She's named after my favorite baseball player, Mickey Mantle.").

"There was a time, after Cat's death, when I never felt an urgency to get home," he admits. "I'd just hang out with the lawyers, watch the trial, maybe even do a little sightseeing for a day or two. But, no more."

On the day New York's World Trade Center buildings collapsed after the infamous 9/11 terrorist attack, Hirschhorn was in Brownsville, Texas, helping to pick yet another jury. "All the planes were grounded, of course," he says, "so I immediately rented a car and began driving. For twelve hours, all I could think about was getting home to hug my family and make them aware I would do everything in my power to protect them."

In a sense, then, the professional and personal life of Robert Hirschhorn today are really not that different.

◆*Texas, Houston Chronicle Sunday Magazine*, February 2004

On the Border

Young and nervous, Rogelio Sanchez Brito had driven his red Ford pickup southward, arriving at the Millenium Hotel in the Mexican border town of Ojinaga, where he turned it over to a man he'd never seen. Brito waited at the hotel for two days, then his truck was returned, loaded with 300 pounds of marijuana hidden in its tires and beneath the floorboards in tape-wrapped bundles. For his first attempt at smuggling drugs and delivering them to a dealer in Odessa, Texas, he was to earn $4,000. Had it not been for a drug-sniffing dog named Rufus, he might have made it. Instead, he sits in the Brewster County Jail, awaiting arraignment.

It's one of those starlit summer evenings in the Texas TransPecos when sweet breezes quickly cool the desert, and residents of this vast and stark Texas landscape are enjoying their simple pleasures. In Alpine, locals are gathering at the Front Street book store, awaiting a slideshow presentation by celebrated photographer James Evans, while over in tiny Marathon, vacationers sit in oversized rocking chairs on the porch of the historic Gage Hotel, enjoying a quiet unknown in the urban rat-race from which they've briefly escaped. An hour's drive to the east on Highway 90, people peer through telescopes toward the darkened mountain range where the mysterious Marfa Lights do their nightly dance. And down in the picturesque Big Bend National Park, campers young and old sit around their campfires, planning the next day's adventure. Ranchers who tend spreads that often exceed 200,000 acres are already sleeping, one hard day's work ended and another soon to arrive.

The region is peaceful, pastoral, and isolated. The nearest Wal-Mart is 80 miles away in Fort Stockton, the closest shopping mall a three-hour drive to Odessa.

To the immediate south, however, hidden in the darkness, another world, dangerous and deadly, thrives. Along the Rio Grande, which marks the winding border that separates the United States and Mexico, smugglers of drugs and illegal aliens go about their endless work. On this night alone, Border Patrol and Drug Enforcement Agency officials will make six drug seizures and arrest 42 undocumented aliens. They will confiscate 1,340 pounds of marijuana, two and a half pounds of cocaine, and one loaded pistol. A few miles away, fellow agents will stop four alien "backpackers"— smugglers who walk drugs across the river and into Texas—but they will disappear into the rugged foothills and avoid capture. They will, however, leave 400 pounds of marijuana behind. Meanwhile, at a checkpoint near Presidio, twelve other drug smugglers are being taken into custody.

On the border, away from the soft city lights and serene lifestyle, it is dirty business as usual.

A few nights earlier, agents stopped a suspicious-looking moving van just west of Pecos and, after removing a wall of furniture stacked in the rear, found 19 illegal aliens—men, women, and several children—who were to be delivered to a "stash house" drop-off in Dallas. In the truck, agents found just two gallons of water for the two-day trip.

And despite the collective efforts of the region's law enforcement— Border Patrol, Customs, DEA, U.S. Marshals, Park Rangers, sheriffs, and police departments—the illegal flow continues along the 420 miles of border they watch over. "We aren't stopping it," says Brewster County sheriff Ronny Dodson. "On the best of days, we might just slow it down a little. If someone tries to tell you the situation is getting better, he's blowing smoke. Actually, most of what we catch is by accident." It's an understandable statement when one considers Dodson and his six deputies patrol the state's largest county. Stretching across 6,128 square miles, it is larger than the state of New Hampshire.

The official assignment of DEA agents stationed in the region is to "disrupt and dismantle." Even at their best, they can only disrupt. The other part of their marching order seems impossible. There's simply too much money, too many smugglers, and too much geography involved.

At the federal courthouse in Pecos, the Western District docket is so crammed that calls have gone out to visiting judges from as far away as New York, Vermont, and Mississippi to help keep the judicial system from being completely overwhelmed. The 90-bed Pecos jail stays filled to capacity while detention hearings, arraignments, indictments, jury trials, and plea bargains drone endlessly in nearby courtrooms. "I was on the bench there for eight years," says U.S. District Judge Royal Furgeson, who now presides in San Antonio, "and by the time I was ready to leave, I thought I'd put everyone in the world in jail. Truth is, I hardly made a dent."

Records for the past three years indicate no fewer than 500 criminal cases—the majority of them smuggling-related—are filed in Pecos annually. In one of the most sparsely populated areas in the state.

This sprawling and barren region, understand, is different from the high traffic drug routes that lead to El Paso or Laredo, through which trailer truck-loads of drugs and aliens are being smuggled. In the desolate six-county desert that stretches from east of El Paso to Del Rio, smaller cargos flow with remarkable—and, for authorities, frustrating—ease.

"The fact that arrest and seizure statistics are down slightly in some areas," admits Marfa Sector Border Patrol spokesman William Brooks, "might—and I emphasize the word 'might'—mean we've slowed the traffic." Or, he admits, it could mean that the approximately 200 agents working out of his office are simply being skirted by the inventive new ways smugglers slip their illegal wares into his jurisdiction.

Most recent statistics show that in the fiscal year of 2002, Border Patrol agents headquartered in Marfa alone seized 84,595 pounds of marijuana and 295 pounds of cocaine and apprehended 11,374 aliens. While cocaine seizures and alien arrests are down slightly from previous years, smuggling of the high-grade marijuana grown in central Mexico has reached a record high.

So frequent are the drug busts in his circulation area, says Marfa's Robert Halpern, editor of the weekly *Big Bend Sentinal*, that not all are reported in his paper. "The joke here in the office," he says, "is if they seize only fifty pounds [of marijuana] we considered it to be 'for personal use' of the guy arrested."

On a more serious note, he admits the cases his paper has reported on quickly become a blur. "They got 2,000 pounds on one stop a few weeks ago," he says, "and that got my attention. But next week, or the week after, they'll catch someone with 3,000, 5,000. And on and on it will go."

What troubles Halpern is the fact a few local youngsters have recently become involved in trafficking. "It's sad," he says, "but they've decided to become big-time smugglers and are winding up in jail, their lives ruined. All to make a quick, easy dollar."

The big bucks, acknowledges Larry Leon, the resident DEA agent headquartered in Alpine, are in the trafficking of marijuana. "The profit margin is incredible. On the other side of the border, the going rate is $100 a pound. In Dallas, the sale price is $600-$650. Farther north, in Chicago and New York, it goes up to $800-$900."

That's not to say the smuggling trade in heroin, cocaine, and amphetamines has waned. "Actually, the other drugs are easier to get across because they're not as bulky. A pound of heroin, for example, is no bigger than a baked potato. And cocaine and pills are much easier to hide. But the fact remains that the greatest profit margin is with marijuana. And profit is what drug smuggling is all about," Leon says.

Will his agency and the Border Patrol, more high profile than ever since Homeland Security became an everyday concern, ever get the upper hand on the matter? Not likely, everyone from officers in the field to jurists in the courtrooms candidly agree.

Alpine-based defense attorney Mike Barclay, who has lost track of the number of traffickers he's represented, echoes the disturbing litany. "The situation is not getting any better—and it isn't likely it ever will," he says.

"The technology the smugglers are using," says Leon, "continues to improve. And many of them seem to be getting smarter." Time was, he points out, when the drug dealers were comfortable with the high-risk of bringing in their contraband in large, truckload amounts. When, however, more and more checkpoints were established along the busiest highways, equipped with X-ray machines, drug-sniffing dogs, and well-trained lawmen, the smugglers began looking for alternate routes.

Among their favorites today is the mesquite and cacti region just south of the Alpine-Marfa-Presidio area.

* * *

They come, not in huge trucks, but in automobiles, pickups, and RVs, each transporting only 50-60 pounds of marijuana. "Basically, they're still trying to get the large amounts into the States," Leon explains, "but they feel their chances are better if they split it into smaller loads. The thinking now, in fact, is that there is a very good chance some of the vehicles they're sending up will be caught. But they're playing the odds, hoping they can make it through with six or eight out of ten or twelve loads."

Drugs are hidden in door panels, dashboards and headliners, false gas tanks, metal containers inserted into the tires, and the space where the passenger side airbag would normally be. Recently, a fake battery was found to be filled with Mexican black heroin (the real battery was mounted beneath the car). Cocaine is being found hidden in a motor's manifold since smugglers have learned that the engine heat will not melt or damage the drug. "I had one guy," says attorney Barclay, "tell of driving straight through from Chihuahua City [Mexico] to Wichita, Kansas with his manifold packed with coke. The only problem he had was the need to wait several hours for the engine to cool before he could make his delivery."

And now even law-abiding citizens have become unwitting accomplices. Mexican dealers will spot the parked vehicle of a vacationing family from Texas or New Mexico and wait until night to place a cargo of drugs into some hidden spot. That done, they take down the license plate number and do a computer check to determine the owner's home address. "An innocent-looking family isn't going to have much trouble getting back across the border," says Barclay. "They get home, park their RV in the driveway, and while they're sleeping, the dealers sneak up and retrieve the drug shipment."

More and more, he says, innocent victims are being lured into the trade. He tells of an independent Garland truck driver who responded to a *Dallas Morning News* classified ad last winter, seeking someone to haul a load of cattle from Presidio to Fort Worth. After calling to enquire about the job, he was informed a loaded trailer would be waiting for him. What he was not told was that, in addition to cattle, he would also be hauling over a ton of marijuana. Nor, supposedly, did he have any idea he would be stopped, arrested, and ultimately jailed.

Then there are the backpackers, young men familiar with the rugged terrain and willing to hike across the border with 50-100 pounds of marijuana. Often equipped with night vision goggles and two-way radios, they may travel 80-90 miles on foot before reaching their assigned drop-off point.

"Not only are they familiar with the region," says Sheriff Dodson, "but they're in constant contact with scouts on this side who alert them to where we [law enforcement] are. I can assure you that every time I pull out of the parking lot in front of my office and start driving south, someone is on a cell phone or walkie-talkie, letting the smugglers know."

Getting illegal aliens across is only a bit more difficult. In some cases, the trucks hauling them northward simply pull over a few miles before reaching a Border Patrol checkpoint, allowing them to walk through the desert and around the inspection station and be picked up a few miles beyond it. In other instances, they are picked up by all-terrain vehicles and driven through the darkened desert to a waiting truck.

"If," says Leon, "they can make it up to Interstate 20, they're pretty much home free. From there, they can go to New Mexico, Lubbock, or Dallas."

TransPecos law enforcement typically target the "mules" who transport the drugs and the "coyotes" who move human cargo from abject Mexico poverty to the promise of minimum wage jobs in the U.S. While the drug lords and slave traders wait safely on their ranches and in plush villas, counting their money, and the U.S. dealers ply their trade in hiding, the smugglers are the high risk-takers, often desperate and destitute men from the poverty stricken Mexican border towns.

They are the men 73-year-old Mike Barclay, called by many the "dean of West Texas trial lawyers," has come to know well.

* * *

He began his legal career in Dallas a half century ago and over the course of 30 years earned a reputation as one of the city's premier criminal defense lawyers. Thieves, murderers, and rapists were his stock-in-trade, and those in the judicial system viewed him as a gifted, learned, and always-prepared litigator. His good humor and courtroom theatrics served as an entertaining and legendary bonus.

Once, while cross-examining a witness who could not remember if his client was, in fact, missing an eye, Barclay removed his own prosthetic eye that he'd worn since 1947 and placed it on the witness stand. "If he looked like this," he said, pointing to his own vacant eye socket, "don't you think you would recall it?"

He was clearly devoted to his work, always quick with an amusing story to pass along to colleagues, a man to whom laughter came easily. Then, as the '80s approached, the plague that often befalls defense lawyers hit. Losing three consecutive court-appointed capital murder cases didn't help. "I finally realized I was burning out," he reflects, "and began looking for a way to escape everything—the violent crime, the Dallas traffic, the whole big city rat-race."

Years earlier, he'd begun the habit of vanishing into the Big Bend area for Christmas vacations and became enamored with the open spaces and slow pace of the region. By the time he made the decision to close down his Dallas practice and semi-retire, he'd decided that Alpine, with a population just shy of 6,000, would be his new home.

"My thinking at the time was that I'd keep my license and maybe help draw up a will or two now and then," he says as he sits in his small office behind the home he shares with artist wife Barbara. Originally the Alpine hospital, built in 1907, it was remodeled into a bed-and-breakfast during World War II. "Now," Barclay brags, "I'm the only lawyer in Alpine with 14 rooms and seven baths."

And a case load far greater than any he ever juggled in Dallas.

"I wasn't here long before I realized that the courts were literally inundated with cases of drug and alien trafficking." Soon, his phone began ringing non-stop, calls coming from weary judges asking that he take court appointments and an occasional client who could even afford to hire counsel for his own defense or that of a family member.

It didn't take long for the old flame to reignite. Today, Barclay spends much of his time making the 100-mile trek to the federal courthouse in Pecos, where, at times, he might have as many as a dozen cases on a single docket. The "rocket docket," they call it.

The phrase was born during the tenure of late U.S. District Judge Lucius Bunton. Because of the flood of cases arriving in his court, he made it clear to attorneys—defense and prosecution alike—that two witnesses were not to be called when one would do. His courtroom opened early and often didn't close until late into the night. While jurors might be excused for a quick lunch, lawyers were instructed to remain and eat the same sack lunch served to inmates at the nearby jail. "I soon got pretty good at making a motion with a bite of mystery meat sandwich in my mouth," Barclay says.

And that treadmill style of justice continues today. "It's the only way to keep your head above water," says Judge Furgeson, who replaced Bunton and adopted his practices. Barclay, he says, is one of the few who can keep up the pace and still do a good job defending his clients.

"He's a throwback to the lawyers of bygone days," Furgeson says. "For him, making certain our justice system works is more than a job; it's a calling. And over the years, he's reached a status where he probably gets away with more in court than he should. Prosecutors often defer to him and rarely object, he's friends with everyone in the courthouse and, most important, he commands great respect."

He's also resourceful. Several years ago, he was hired to represent a man from Philadelphia who had been caught smuggling a load of Chinese illegals through the Sierra Blanca crossing. "These people," he recalled, "had paid $38,000 apiece and had traveled from mainland China to Hong Kong, Korea, France, Tokyo, and Mexico City in hopes of finally making it to Phoenix. I badly wanted to hear their story." To do so, Barclay located the only Chinese national living in Brewster County—where census statistics show there are but 1.4 people per square mile.

Judge Furgeson says he has Barclay's voir dire questioning to potential jurors memorized: "He'll smile at everyone and then tell them how he moved out here years ago from Dallas. He'll say that after he'd been here a while he phoned his mother to tell her how friendly everyone in this part of the country was. He tells them she just laughed and said, 'Honey, they're not friendly; they're just lonesome…'"

More than once, Barclay has resorted to authoring his own poetry in an attempt to deflect a judge's anger over the fact a client has unexpectedly skipped a court date. Like the time defendant Hernando Felix-Yague (pronounced "yah-gee") failed to appear:

> *Hernando Felix-Yague*
> *Has a mind that's now become foggy.*
> *On a search for his person*
> *Pre-trial is still cursin'.*
> *But I just learned this day*
> *He's down Mexico way.*

"I can't tell you how many times I've thought I ought to cite him for contempt or at least reprimand him," says Furgeson, "but I knew if I opened my mouth I'd start laughing. "

* * *

Despite the free-spirit and levity Barclay brings to his work, it's obvious he's well-regarded by his peers. Fellow defense lawyers and an occasional prosecutor routinely come to him for advice. Even members of law enforcement begrudgingly applaud his encyclopedic knowledge of the law.

"He came out here," says Sheriff Dodson, "and taught us how to do our jobs." A member of the Alpine police force when he first became acquainted with Barclay, Dodson admits that the day-to-day details of such matters as showing just cause for a search warrant were often overlooked. "The first half dozen cases Mike defended were dismissed because he was able to easily show that law enforcement hadn't done everything by the book. Thanks to him, we learned quickly to dot the 'i's and cross the 't's."

Dodson, in fact, now laughs along when Barclay insists on retelling a story he heard about the sheriff shortly after settling in Alpine. Dodson, it seems, was sworn in as an Alpine PD patrolman almost a year before his 21st birthday. "He was issued a badge and a gun," Barclay says, "but, by law, he was too young to purchase ammunition. So for the first year of his law enforcement career, he had to take his wife with him down to Morrison's True Value so she could buy him bullets."

Little of what Barclay deals with, however, is a laughing matter. His clients range from frightened young men to older, more hardened criminals with nothing more than greed as motive for their crimes. Yet for the majority of those he defends, the veteran attorney feels a noticeable degree of sympathy.

"They're desperate," he says, "because they're hungry. Their families are hungry. They've reached a point where they'll do anything to improve their hopeless situations." And so they risk arrest for paltry sums. The going rate for a drug mule, Barclay says, is $100 per pound of marijuana they can successfully smuggle in. No up front payment, no promise of legal help if arrested, no knowledge of the English language, and no assurance against bodily harm.

The key link in the Mexico-to-U.S. drug chain, they are the most expendable and the most poorly compensated.

The same applies to the "coyote" who receives in the neighborhood of $150 per illegal alien he smuggles across the border; Mexican kingpins like Ruben Valdes (who recently received a 27-year prison sentence for practicing the illicit trade) earn $1,500 and more from each person jammed into the back of a trailer.

"More than once," Barclay points out, "I've seen cases where one of the mules, carrying, say, 50 pounds of marijuana, will be sent across when the people hiring him know he's going to be caught. He's just a decoy, there to divert attention from another mule close behind with 500 pounds."

Even the courts, he says, are generally prone to view his clients' crimes with some degree of leniency since it is not the endless reserve of downtrodden and defeated middlemen the authorities are really after. "The judges know that, in most instances, these people are just being used," DEA agent Leon acknowledges. "For the most part," he says, "these are sad people, down on their luck. They need money so badly they're willing to take the chance of going to jail for a long time." Law enforcement's primary interest in them, then, is any information they might provide about where the drugs they're smuggling originated and where and to whom they are to be delivered.

Rarely, however, do the mules know. "The dealers are smart enough not to expose themselves directly to the smuggler," Leon explains. "On both sides of the border, the transaction is filtered through several layers. "

The repeat offenders who smuggle dope and aliens, however, are a different matter. Having had a taste of the excitement and easy money, alluding capture has become a game. "Some," Barclay admits, "have become quite smart, very inventive." Others, he says, prove to be several cards shy of a full deck.

A recent Barclay client made it through the border checkpoint only to be stopped by a state trooper north of Alpine for a defective taillight on his truck. The frightened driver immediately jumped from the cab, his hands stretched into the air, and yelled out, "You've got me, don't shoot!" Stunned by the quick admission, the trooper investigated and found 750 pounds of marijuana and a drunken woman in the trailer the man was pulling.

Then there was the smuggler whose pickup engine began to heat after he'd reached the American side of the border. While the truck was pulled over to cool, an off-duty Border Patrol agent stopped to lend a hand. During casual conversation as they tinkered with the engine, the good samaritan asked what the driver was hauling. When the man boasted that he was taking a 1,400 pound load of marijuana to Dallas, the agent placed him under arrest.

Which is to say a lot of cases Barclay doesn't have much chance of winning. "But, what impresses me about him," says Judge Ferguson, "is the fact that once he's in the courtroom, there is no way to tell if his client is court-appointed or one who is able to pay for counsel. Mike works equally hard for them all."

When the compliment is passed along, Barclay only shrugs. "My role is that of any other defense attorney. If my client is innocent, I've got to do everything I can to prove it. If his arrest or the investigation wasn't conducted properly, I'm going to raise hell about it."

While he doesn't admit it, those young, ignorant, out-of-work men caught in their first, desperate smuggling attempts are who Barclay wishes most to help. After 45 years of practice, he holds to a belief that one illegal act does not make a person forever evil.

"These people's lives," he says, "are bad enough already."

* * *

The end of another day nears, and in the distance, dark, purple clouds roll over the mountains. Fingers of lightning signal a welcome summer rain approaching parched Brewster County. Sheriff Dodson has left his office to help a neighbor erect a tent for a child's birthday party. And Barclay, having argued two drug cases earlier in the day, is back home. Ever the optimist, he's looking forward to watching the Texas Rangers game on cable. In downtown Alpine, the parking lot of the Food Basket grocery is filled with after-work shoppers, and the evening buffet at the Pizza Hut is drawing a good crowd.

Soon the city will be quiet, sleeping.

A short drive south on Highway 118, the shift has changed at the barn-like Border Patrol checkpoint. The agents have pulled their rain slickers from lockers in preparation for the fast-approaching storm.

The mules and coyotes, they know, are not fair weather travelers.

◆*Dallas Observer*, July 2003

Deadly Drug

There is a grim, thought-provoking irony to the fact that 18-year-old Rob Hill died in the same hospital in which he was born. In the years between those two milestones, the handsome youngster lived an enviable life that seemed to comfortably fit the American Dream. Raised in the upscale town of Plano in north Texas, Rob grew up in a comfortable home with a loving family. He raised his golden retriever Peaches from a pup and drove his own Jeep Wrangler. Filled with ambition, he was on the football team and planned to enroll at Texas Tech University.

But Rob was also experimenting with chiva, a powerful mixture of high-grade heroin and antihistamines that users say creates a warm, carefree feeling that lasts about an hour. Usually snorted like cocaine, the light brown powder (which sells for $10-$20 a hit on the streets) has been gaining popularity in recent years. In August of 1997, after a night out with friends, Rob accidently overdosed and died. Tragically, his premature death is one of many in Plano. In the past two years, chiva has claimed the lives of eleven of the community's best and brightest youths. Two college students, a former alter boy, a dedicated young Marine, and a 17-year-old girl looking forward to a summer in Europe all fell prey to the drug's sinister allure.

Hardly an urban ghetto, Plano, population 192,000, is a town of sprawling brick homes with neatly manicured lawns. It was recently rated one of the best places in the country to raise children, and its schools are well-known for the quality of education they provide. There are 22 alcohol- and drug-prevention programs and resource centers available in the school system alone. The police department employs eight narcotics investigators and has 12 uniformed officers assigned to local campuses. The nightmare plaguing Plano wasn't supposed to happen.

But the tragic reality and the shattered lives are too real, too darkly evil, to ignore.

At the House of Isaiah, a rehab facility near Dallas run by former NFL linebacker Isaiah Robertson, ten of the young people in residence are from Plano. All are recovering heroin addicts whose drug use has destroyed their lives. "They come here from successful, caring families," says Robertson, "but by the time they arrive, they're full-fledged addicts who have already been through two or three other rehab programs." His rural, isolated facility is often their last chance.

The stories of the teens at the House of Isaiah and elsewhere are desperate. According to Sabina Stem, coordinator of the Collin County Substance Abuse Program, one 16-year-old stole $10,000 worth of valuables—including his mother's wedding ring—to support his habit. Adam Craighead, 18, a recent Isaiah graduate and son of an oil field equipment salesman, used his parents' ATM card, wrote bad checks and pawned $15,000 worth of family jewelry before being thrown out of the house. "I had a family that trusted me and friends who warned me that I was getting into big trouble," says Adam, who was homeless when he finally found help. "But I was convinced the feeling I got from chiva was what I was looking for."

"You get this warm, wonderful feeling, and all of your problems just go away," says Isaiah House graduate J.J. Mayer, 18, whose father sells insurance. Chris Cooper, 19, a former Plano High student, stayed straight for two months after a close friend died of an overdose of chiva. "But my willpower ran out," he admits. "You know that it can kill you, but you just don't care."

And so the heroin-related death count continues. Some feel that the town's privileged lifestyle—and a lack of real family values—is partly to blame for the crisis. "There's an attitude here that money takes care of any problem," says former FBI agent Larry Wansley, who lives in Plano. "It doesn't work that way."

Making matters worse, the north Texas area is rapidly becoming one of the busiest drug corridors between Latin America and the United States. In March, a Plano-based sting operation resulted in the arrest of 37 suspected drug dealers, fourteen of them local high school students. Yet despite these and other arrests, buying drugs is still almost as easy for regular users as purchasing a pack of cigarettes. Says Brent Smith, a 21-year-old recovering addict whose best friend died of an overdose, "In Plano, dope is always just a beeper number away."

"If Plano is looking to us to win this war, we've already lost it," said police chief Bruce Glasscock last year during the department's undercover efforts.

Troubling, but all too true, given that many kids ignore the warnings and dismiss the deaths and heartaches left in chiva's wake. Dr. Larry Alexander, who was an emergency room physician at the Medical Center of Plano in 1997, says the hospital treated over 70 heroin overdose victims last year alone, some more than once. "Their friends drive up to the door and leave them, yelling, 'He's not breathing!'" the doctor says. "Then they just take off." Often, the youngsters return to a party for more drugs. "They don't believe they can die," Alexander says. "It's frightening."

* * *

Lowell and Andrea Hill sit in their living room, remembering their son Rob and the night he died. For the Hills, the ordeal hasn't ended.

Lowell, a 58-year-old former insurance executive, was in bed when he heard Rob return home at around 1:30 a.m. "He stuck his head into our room and said he'd gone out to a party with some of his buddies who were getting ready to go off to college," the father remembers.

Not long after, Lowell noticed the light and television were still on in Rob's room. "When I looked in, he was half-sitting on his bed, fully clothed, with his hands and head buried in a pillow," he says. "I thought he'd fallen asleep, so I went over and shook his shoulder."

Rob wasn't sleeping. He was in a coma, barely breathing. His lips were blue, and he'd vomited. Lowell yelled for his wife and frantically began trying to revive his son. Andrea rushed into the bedroom, taking her son into her arms while her husband dialed 911.

Arriving minutes later, paramedics could barely find Rob's pulse and rushed him into an ambulance. "It was an hour or so later, as we stood in the emergency room waiting area, that a doctor came out and told us that Rob had died of a heroin overdose," whispers Lowell. "I told him my son didn't do drugs, that he had to be wrong. I know now that he wasn't."

While it is too late for Rob Hill, other kids are now reaching out for help. "If there is a positive right now," says Sabina Stem, "it is that more kids are voluntarily going into treatment than was the case a year ago."

Others are trying to fight back. "For a long time, kids around here just didn't want to talk about it," says Kaelin Weiler, 17, a junior at Plano East High School. "The attitude was that it was somebody else's problem—it couldn't happen to me." Kaelin herself had a rude awakening last year when a friend was jailed for possession of heroin. "I was very naive," she says. "Suddenly, I realized a lot of my friends who I never thought could be involved in drugs actually were."

As a member of her school's Student Senate, Kaelin urges others to take action. Their efforts became visible this past spring during Plano's student-organized anti-heroin campaign. They tied white ribbons signifying their concern around town traffic lights, created a memorial wall of pictures for the families of kids who had died, and organized assemblies featuring a student-produced video on the dangers of drugs.

But even as they planned these events, yet another tragedy unfolded nearby. Seventeen-year-old Natacha Marie Campbell, a former Plano student, was rushed to the emergency room after overdosing on a combination of cocaine and heroin. She had stopped breathing and had no pulse.

As Natacha lay in a coma, dozens of her friends stopped by to lend their support. But her grieving uncle, Michael Graham, felt something more needed to be done. "I'd like to call the Plano schools and have them send all their students here to the hospital," he told *Dallas Morning News*. "I want them to come walk by Natacha and see what a child looks like on a respirator." Two days later, Natacha's relatives said their goodbyes and took her off life support.

"We're tired of seeing people die," says Plano East junior Kelly Smithy, 17, another Student Senate anti-drug activist. "We've got to do whatever we can to stop what's going on, to make people aware that we're concerned. If we can just help a few of our friends, we'll consider our efforts a success."

◆ *Teen People*, August 1998

POSTSCRIPT:

Over three years, the number of heroin-related deaths in Plano climbed to eighteen before the statistics finally stalled. Some cheered public awareness and active participation in anti-drug programs and rallies as the cause. Others, less optimistic, say the problem has only gone farther underground.

Lips to Die For

[B]eauty, though injurious, hath strange power...
  ▪ Milton, *Samson Agonistes*

It began with whispers in beauty salons, in spas, and over lunch dates, spreading to women young and old who were eager to have wrinkles erased, frowns turned upside down, and lips made to look like Hollywood stars'. There was, according to rumor, an easy, quick, and inexpensive treatment only a clandestine appointment and a few hundred bucks away. All one needed was a phone number, a referral, and the right amount of cash. A Florida doctor who had been regularly visiting Dallas for six years, appealing to the vain desires of modem culture, was offering a seductive promise that was simply too good to ignore.

The miracle doc, based in Miami but scheduling monthly patient appointments at two Dallas spas, insisted to one client that his entire 20-year medical career had been driven by the solitary desire "to make women pretty."

Dee Myers, a 36-year-old divorcee who has worked as a nurse for two cosmetic surgeons since coming to Texas from her native Georgia, was one of his many patients. Sitting outside a north Dallas Starbucks recently, she reflected on how it all began, reviewing the sequence of events that led her to the man she knew as Dr. Luis Manuel Sanchez.

On an April evening two years ago, while having dinner with a friend, Myers learned of the remarkable beauty treatment. Her friend talked enthusiastically of a Cuban-born doctor she'd seen and of the product with which he'd injected her: New-Fill. She explained that, though still not approved in the U.S. by the Food & Drug Administration, it had been successfully used throughout Europe for two decades. For the bargain price of $300, Myers' friend told her, she too could have the same full and beautiful lips as her dinner companion.

Myers, who freely admits to being a "huge fan" of anything that will make her look younger and swears by age-erasing chemicals like Botox, collagen, and Restylane, remembers telling her husband even before they married, "Be prepared; I'm going to do whatever it takes to stay young."

She, Dr. Sanchez, and his New-Fill were meant for each other.

Returning home, Myers immediately logged on to the Internet and began researching the non-approved drug. She found it is a biocompatible, biodegradable, and immunologically inert synthetic polylactic hydrogel safely used for twenty years by European orthopedic and reconstruction surgeons and held in good standing by the European Drug Agency and the watchdogs of the European Good Laboratory Practice. The increasingly popular liquid polymer is, she learned, intended for the treatment of age lines, wrinkles, and scars and the augmentation of chin tissue, cheek bones, and lips.

Even the plastic surgeon she worked for told her he'd heard great things about New-Fill, despite the fact it hadn't yet been approved for use in the U.S.

Then the blond, hazel-eyed Myers contacted her friend and asked for the number she should call. Phoning a woman named Jheri McMillian, whose business card identifies her as a skin practitioner at a spa called Essence of Well Being, Myers made her much anticipated appointment and began spreading the word. She told her hairdresser about the doctor and his New-Fill injection treatments. Her hairdresser passed the word along to dozens of clients. Those clients told friends. Word from Myers and other Sanchez patients spread west as far away as Wichita Falls and eastward into Louisiana. One woman who made an appointment immediately after hearing about the Miami miracle-worker scheduled a visit for her mother as well.

Myers remembers arriving in the small upstairs office in a gray brick building that was "kind of old and shabby-looking." In the hallway, several women sat in folding chairs, their lips covered with a thick white cream they'd been told would deaden the areas to be injected.

Yet even after learning she'd be expected to pay cash for her treatment, making it necessary to rush out to a nearby ATM, Myers says she was reasonably comfortable with her decision to have the treatment. "Still, it did seem a little strange," she admits, "a little hush-hush—everything but a secret handshake—but I just let myself believe it was all related to the fact that New-Fill was not FDA approved."

By the time she was finally escorted into the 59-year-old Sanchez's mirrored procedure room, a syringe filled with clear liquid lay on a nearby table. The series of injections and the gentle massaging of her lips took only a few minutes. She was given an ice pack to reduce what she was told would be slight and temporary swelling and briefly discussed a follow-up visit.

"It was a few days later when I became concerned at the unevenness of my lips and the fact they remained more swollen than I'd expected," she says. When they became chapped and blistered, she attempted to contact McMillian to schedule another appointment as soon as the doctor returned to Dallas.

And the runaround began. Several calls to McMillian went unreturned. Finally, a woman named Gail Burch, owner of The Aesthetic Center, another spa where the beauty doctor saw patients, phoned to say it would be some time before Sanchez returned to Dallas.

"By then," Myers says, "I was getting pretty fed up with the whole mess and decided I needed to see a doctor who could help me with my problems immediately." Typing the words "New-Fill Dallas" into her computer one evening, hoping to find a doctor familiar with the product, she found instead a strange site that included a stream-of-consciousness diary written by a young Dallas woman. As she read, Myers feared she might become ill.

Recounting a visit to "a Miami doctor I'd heard about," the writer described the same run-down building to which Myers had gone, an unnamed doctor whose physical description sounded quite familiar, and seeing "hot Dallas women in their 30s and 40s lined up in the hall like they were visiting a back alley abortionist." The diarist told of reaching a point where she was actually in the chair, awaiting her injections, when she noticed a bottle on a nearby table. The label indicated it was not New-Fill but, instead, Silicex, "which sounded too much like silicone to me...the whole thing suddenly felt wrong."

The woman wrote that she'd asked the doctor if he was planning to inject her with silicone, and he'd assured her he wasn't. Still, she became uneasy and left without receiving her treatment. Once home, she looked up Silicex. "It was silicone, " she wrote.

Concerned for her own well-being, Myers says she also felt an overwhelming guilt for recommending the doctor to others. "I went into a three-day depression; didn't even go in to work. All I could think about was if he was injecting women with silicone and not New-Fill, I wanted him to be stopped."

Soon, she was asking herself why she hadn't been able to put vanity aside and heed the numerous warning signs, such as the secretive manner in which the doctor conducted business, the cash-only demand, the decrepit location where he gave treatments, and the fact she never had to give her medical history or sign any kind of consent form.

And where had the framed medical diploma that is standard decoration in any doctor's office been?

In retrospect, even though he wore the traditional lab coat when he had greeted her and had conversed in all the proper medical jargon,

Sanchez hadn't even looked like a doctor with his gold chains, diamond stud earring, and Caesar-style haircut.

Yet the alarm bells went unheard, muted by what Myers and others now admit was a vain desire to reverse nature's course.

"I was an idiot," Myers laments. She quickly began contacting women to whom she'd recommended the doctor and his treatment, warning them to stay away.

* * *

Myers wasn't the only Sanchez patient having second thoughts. Sandy Devine, a retired nurse, had also longed for a fuller upper lip and paid three visits to the doctor on the recommendation of a friend. Ultimately, she decided to have New-Fill injections not only to her lips, but also to the lines forming around her mouth and eyebrows. Total cost: $700. "In today's society," she says, "women are always wanting to find ways to look a little better. In my case, I'd always felt my upper lip was too small. So, when I heard about this doctor, I locked on the blinders. People in my income range can't afford the really expensive treatments or plastic surgery, so when they hear about something like this..."

Her voice fades to a whisper, and she shakes her head.

Today, as a result of the injections she received during her appointments with Sanchez, her life has become torturous. Her mouth is now so sensitive she can no longer eat or drink extremely hot or cold things. If she does have coffee, she sips it through a straw. She is now embarrassed to drink from a glass in public since she often drools when doing so. The areas where she was injected have hardened to a point where she has trouble forming certain words. Once outgoing, she rarely smiles these days because of the swelling and distortion of her lips. Since Sanchez's treatments, her immune system has begun to malfunction, and she suffers from oral Herpes.

And she says there's another thing: "I feel ugly."

But while Devine suffered in silence, Myers turned detective. Despite growing reservations, she decided to keep the follow-up appointment she'd made. This time, however, the purpose of her visit was to find answers.

As she entered, she immediately noticed a large bottle bearing a New-Fill label sitting on a tray beside several already-filled syringes. "I immediately knew what the woman had meant when she'd written that things felt wrong," she says. "The label on the bottle was old and soiled, as if it had been Xeroxed and just pasted on. When I told Sanchez that I would be more comfortable if I could see him draw up the New-Fill from a new bottle, he dismissed me, saying that he'd already made preparations for the day. He told me he would promise to draw from a new bottle the next time

I came in.

"At which point I walked out, devastated, knowing what I had to do." Her new role in life would become that of whistle-blower.

Finding a sympathetic ear, however, wasn't easy. The doctor for whom Myers worked made calls to the American Medical Association and the Texas Attorney General's Office but sensed little interest. Myers says when she contacted the Dallas Police and Sheriff's Department she "got the impression that their attitude was that I got myself into this mess and they weren't interested in getting involved."

Help, ironically, finally came from Sanchez's home state. Myers had watched an MSNBC expose on the back alley beauty business in Florida and saw Enrique Torres, head of a Department of Health Unlicensed Activities Office task force, describe myriad scams and illegal procedures used by the so-called "beauty doctors."

Online, she read an article written by *McAllen Monitor* (Texas) reporter Bradley Olson who had been investigating the illegal beauty trade across the border in Mexico. In it, Olson quoted Torres saying such illegal activities were "prolific, a national problem." The article indicated that Miami, Sanchez's base of operation, seemed to be the breeding ground for the spreading industry. Torres pointed out that in the last three years, he and his six-man task force had made over 150 arrests of phony doctors. "And we're just scratching the surface," he said. He went on to point out that it's not unusual for practitioners to earn as much as $1 million annually performing illegal cosmetic procedures.

In U.S. beauty salons and hotel rooms, even in private homes, an ever-growing number of women put their health at risk. *ABC News* reported on Tupperware-like parties throughout the country where women gather to sip wine, hand over their cash, and receive beauty enhancement injections. According to Olson, those who have visited back alley Mexican doctors have been injected with everything from liquid silicone to mineral oil, even candle wax and paint thinner.

Authorities in China say the problem there has reached an epidemic level.

Myers telephoned Torres and told him what was taking place in Dallas. Hearing what sounded like an all-too-familiar scenario, he immediately promised to contact the proper authorities. It was likely, he guessed, that Sanchez wasn't licensed to practice medicine in Texas. And, he acknowledged, the possibility that Sanchez was injecting women with some form of silicone was very real. It wouldn't be the first such case Torres had encountered.

Soon, an investigative chain-reaction was underway. A uniquely cooperative effort on the part of the Austin-based Food & Drug Administration, the Texas Rangers, Dallas County Sheriff's Department, and the Dallas County District Attorney's office stretched over an eight-month period.

* * *

Putting together a biography of Luis Sanchez is like trying to bottle smoke. His resume is a Gordian knot of truths, half-truths, and outright lies. If you believe what he told Sandy Devine, he's married with a family. Myers' first impression of him was that he was single and likely gay. He says he was born in Cuba, came to the United States in 1961, served in the Army during the Vietnam conflict, later earned U.S. citizenship, and is the sole provider for aging parents who live near him in Miami, which, according to authorities, appears to be true.

His professional history is more difficult to verify. He says after being discharged from the service, he attended and graduated from medical school in the Dominican Republic then returned to Miami and opened his practice. Later, to an undercover officer, he said he'd actually gone to med school in Spain. To one patient, he talked of plans to soon open a new clinic there.

Yet he had no records to prove he was, in fact, licensed to practice medicine anywhere. His explanation: he'd "run out of money" and thus never applied for board certification or fulfilled the routine residency requirements.

Whatever is real or not, true or false, Luis Sanchez had Dallas women—and a few men—lined up in the halls, waiting to purchase his sale-priced injections. And more than one investigator now familiar with the pieces· of his career they've been able to put together stands ready to bet a steak dinner that Dallas wasn't the only city where he plied his fly-in trade. Their estimates of the number of women he's treated run into the thousands. .

Yet making a criminal case against him was hardly a slam-dunk. When Dallas-based Texas Rangers sergeant Richard Shing took Dee Myers' statement, his immediate concern was finding a statute to charge Sanchez with violating. "One of the things I quickly learned," he says, "is that the laws that address this kind of criminal activity aren't what they need to be."

Finally, with the help of William Brannon, a special agent with the Texas FDA in Austin, it was determined that Sanchez was in violation of the relatively obscure Texas Occupations Code, which regulates the licensing of everyone from plumbers and electricians to doctors. They could not, however, find any state law that judged injecting patients with something other than what they agreed to as a felony that would earn the offender jail time. "In fact," says Shing, "after we figured out what we were up against, we had to figure out if it was best to take the case to the D.A.'s office or the U.S. Attorney. After becoming convinced of the severe nature of the crime, we felt the sentencing guidelines offered at the federal level— basically nothing but a fine—wouldn't be just punishment for what was done to these women." The maximum state penalty, they learned, was ten years in prison.

Thus, the case was delivered to prosecutor Bridget Eyler in the D.A.'s Public Integrity Division. Soon, she was interviewing a lengthy procession of women treated by Sanchez. "What he did," she says today, "was egregious."

On a May afternoon in 2002, a sting operation targeting Sanchez was finally set in motion. A female Dallas Police Department undercover agent agreed to pose as a potential Sanchez client and made an appointment for his next visit to Dallas. When she entered the salon, she wore a hidden microphone that law enforcement officers Shing, Brannon, and Dallas County Sheriff's deputies, armed with arrest and search warrants, monitored from the parking lot.

Another patient had already been prepped with the numbing cream when the undercover officer arrived and asked if she might watch the procedure she was scheduled to later receive. When Sanchez agreed, the officer struck up a casual conversation, ultimately asking how long he'd been in practice and where he was licensed. Sanchez acknowledged that he'd practiced medicine for twenty years and was licensed in Florida. But not in Texas. Hearing that admission, Shing and the other officers quickly entered and made the arrest just moments before Sanchez injected the patient.

"He was very calm about the whole thing," Shing recalls. "What we saw was the kind of charming, disarming demeanor that you often see from con men. He was playing his game, right up to the time we took him off to jail."

During the search of The Aesthetic Center, the investigation took on an even darker note. Though arresting officers say Sanchez had seen several other patients earlier in the day, searches of a biohazard box and other trash receptacles revealed no discarded needles.

Sanchez, they believe, reused needles on his patients.

"He wouldn't admit it, wouldn't say that he was using contaminated needles," recalls Shing, "but it was pretty obvious."

Sanchez's lawyer, Andrew Chatham, refutes the claim. "The woman he was preparing to inject when he was arrested was the first patient he was to give a treatment to that day. So, it stands to reason there would be no discarded needles at the time." Additionally, he points out that among the items confiscated from the room that afternoon was Sanchez's backpack filled with "hundreds of unwrapped needles."

Whatever the case, FDA lab tests conducted on the vials of what Sanchez referred to only as "product" taken from his office revealed they contained industrial strength silicon-based dimethylsiloxane.

"This," says Shing, "was all about greed. All about money." And, adds prosecutor Eyler, endangering the lives of his patients. Not only was there a real chance the injected silicone presented a variety of potential physical and health problems, but a new possibility emerged during the course of the investigation.

In the process of seeking out those duped by Sanchez, Eyler interviewed a young man who confided he'd been diagnosed with the HIV virus prior to receiving lip injections from the phony doctor.

"Normally, in the process of interviewing witnesses," says Eyler, "you do a lot of the work by phone. But because of the nature of the crime and the possibility that there might have been those who were infected by contaminated needles, I felt it my responsibility to talk with each person face-to-face." During each of those interviews, she urged the women to be immediately tested for AIDS.

To date, she says, all tests have been negative. But the prosecutor admits she now wonders how many women there are who, for whatever reason, have not acknowledged that they received treatments from the fake doctor and remain unaware of the danger they may face.

"One of the things that puzzled all of us," says Shing, "was how angry some of the women we contacted got when we tried to explain what we'd learned. Many were very happy with their results and told us how wonderful they thought Sanchez was."

Despite such endorsements, Sanchez pled guilty to the charge of practicing without a license.

* * *

Asked last March to testify about her experiences during Sanchez's sentencing hearing, Sandy Devine arrived in District Judge Mark Nancarrow's courtroom to find it filled with women—all of whom had been patients of the fake doctor. The hard wooden benches were occupied by housewives, corporate executives, and even a couple of psychiatrists, ranging in age from their early 20s to 60s. "I was stunned," Devine admits.

Yet those present, Eyler says, represented only a small percentage of the victims she'd become aware of during the course of the investigation. Admitting she became more personally involved in the case than any she'd ever prosecuted, she says, "I've never had a case that affected so many people. These women were not only lied to and put in danger, but ultimately made to feel as if they had done something wrong, that somehow they were to blame for what had happened."

The day-long hearing, at which Sanchez was sentenced to five years in prison, painted a disturbing picture. Dr. James Thornton, a plastic surgeon and faculty member of the University of Texas Southwest Medical Center, took the witness stand to explain the dangers to which the women had been exposed. He reminded the court that the use of silicone for breast implants had been banned in the U.S. after it had been shown to dissipate over time and spread to other parts of the body. The liquid form, he testified, does the same and is virtually impossible to remove once injected. It can, he said, cause scarring, pain, and disfigurement.

Even now, there is emotion in Eyler's voice as she discusses the case. She tells of the woman who has undergone two surgeries in an attempt to remove the painful knots that formed in her mouth, of another who deals with irritating rashes for which she's found no cure, others too embarrassed to confide even to husbands and friends what they had done, and of her ongoing concern that the results of some woman's next HIV test might be bad news.

Still, throughout the hearing, Sanchez repeatedly insisted he is, in fact, a doctor. "Just not a licensed doctor," he said. And, he testified, his unnamed Brazilian supplier assured him he was purchasing New-Fill, never a silicone-based product, for his patients.

Defense attorney Chatham, who advised Sanchez not to talk with D, says his client feels badly that women have been hurt yet insists he never intended to harm anyone. "He got conned. What unfortunately happened was that Sanchez was sold counterfeit New-Fill by his supplier and unintentionally used the silicone product on his patients. For years, he'd been doing the procedures without any problems or complaints. But after 9/11, it became increasingly difficult to get things shipped into the country. In dealing with that situation, he got duped by the people he was buying from."

Noting Sanchez had no previous felony record and his sentence was less than ten years, Chatham says he is now free to explore the legal option of applying for "shock probation" for his jailed client. Were it to be granted, Sanchez could soon be a free man. Meanwhile, there is also talk that he may soon hire an appellate lawyer to contest the length of his sentence.

For prosecutor Eyler, then, the fight isn't over. She's prepared to argue against a motion for any form of probation or sentence reduction and, while reluctant to discuss details, admits Gail Burch and Jheri McMillian, the women who arranged appointments for Sanchez at their spas, are currently under investigation by her office.

Burch, who is now listed along with Sanchez in a civil lawsuit filed by Dallas attorney Donal Schmidt, Jr., on Devine's behalf, did not return *D*'s calls for comment. McMillian offered only a cryptic prepared statement on the matter: "I'm deeply saddened and angered at his [Sanchez's] misrepresentation," she says. However, she went on to say Sanchez injected her lips and that she's very pleased with the results. "His work was impeccable, and I have no fear of any untoward effects."

Meanwhile, Sanchez retains his innocent posture. As he prepared to testify during his sentencing hearing, he looked out into the gallery after taking the stand, spreading his arms in a gesture to demonstrate bewilderment at his legal difficulties.

"You're all beautiful women," he said. "All I see is beautiful women."

From those who had sought him out with beauty as their goal, he received only cold, angry glares.

◆*D Magazine*, June 2004

The Miracle of Kevin Curnutt

The polished tile hallway outside the Arlington Community Hospital emergency room echoed the doctor's whispers as he stood, grim-faced, trying to comfort the parents of a dying 13-year-old boy. For Jerry and Gail Curnutt, the past few hours had dissolved into a sequence of bizarre events borne from nightmares. Suddenly, nothing made sense.

That bright Sunday afternoon in January of 1981, so full of activity, so carefully planned, was not supposed to end in a strange hospital with a doctor talking of death.

Jerry and Gail had attended church services that morning, had lunch, and planned to spend the early part of the afternoon back at the church, giving country and western dance lessons to a group of junior high students. The lessons would be cut short, everyone agreed, so they could get back home in plenty of time to watch the Super Bowl later that day.

Kevin, the Curnutt's youngest son, would visit friends nearby. They planned to ride motorbikes on some trails in a wooded pasture across from the south Arlington church.

Then, just minutes before 3 p.m., a carefree day turned into a pitch black horror in which the family still lives. A quiet mystery man who lived a reclusive life near the property on which the youngsters were riding, shot and killed 14-year-old Trey Shelton and seriously wounded Kevin Curnutt.

"I have to be honest with you," the doctor told Gail. "Your son has been mortally wounded and is unconscious. He won't know you're here." The doctor went on to explain Kevin had been shot in the head. A piece of buckshot fired from a 12-guage shotgun entered above the right temple, traveled completely through his brain, and exited on the left side. The exit wound, located in the area of the most severe damage, was roughly the size of a silver dollar. Her son, he said, would not live more than another half hour. The doctor examined Kevin, then simply wrapped a towel around his head to cover the wounds. The situation seemed hopeless.

As afternoon crept into evening then night, Jerry Curnutt paced the hospital corridors in shock. It was, he recalls, as if his own brain had overheated. "The only way I can describe it is to say it was as if I had spent a lot of time looking directly into the sun," he says.

Dazed and desperate, he tried to bring reason to what occurred just hours earlier. There had, he realized, been warning signs such an insane tragedy might occur. The previous fall, his son returned home to tell him of "some old guy" who lived near the Sheltons chasing him and Trey with a shovel. Jerry listened to the story, made certain the boys hadn't been on the man's property, then dismissed the incident as a case of teenage exaggeration.

Later, he overheard a conversation between Kevin and Trey about a $25,000 quarter horse owned by Trey's father, former Arlington city councilman Ralph Shelton, being killed by a shotgun blast "down at the barn" on the previous New Year's eve. Jerry Curnutt, who had never visited the Shelton home, didn't realize the barn sat on the same 17-acre plot as the family's residence.

Shortly after 10 p.m., the distraught father passed a waiting room television set and heard a reporter giving details of the shooting of Trey and his son. Both youngsters, the reporter said, had been killed. Still not certain he wasn't trapped in a bad dream, he turned and ran back to the intensive care unit with tears in his eyes. He felt a small rush of relief when he saw his son, defying all odds the medical staff gave him, still clung to life. There was little evidence that night, however, that Kevin would still be alive twelve years later, mentally alert and making a slow-but-sure physical recovery that goes beyond all medical logic.

* * *

The friendship of Kevin Curnutt and Trey Shelton developed soon after they enrolled for the eighth grade at Arlington's Floyd Gunn Junior High in the fall of 1980. They shared several classes and were teammates on the football team. Soon, they began to spend time in each other's home, often staying overnight and occasionally taking trips with Trey's father to attend cutting horse competitions.

The Saturday before the shooting, in fact, Trey spent the night with Kevin. "I remember them being back in Kevin's room, laughing and talking until late in the night," Gail Curnutt says. "In fact, I finally had to go in and tell them to quiet down and get to sleep because we were going to church the next morning."

The following afternoon, the Curnutts and another couple were busy with the dance instructions when a man Jerry didn't know entered the back door of the church and spoke briefly with one of the other instructors. He, in turn, walked over to Jerry and informed him there might be a sniper in the woods across the street.

After advising all those in the church not to leave the building, Jerry walked out onto the front steps and saw several police cars lined up along South Bowen Road. An ambulance and a paramedic team had also arrived. A police officer, seeing the lanky man standing on the church steps, yelled for him to get back inside.

Panic tight in his chest, Jerry Curnutt ran immediately to his car and drove it the 50 yards to where police officers were assembled. He parked near the ambulance and took cover behind a telephone pole.

A paramedic told him two boys had been shot and a sniper was barricaded in the house across the street. One of the victims had been picked up and taken to the hospital. They hadn't yet been able to reach the body of the other youngster.

Curnutt drove back to the church to tell his wife what he'd learned. Standing on the porch, the hectic police activity in full view, he repeated to her what the paramedic had said. Gail Curnutt, her mouth suddenly dry, listened silently. Then she fainted.

While others tended Gail, Jerry telephoned the Shelton house. It was Trey's oldest sister's birthday, he knew, and some sort of celebration had been planned. The sister answered and said her mother was out walking with a neighbor. Curnutt briefly explained the possible danger in the woods and urged her to remain in the house.

In a matter of minutes, a call came to the church from Arlington Community Hospital, asking that the Curnutts get there as quickly as possible.

It would be some time before they learned the full details of the tragic event that brought them to the emergency room on that suddenly dreary Sunday afternoon.

Only after talking with Arlington police investigators did they find out their son had been ambushed by a man named Richard Wade Tiedemann, a 32-year-old aerospace engineer employed by the Vought Corporation. For four years Tiedemann had lived alone in the two-bedroom house adjacent to the Shelton property. Others in the neighborhood described him as a loner who rarely spoke to anyone and always kept the gate to his property locked. Born in Texas City, he graduated with honors from the University of Virginia and earned a master's degree from Princeton. He spent a great deal of his time raking leaves in his oak-shaded yard or working on the sailboat he'd recently purchased. No one seemed to know him well or call him friend.

A search of Tiedemann's house later revealed he also owned an arsenal of guns. In fact, when he'd paid a Christmas visit to his parents' home in Texas City a month earlier, he took all of his guns with him, explaining to his father that he feared someone might break into his house and steal them while he was away.

Two months before, Tiedemann called the Arlington police to complain about the noise made by kids riding dirt bikes on the property next to his house. Police records indicate an officer drove to the area and spoke to young Trey Shelton and several of his friends about the matter. Neither the police nor Tiedemann ever spoke with Trey's parents about the complaint. No action was taken; the bikes were being ridden on the Shelton's property, and no one else in the south Arlington neighborhood had complained about the noise.

On that Sunday, however, Richard Tiedemann decided to take the law into his own hands. He loaded his 12-guage shotgun then stepped over the barbed wire fence separating his property from the Sheltons' and positioned himself behind a concrete outbuilding.

He waited until young Shelton, riding ahead of the inexperienced Curnutt (who had been riding his friend's bike for only a couple of weeks), topped a small rise on the dirt road running adjacent to the fence line. Tiedemann fired two shots, knocking Trey from his bike. Hit in the back of the head, the boy died almost immediately.

The third shot was aimed at Kevin Curnutt and struck him in the head. He fell, and the red dirt bike he'd been riding toppled over onto him.

Tiedemann then rose from his kneeling position, his shotgun at his side, and slowly walked back to his house without even looking back at his fallen victims.

Arlington detectives R.A. Puente and T.C. Ingram, in the vicinity at the time, received word from dispatch of a possible sniper shooting and reached the scene in a matter of minutes. From their vantage point, they could see Kevin Curnutt was still alive but convulsing.

As soon as the medical unit arrived, Ingram drove his police car through the gate to shield the EMTs who made their way to Kevin and hurriedly lifted him into the ambulance. Getting to Trey Shelton was impossible; the gunman was evidently watching from his house and likely to start firing again at any time.

Within minutes, the police department's tactical unit arrived and took up positions while attempts were made to talk Tiedemann into surrender. Once, as the surrounding officers waited, the gunman walked, almost casually, from his house to the garage. He stayed only a few minutes, then walked back to his front porch. As he stepped up onto the porch he turned suddenly and fired in the direction of the officers. Several return shots were fired and Tiedemann screamed, reached for his leg, and fell. In obvious pain, he crawled back into the house.

Sometime after 6 p.m., officers fired tear gas canisters through the front windows of Tiedemann's home. Soon, a small fire blazed inside. Moments later, Tiedemann lunged out the front door and into the front yard, where he fell and started shooting. Marksmen from the tactical unit returned fire. In minutes, Richard Tiedemann was dead .

* * *

For almost three weeks, Kevin lay in a coma. Despite an endless stream of relatives and friends who came to the hospital, offering help, the Curnutts rarely left their son's side. They attended Trey Shelton's funeral and occasionally made quick trips home for clean clothing and to check their mail, but they always rushed back to the hospital, feeling guilt for their brief absences.

Their ordeal seemed endless. Jerry tried to comfort Kevin's distraught friends, who could be found in the hospital waiting room at all hours. For Gail, one of the greatest difficulties was telling her mother about her grandson's misfortune.

"I called her the night after it happened," she remembers, "and told her that Kevin had been shot and wasn't expected to live. As soon as I mentioned he'd been shot, she'd wanted to know where. I told her he'd been shot in the woods. She asked the question again. And again, I said he'd been in the woods. Finally, she said, 'Gail, what part of his body?' I said, 'Mother, he's been shot in the head.' For some reason, it was really hard for me to say that Kevin had been shot in the head. But once I did, I found that I was able to talk more openly about what had happened. Since that time I've never had any trouble talking about the details of the shooting."

Jerry and Gail and their oldest son, Kelly, constantly talked to Kevin. They told stories, read aloud, sang songs, and prayed, hoping they might be heard by the youngster who lay motionless. Even if Kevin lived, doctors believed, he would likely be in a vegetative state for whatever time remained to him. The swelling in his brain was still too severe to determine the full extent of the damage, but no doctor was optimistic.

As the days passed, the Curnutts were told the heartbreaking list of problems that could plague their son for the rest of his life: paralysis, blindness, inability to speak, loss of memory. And, of course, there was a very real chance Kevin might never wake from his coma. The doctors tried to prepare them for the worst. They didn't realize the Curnutts were preparing for something entirely different.

For parents who had gone so far as to sign organ donor agreements on that first dark night, the fact Kevin remained alive was all the reason they needed to hope. "We had talked to the doctors about donating Kevin's organs," Gail says. "At first, the idea bothered me a great deal, but then I began to think maybe it would be a way a part of him could live. At that time, I think we were resigning ourselves to his death. I remember looking at the form and the list of things on it: eyes, liver, heart, and skin. The thought of someone else with Kevin's skin really troubled me. I kept trying to imagine someone with his freckles."

* * *

Kevin hung on, but each day presented some new crisis. Following surgery, his temperature rose dramatically and would not subside for several days. And there was no indication he was responding to any of the stimuli provided him. The family continued to talk, to sing, to read, but there was no evidence Kevin could hear them. The doctors grew even more certain of their earlier diagnoses. The longer Kevin remained comatose, the greater the possibility he would never regain consciousness.

On a Sunday afternoon, three weeks after the shooting, a nurse stood feeding Kevin small spoonfuls of ice cream, carrying on a one-sided conversation with the patient. "I'll bet you're getting tired of ice cream," she said. "What you probably would like is a big ol' pizza with everything on it."

Nearby, Gail Curnutt smiled. The mention of pizza, she told Kevin, reminded her of the time he and one of his friends climbed through some cubicles designed for smaller children at one of the pizza restaurants the family regularly visited. Kevin had become stuck while attempting to crawl through one of the small boxes.

The nurse, joining in, said to Kevin, "You must have really been a sight. Your rear end must have been a foot in the air."

Suddenly, Kevin Curnutt was laughing. His mother laughed with him, then began to cry. It was, she says, a miracle. Doctors, admitting surprise that he'd come out of the coma, still refused to offer the family any real hope their son would recover. One of the nurses, apparently concerned that the Curnutts might get their hopes too high, again used the words that chilled them: "In all likelihood," she said, "he will be a vegetable for the rest of his life."

No longer comatose, Kevin was transferred from the intensive care unit into a private room the following day—Valentine's Day—and his condition was upgraded from critical to serious. Though still immobile, the youngster was alert and aware of those around him. His speech had not yet returned, but with the use of an alphabet board designed by his brother, he was able to communicate. His greatest response was to the steady flow of taped messages from his former classmates who kept him updated on what was happening at school. "Seeing his eyes light up as he listened to those tapes," says his father, "was worth a million dollars." Two weeks later, Kevin was transferred to Baylor Medical Center in Dallas for a battery of tests and physical therapy. After three more weeks, doctors told the Curnutts they could take their son home .

* * *

For eight years, Gail Curnutt had worked as an elementary school teacher. She loved her job, but now her course was clear. She resigned to stay at home, tending to the constant needs of her injured son.

Waves of frustration washed over her as she did everything she could to see that Kevin was comfortable, yet his condition soon took a mysterious turn for the worse. For reasons more than twenty doctors could not determine, Kevin couldn't keep food down. In time, even the mention of food caused him to become violently ill. He had weighed 155 pounds at the time of the shooting and was down to 130 when he returned home from the hospital on June 1, 1981. Once a husky youngster with full cheeks and developing adolescent muscles, Kevin had begun to look as ill as he actually was. Pale and drawn, there was a distressing listless quality about him. He looked somehow older and weary. If there was a sign he had the strength to continue his battle for life, his family was unable to see it.

After just a month at home, Kevin's weight dropped to 100 pounds. Baffled, the doctors even called in a psychiatrist to determine whether Kevin was actually trying to starve himself to death.

"I think," Jerry Curnutt says, "that there is an inclination in the medical profession to lean on psychological explanations any time they are unable to come up with a medical answer. There was no way they were going to convince us that our son was trying to commit suicide. That just didn't fit Kevin's personality. Maybe he was too sick and too weak to put up much of a visible fight, but we knew if we could find out what the physical problem was, he would battle back."

Kevin was admitted to Arlington Memorial Hospital on July 4th and for the next several weeks was intravenously fed a mega-calorie liquid diet while doctors wrestled with the problem. Eventually they discovered Kevin was suffering from hypercalcemia (excessive calcium in the blood), an ailment common to young males who are immobile. Medication controlled the problem, and soon he was again eating normally, regaining the lost weight.

But the good news, it seemed, was always mixed with bad. A neurosurgeon reviewed Kevin's brain scan and told Jerry and Gail that there was little hope their son would ever be able to move. The gunshot injury had damaged the area of the brain that controls motor skills.

On the advise of the doctors, the Curnutts took Kevin to Denver for a two-month stay at the Craig Rehabilitation Hospital. There, the family went through a training program on the care of quadriplegics. Gail stayed the entire two months, living in an apartment near the hospital.

Miraculously, Kevin was mentally unimpaired, and his speech, which had slowly returned, and eyesight were not affected. There had been no nerve damage, and he'd retained his sense of touch. But, he and his family were told, walking or using his arms and hands were out of the question.

"The people telling us these things," Jerry remembers, "were highly trained professionals for whom we had a great deal of respect. But we simply could not accept their conclusions. We had no idea when or how, but we felt strongly that the day would come when Kevin would be able to walk again. We just had to keep searching and praying that we might find the way."

In the meantime, they tried to provide their son with as normal a life as possible. One of the first orders of business was to solicit the service of an in-home teacher so that Kevin might continue his education. The Curnutts had their van equipped with a lift and, strapped into a wheelchair, Kevin enjoyed occasional weekend outings for chicken fried steak and a movie with friends or his brother.

But for almost a year there was little, if any, sign of physical progress.

* * *

In the fall of 1981, almost a year after the shooting, Jerry Curnutt heard a news item on his car radio about an anti-gravity platform created by NASA to help brain-damaged children learn to walk. He immediately began placing calls, trying to learn more about the device. The radio station directed him to the CBS offices in New York. They, in turn, put him in touch with NASA's Ames Research Center in Mountain View, California. A dozen or so calls later, Jerry spoke with a staff member of The Institute of Human Potential in Philadelphia, a facility specializing in the treatment and rehabilitation of brain-damaged children.

The next stop in the Curnutt family odyssey was Philadelphia. There, finally, they found the hope they'd long sought.

The institute operates on the philosophy that a very small portion of the brain controls all the body's physical movements. Another, still healthy part of the brain can be trained to take over the motor function responsibility of the damaged part through a reteaching process. To help stimulate activity in the untapped areas of the brain, a series of daily breathing exercises (called "masking"), designed to send additional oxygen to the brain, is part of the rehabilitation program. An agonizingly slow process, it is much like training an infant to first crawl, then support his own weight on all fours, and finally stand. In a sense, then, the previously unused portion of a patient's brain has to grow from neurological infancy.

Facing a year-long waiting list, the Curnutts repeatedly contacted the institute to check for cancellations. In March of 1982, five months after their first contact, they were at the facility with Kevin. Tests were performed, and the Curnutts, including son Kelly, spent five 14-hour days being instructed in the program and the procedures it involved. The basis of the still-controversial Philadelphia program is "patterning," which involves five people working together, moving the patient's body in a crawling motion. The concept, originated in the '50s, is that repeated physical movements develop new motor pathways that signal to the brain what's expected.

Jerry and Gail returned home to make preparations to begin the program in their home. They converted their garage into a bedroom/therapy room, and, with the help of his father, Jerry Curnutt began building the necessary equipment (designed by the institute) for the patterning procedure.

The institute outlines the therapy program, then turns the administration over to the parents. Progress reports are sent at regular intervals and return trips to the facility are scheduled only after the patient has reached a certain level of recovery. It is a three-times-a-day workout, seven days a week. If patients fail to adhere to the rigorous demands of the schedule, they are dropped from the program to make room for another who is waiting.

For the experiment to have a chance at success, the Curnutts realized, they would have to make Kevin's recovery their full-time jobs; Jerry would have to give up his position with the Department of Energy, and Gail would have to dismiss the idea of returning to teaching. They would rely on their respective retirement funds, a modest settlement granted by the courts from the estate of the man who shot their son, and aid from the Victims of Violent Crimes program. Careful budgeting, they felt, would enable them to devote full time to the program for two years before Jerry would have to return to the workplace. That original estimate has been extended, he said late in 1985. "I think we can make it another eighteen months."

Though there have been offers, the Curnutts have refused charitable help. "We decided when we got into the program that we wouldn't look too far down the road," Jerry says. "Our approach, much like Kevin's, had been to take things one day at a time."

With volunteer aid from friends throughout Arlington, Kevin's rehabilitation program began in April of 1982. Three sessions, lasting almost two hours each, were held daily. Repeatedly, the five volunteers who came to the Curnutt house gently moved Kevin's limbs through crawling motions, according to Jerry's instructions. With the aid of a specially designed canvas harness and hydraulic lift, Kevin was hoisted and placed in an all-fours position so he could begin to get the feeling of , "walking" on his hands and knees. That's still the daily routine in the Curnutt home.

The patterning aides talk with Kevin, lending constant encouragement. Trey Shelton's mother and father are two of the more than 80 people who call themselves "Kevin's Team." Teachers, airline pilots, bankers, and housewives are among the volunteers who give their time and their hearts to Kevin.

"I have never been exposed to such a positive, upbeat, loving atmosphere in my life," says Katheryn Toxey, who for four years doubled as Kevin's home teacher and a member of one of the patterning groups. Today, another teacher instructs him in his high school studies, but Toxey continues to work with the Tuesday evening patterning team. "I think of Kevin as my own," she says. "I love him dearly. He has a wonderful attitude and has remained optimistic throughout all this. To see him progress has been one of the most rewarding experiences of my life."

To the casual observer, the progress might seem minimal. Kevin still can't walk or turn the pages of the books he enjoys reading. But he can now crawl on his stomach as far as 1,000 feet a day on the carpeted floor of his room. And while he still uses the harness and lift, he is able to support himself on hands and knees. On the afternoon of October 22, 1985, he established a new personal "record" by moving forward on hands and knees nine inches—five inches farther than he'd ever gone before. His balance has also shown marked improvement in recent months.

"The light at the end of the tunnel is getting much brighter," his father says. "Perhaps it's like first learning to ride a bicycle. Once you get the balance down and get some momentum, you really start to pick up speed. We're more encouraged than ever now. When you say it, nine inches of movement doesn't sound like that much. But when you stop to think that what he's done is considered medically impossible, it is really something.

"When you understand that he couldn't even hold his head up alone or move an inch along the floor when he started," says volunteer Dolly Wadlington, "then you realize the amazing progress he's made. There aren't many kids who would have the strength and courage that he has shown day after day. And the attitude of Jerry and Gail is incredible. They know Kevin will again walk one day and they are devoting themselves to seeing that happen."

* * *

Today Kevin Curnutt is 18 years old. Currently a high school senior, he is aware of the time his injury has cost him. Taking just two courses a year, he is still four credits shy of graduation at a time when most of his friends have gone off to college.

Visits from youngsters his own age are less frequent now. "I miss seeing a lot of my friends," he admits, "but they're pretty scattered now, going to different colleges and all." Troy Jackson, one of his closest buddies and once a regular companion on his weekend outings, is now a student at Stephen F. Austin State University. "We haven't been together in a couple of months now," Kevin says, "because he doesn't get home that much. But he calls now and then to say hello."

Someday Kevin hopes to also attend college. And if he can fight his way back, he would like to train to be a pilot. His dreams are still intact. Despite the fact he cannot feed or clothe himself, that he has to be lifted from the bed and carried to his specially designed shower, and that the simple desire to sit outside in the sun means being strapped into his wheelchair, Kevin holds firmly to his ambitions.

And he's not bitter about life. "There are times when I get frustrated," he admits. "Just keeping on with the program gets hard some days, particularly when I reach a plateau and don't see much improvement.

"See, everything happens so slow—too slow. There have been times when I've wondered if I really was getting any better, but then something always happens to show me that I was and I'd be okay. It hasn't been that much of a battle because I know this is what I have to do to get well. I really feel like I'm making progress now. It may take another year, maybe two. But I've just got to keep telling myself to be patient."

Kevin rarely thinks back on that January day years ago. "I really don't remember anything about the shooting," he says. "One minute I was riding a bike, and the next thing I knew I was waking up in the hospital. Thinking about it won't do me any good."

On his bedroom wall, near a collection of gimme caps and souvenirs give to him by friends, hangs a photograph of Trey Shelton, forever an eighth grader. Kevin still thinks of his late friend. But the dreams that once came regularly are now gone.

"I used to dream about him a lot," Kevin says. "Not nightmares, nothing scary. Just dreams. I would dream that I was in the school lunchroom and see him. I would go over to him and say, 'What are you doing here? I thought you were supposed to be dead.' Dreams like that. But not anymore. All that is in the past now."

Kevin is well aware of the time, effort, and sacrifice his parents and his brother have devoted to him. "I know that Mom and Dad get frustrated, just like I do. But they're great. So is Kelly. A lot of people would have quit this program a long time ago or just taken off somewhere. But they believe in what they're doing, just like I do. They go to bed exhausted every night, and they're ready to go again the next morning.

"And they're fun to be around. I'm lucky."

With that he falls silent for a moment. "Back before I got hurt," he says, "Mom and Dad used to go dancing all the time. They both love to dance. But now they don't have the time. Sometimes I feel bad about that. I wish sometimes they could go dancing."

◆*D Magazine*, December 1985

POSTSCRIPT:

In a world neither harsh nor real, this story would have a more satisfactory ending. But despite determination and all heroic efforts, Kevin Curnutt has never again walked. Today, he is 42, and a website designer who operates an online business He continues to live in his parents' home yet has an active social life, friends, and a wide range of interests.

Jerry and Gail Curnutt, proud and still amazed by their son's accomplishments, occasionally go dancing.

Burden of Proof

The young bricklayer peered out the window into a gray January morning, sipped from his coffee cup, and resigned himself to an idle weekend. No construction crews, he knew, would brave the bitter temperatures and frozen roads to work. The previous night's blizzard, which left a 12-inch blanket of snow, had been the first of 1985, signaling to those who call North Texas home that their world would stand still until the thaw. He turned his thoughts to spending time indoors with his wife and newborn son. While they slept, he poured himself more coffee and turned on the television.

Minutes later, he was in the bedroom, gently shaking his wife. "You aren't going to believe what's happened," he told her.

A solemn-faced newscaster reported a young nurse who worked the night shift at the local hospital had been reported missing. Even before the her name was mentioned, the bricklayer recognized the woman in the photograph shown on the TV screen. Her name was Toni Gibbs, and she and his wife had once been members of the same college sorority. He remembered being invited to a party at the woman's house, and though he'd not known his hostess well, he'd liked her.

And now there was clear concern that something horrible might have happened. She hadn't reported for work and was not at the apartment where she'd been living since she and her husband divorced. "This doesn't sound good," the young man told his wife.

It marked the first time in his life that a person he knew was the focus of such ominous attention, and it made him uncomfortable. He felt a sudden need to do something.

By mid-morning, local police announced they were organizing search parties in the parking lot at Midwestern University, urging anyone willing to help to report. The bricklayer telephoned his brother. For the remainder of the day, they walked side-by-side with somber strangers, across frozen fields near Gibbs' apartment, along the muddy shoreline of the lake, up and down alleys, and through deserted parking lots. They found nothing.

When the woman's abandoned car was discovered two days later, little doubt remained that something unthinkable had happened. But, as days turned into weeks, the urgency of the search dissipated. Reporters rarely mentioned her name, the volunteer search parties no longer gathered, and the bricklayer returned to his job.

Then, one mid-February evening when he returned home, his wife met him at the door, her face ashen. "They found her," she said.

Earlier in the day, an electrician checking a faulty transformer discovered Toni Gibbs' nude body lying in a scrub-brush field less than two miles from the bricklayer's suburban home.

News of the death hit his wife hard, but he thought the story would end there for him. Little did he know how the grim discovery would change his life, how involved he would one day become in the case. He had no idea that the murder of Toni Gibbs would take him on a journey marked by high-tech investigation, old-fashioned sleuthing, and horrific discovery throughout North Texas. He was unaware that he would become a major character in a story line that more resembled a *Law & Order* episode than it did real life. How could he know? He was just a bricklayer.

* * *

Toni Gibbs' death was part of a long nightmare that began in the bone-chilling winter of 1984, just a few days before Christmas, and stretched into the dog days of late summer in '85, spreading a palpable fear among the 100,000 residents of Wichita Falls. During an 18-month span, three women—a college student and part-time hospital worker, the nurse, and a waitress—had been stabbed, strangled, and, in two cases, raped, their bodies left in the most unlikely places.

The first victim had been 20-year old Terry Sims, a pretty Midwestern student who also worked as a technical assistant at the Bethania Regional Health Care Center. Her body was found lying in her own blood on the bathroom floor in the house of a female coworker with whom she planned to spend the night. She had been bound with an electrical cord, stabbed repeatedly, and sexually assaulted.

In January, Toni Gibbs, the Wichita General nurse, disappeared and died. She, too, had been stabbed and raped.

And in October, the nude and decomposed body of 21-year-old Ellen Blau, a Midwestern student and waitress who had moved to Texas from Connecticut, was discovered by a county· employee mowing alongside a rural road.

While whispered concerns that a serial killer might be on the loose swept through Wichita Falls, officials from three law enforcement agencies— the Wichita Falls Police Department, which had jurisdiction over the Sims homicide; the Wichita County Sheriff's Department, which was in charge of the Blau case; and the Archer County Sheriff's Department, which was investigating the Gibbs murder—quickly developed different suspects in each death. Surprisingly, investigators made no link between the three murders. Instead, they focused on a suitor whose advances Terry Sims had repeatedly rebuffed, coworkers of Ellen Blau's who had acted suspiciously since the day she disappeared from the parking lot of a convenience store, and a 24-year-old employee of a nightclub Gibbs frequented.

In time, in fact, a troubled young bartender's assistant named Danny Laughlin was indicted and tried for the Gibbs murder. He talked of his romantic interest in the nurse, seemed to know unpublished facts about her disappearance, and, according to an eye witness, was seen, just days before her body was discovered, walking his dog in the field where Gibbs was killed.

A jury eventually voted 11-1 for acquittal, but for many who had followed the case, there remained a strong belief that Laughlin simply managed to beat the system, that he had, in fact, gotten away with murder. That cloud of suspicion followed him long after he took leave of Wichita Falls, even beyond the day in 1993 when he died in an automobile accident.

Not until 1996 did advancement in forensic technology allow the testing of a small DNA sample taken from Gibbs' body a decade earlier and stored away in the Texas Department of Safety laboratory. Matching it against a blood sample taken from the suspect while he was in custody, the results finally proved Laughlin—who long insisted his only knowledge of the case had come from watching news reports and reading portions of a case file inadvertently left in a police station interrogation room where he awaited an interview—hadn't sexually assaulted the nurse or killed her.

Officially, the Gibbs murder investigation was reopened. In reality, it only gathered dust, awaiting some new lead few expected would ever come.

* * *

Grieving and angered families of the victims aside, the memories of Sims, Gibbs, and Blau grew faint. Yet the murders continued to haunt longtime Wichita County District Attorney Barry Macha, who had been sworn into office just ten days after the first killing. Privately, he found himself troubled that his career might one day end with three of the most high-profile cases of his tenure still unsolved.

With that in mind, Macha summoned a relatively new investigator, John Little, into his office in the final week of 1998 and handed him three timeworn files, asking him to read through them. "See if you can find anything that's been overlooked," the district attorney instructed.

Macha made no mention of it at the time, but in the years that had passed since the crimes occurred, he'd often taken solitary drives past key sites that had been visited during earlier investigations—the house where Terry Sims was murdered, the street where Toni Gibbs' abandoned car was discovered, an apartment where Ellen Blau briefly lived. They were all in a relatively confined area. Privately, he'd long suspected the person or persons responsible for the murders had some connection with that section of the city.

In time, his investigator, the former bricklayer, agreed.

John Little was a lifelong resident of Wichita Falls. He began his career in law enforcement later than most, joining the District Attorney's investigative team in 1993 at age 30. His first choice for a new career had been service with the Wichita Falls Police Department, but after completing the rigors of police academy training, he failed an eye exam. So he approached Macha about becoming an investigator. When offered the position, Little immediately accepted, leaving behind all thought of being a cop and bidding his old livelihood good-bye. His days as a bricklayer had come to an end.

* * *

Soon after the new year began, Little sat at his dining room table, the files spread in front of him, comparing them, setting to memory the names in each report. Only after he reread the file on the Ellen Blau case several times did a name suddenly stand out. An interview with a female coworker with whom Blau had been living mentioned a man who lived in a downstairs apartment. His name was Faryion Wardrip, and he had "given me the creeps," Blau's friend, Janie Ball, told a sheriff's deputy. The report indicated Ball and her husband had both warned Blau to simply ignore Wardrip if she ever saw him in the yard or hallway.

Little remembered reading Wardrip's name in other reports. He'd been a janitor, then an orderly, at the hospital where Gibbs worked—one of dozens of employees routinely questioned and dismissed. Later, he'd been employed at a fast food restaurant just a few doors from where Blau worked. The apartment where he'd resided with his wife and children was only a block and a half away from the small house where Terry Sims was murdered.

Most telling, a computer check revealed Wardrip had only recently been paroled from prison after serving eleven years of a 35-year murder sentence.

The murder for which Wardrip had been convicted involved a Wichita Falls woman. In May of 1986, the body of 21-year-old Tina Kimbrew, bartender/waitress at a local hotel, had been found in her apartment by her grandmother and cousin. Dressed in a nightgown and robe, the auburn-haired native of nearby Vernon had been suffocated with a pillow.

Police Chief Curtis Harrelson, then briefing the media on the investigation, said there did not appear to be any connection between Kimbrew's death and those of the other Wichita Falls women.

But, three days after the briefing, a sergeant in the Galveston Police Department received an almost incoherent call from a guest at a shore-side motel who said he wanted to confess to a homicide he'd committed in Wichita Falls. "I just wanted to come here and see the ocean before I killed myself," the sobbing caller said. He had walked the beach for two days before stopping into a Wal-Mart to purchase a knife, he said. But, he'd been unable to go through with his planned suicide and wanted to turn himself in.

The caller was Faryion Edward Wardrip.

Returned to Wichita Falls, he pleaded guilty to the murder of Tina Kimbrew in exchange for a 35-year prison sentence.

Eleven years later, it became clear Wardrip was going to be paroled, and Kimbrew's parents finally gave up their ongoing campaign to keep him behind bars and, instead, agreed to participate in the new and unique Victim Offender Mediation/Dialogue program run by the Victim Services division of the Texas Department of Criminal Justice. Designed to benefit those troubled by past crimes, the revolutionary program afforded family members an opportunity to question an inmate about anything from details of the crime to motive to plans for his future. The only criterion was that both the perpetrator and the victim's family members had to agree to participate. Wardrip, a trouble-free prisoner and self-avowed born-again Christian, said he was willing.

So impressed was Tina's father, Robert Kimbrew, that at the end of the emotional five-hour session, he extended his hand to the apparently shaken Wardrip and said, "If when you get out of here and find yourself headed for trouble again and have run out of people to turn to for help, you call me."

A portrait of contrition, the prisoner repeatedly insisted to his visitor that he'd never committed a violent act before and that it had only been his addiction to drugs that triggered the tragic death of Tina. Later, he would say, "I wanted to meet Mr. Kimbrew so I could tell him how sorry I was—that I live every day in memory of Tina. She was my friend."

He even asked the father if he would mind his visiting Tina's grave when he was released from prison.

When he later met with Tina's mother, Wardrip tearfully promised to continue with his Bible studies.

Finally paroled in December of 1997, Wardrip moved to Olney, a short drive south of Wichita Falls, where, with the help of his father, he managed to find employment at Olney Door & Screen. Soon, he was an active participant in the Hamilton Street Church of Christ, singing in the choir and teaching a Sunday school class. Divorced from his first wife since 1986, he soon married a woman he met at church.

Required to wear an electronic ankle monitor and allowed away from home only to work and attend church, Wardrip made no complaints about the conditions of his freedom, nor did he try to keep secret the fact he'd been in prison. The reasons he gave for his incarceration, however, were patently false. To some, he told a story of being charged with vehicular homicide in the aftermath of an unavoidable accident. For others, he fabricated a story of a drunken barroom brawl during which a man he was arguing with fell, hit his head, and died.

All that, the scripture-quoting Wardrip insisted, was in another life. That was the old Faryion Wardrip. Soon, he told coworkers, he would begin studying for the ministry.

Though in truth a high school dropout from of Marion, Indiana, he constantly bragged of stellar academic achievements. He wove elaborate tales of his days in the military, failing to mention he'd been dishonorably discharged for smoking marijuana.

A family member later said, "Faryion is one of those people who would climb a tree to tell a lie when it was just as easy to stand on the ground and tell the truth."

Soon those outside Olney, Texas, learned of his lying and manipulations.

* * *

John Little entered his boss' office, making little effort to mask his excitement, and slid onto the couch that was the only uncluttered spot in the district attorney's workplace. "What would you say," he asked Macha, "if I told you that I think I've got the guy we're looking for, that I can put him in the middle of everything that happened, and that he's already been to prison for one murder?"

Macha silently studied the investigator's face as he outlined Wardrip's proximity to each of the murdered women. Little had tracked Wardrip's checkered employment record, learning that he quit his job at Wichita General just four days after Gibbs' disappearance, and contacted utility companies to verify Wardrip's residences at the time the crimes were committed. He also noted a telling entry into the report written by the officers who drove Wardrip from Galveston back to Wichita Falls following his confession to the Kimbrew murder. During idle conversation with the officers, Wardrip made an off-hand remark that "he knew Ellen Blau."

There was, however, bad news: blood samples taken from Wardrip after his 1986 arrest had been destroyed following his sentencing. His DNA profile was included in no law enforcement data bank.

"Find him," Macha said. "Watch him for a few days, and see what he's doing." Then he added, "And let's figure a way to get a sample of his DNA."

They agreed the best method of securing the needed specimen without alerting Wardrip to what they were doing would be through use of the "abandoned interest" law; rather than seek a subpoena forcing Wardrip to provide a blood sample, Little began following him, hoping he would toss away a cigarette butt, a soft drink bottle, or a cup that would yield enough of his saliva for testing.

Casually dressed and driving a borrowed car, Little started leaving home before dawn so he could arrive in Olney early enough to track Wardrip's routine. Daily, Little watched as Wardrip left home, driven to work by his wife each morning shortly before seven. The investigator was there, ready to follow them back home, when Wardrip got off work at 3:30 in the afternoon. Little followed the couple to church services on Wednesday evening and watched from a safe distance as they sat in their front yard, talking with neighbors. And after five days, the investigator felt the heavy weight of frustration. No opportunity to achieve his goal had yet presented itself.

On the sixth day of his surveillance, Little's efforts paid off. The outpost he'd chosen from which to monitor Wardrip's workday was a cinder block washeteria just across the highway from Olney Screen & Door. In an effort to blend with the in-and-out crowd arriving to wash and dry clothing, Little even borrowed a basket of clothes his wife had left in the laundry room. By mid-morning he'd washed and dried the same load several times.

Shortly before 10 a.m., he saw Wardrip's wife arrive in her green Honda and watched as Wardrip came into the parking lot to spend his morning break with her. Clinched in his teeth was a package of cheese crackers, in his hand a cardboard cup of coffee.

Quickly piling his laundry into a basket, Little walked outside as the Wardrips sat in their car, talking. "At one point," Little recalled, "I thought about just walking over, reaching into the passenger window, grabbing the cup out of his hand, and running with it." Patience, however, won out.

He watched as Wardrip finally got out of the car, walked back into the shipping yard, and tossed the cup into a nearby trash barrel. Stuffing a dip of snuff into his mouth as he ran across the highway, Little approached Wardrip. "Hey, buddy," he said, "you got a cup I can borrow?"

"A cup?" Wardrip replied.

"Yeah, a spit cup."

Wardrip nodded in the direction of the nearby barrel. "Help yourself," he said.

By late that afternoon, the elated investigator had delivered the cup to GeneScreen, a forensic laboratory in Dallas that specializes in DNA testing. "The only way there won't be a match," he confidently told lab technician Judy Floyd, "is if I somehow picked up the wrong cup out of that barrel."

The following week he received a call assuring him he'd made no mistake. Floyd said she performed three tests on the cup and the evidence swabs taken from the bodies of Terry Sims and Toni Gibbs. She could not, she said, exclude Faryion Wardrip as the contributor of the semen found in the murder victims.

After a decade and a half, the time had finally come to get an arrest warrant for the man Little was convinced was responsible for the deaths of the three young women. Barry Macha, amazed that less than a month had passed since his investigator began work on the case, quickly agreed.

* * *

On February 13, 1999, a crisp and sunny day before he was scheduled to read Scriptures during Sunday communion services, Faryion Wardrip drove to Wichita Falls at the request of his parole officer. The purpose of the trip, he was led to believe, was to discuss removal of the ankle monitor that so restricted his freedom. So confident was Wardrip that he would soon be free to go where he pleased that he'd confided to several coworkers that he planned to leave on a short vacation the following week.

Instead, he was met by John Little and taken to the district attorney's office.

There, Little and Paul Smith, an investigator with the neighboring Archer County district attorney's office who had worked the Gibbs homicide, launched into a prearranged interview. With DNA linking Wardrip to two of the murders, they hoped to lure him into a discussion of Ellen Blau, the case for which they had no forensic evidence.

Wardrip repeatedly insisted he hadn't known the victim. "Look," he told the investigators, "you know I've been to prison; you know what I did." With that he began describing the remorse he felt over the death of Tina Kimbrew. "It's a tragedy I'll never get over; a terrible accident. I'd never hurt anybody before that, not even my first wife."

It was soon obvious he wasn't going to cooperate. Finally, he asked whether he was free to go. Little, disappointed they'd gotten no information linking Wardrip to the third homicide, looked at the man seated in front of him. "I'm afraid not," the investigator said. Standing, he stared silently at Wardrip for several seconds then said, "Faryion Edward Wardrip, I have a warrant for your arrest—for the capital murder of Terry Sims and Toni Gibbs."

As the sheriff entered the room and handcuffed him, Wardrip began shaking his head. "I got nothing to hide," he said. "I didn't do this. I know one thing, though. This is going to be a big circus."

Not until the following day, while hearing news reports of his arrest, did Wardrip learn the investigators hadn't told him everything. They hadn't mentioned having DNA evidence linking him to the crimes for which he'd been arrested.

That, the prisoner knew, changed everything. It was, indeed, going to become a "circus."

The following Tuesday morning, Glenda Wardrip sat in the jail visitation room, looking through a Plexiglas window into the tired, empty eyes of her husband. During the half hour they talked, he did not once claim innocence.

Shortly before 10 a.m., jailers escorted Wardrip from the visiting room back to his cell. The prisoner said nothing until locked up; then, as the officers walked away, he called out, "Tell that D.A. guy, John, that I want to talk to him.

"And you better tell him to hurry…before I change my mind."

* * *

Since the weekend, Little had found it difficult to share in the excitement vibrating through the district attorney's office. It gnawed on him that it didn't appear they would be able to link Wardrip to the murder of Ellen Blau.

When the call came from the jail, however, his spirits lifted immediately. He contacted Archer County investigator Smith and urged him to meet him at the jail annex as quickly as possible.

The dejected man escorted into the room where the investigators waited looked nothing like the confident, self-assured person Little previously confronted. Wardrip was dressed in the standard-issue white jumpsuit with "Wichita County Jail" stenciled across the back; his hair was uncombed, his shoulders slumped. Several seconds passed before he lifted his head and his eyes met those of the visitor he'd summoned.

"I had a talk with my wife this morning," he said, "and we agreed that I've got to get right with God."

"You tell her what you did, Faryion?" Little asked.

"Naw, I didn't tell her. I couldn't. But she knew." With that his voice broke and tears welled in his eyes. Taking a deep breath and folding his hands, he said, "I'm ready to talk about it."

With a tape recorder and video camera chronicling the conversation, Little said, "Okay, Faryion, what I'd like to do is just go back to the beginning …in your own words…and start with the events surrounding December 21 of 1984. This would be in reference to the death of Terry Sims."

Wardrip's fist clenched, then opened. He looked toward the ceiling, then at Little. While specific dates escaped him, he recalled it as a time when he was heavily involved in drugs, a time when his life had become a dysfunctional nightmare. He and his first wife fought constantly. His only escape from the hatred he felt for her was to leave the apartment and take long walks.

He said he first noticed Terry Sims on her porch on his way home from hours of walking. He'd seen several people that evening—total strangers—and thought about lashing out at them but had managed to restrain his anger until he saw Sims.

"She was at the door," he said, "I went up and forced my way in. I slung her all over the house in a violent rage. Stripped her down. Murdered her."

Wardrip acknowledge stabbing her, but said he didn't "recall all the details." Little stared silently at Wardrip. Nine stab wounds to the chest, slash wounds on the arms and hands, blood all over the house, and Wardrip didn't remember.

* * *

"Okay," Little said, "let's move to a time approximately a month later—January 19, 1995. Mr. Smith would like to ask you some questions about a case he's investigating."

Silent since Wardrip entered the room, Paul Smith made no attempt at mock warmth. If John Little was understated and soft-spoken, the good cop in the three-man drama, Smith was the bull-charging, no-nonsense bad cop. "We're referring to a nurse who worked at General Hospital. Toni Jean Gibbs. Do you remember that?" Smith began.

"Yeah," Wardrip replied, nodding. "Again, I was out walking. Been walking all night and somehow wound up downtown. By the time I started home, it was almost daylight. I was walking up by the hospital and Toni saw me and asked if I wanted a ride. I told her yeah.

"When I got in the car, I started seeing these images of anger and hatred and started in on her. I told her to just drive. I don't remember which direction we were going. As she was driving, I grabbed her and started slinging her around. She swerved off the side of the road and stopped. I had her by her jacket and told her to turn down this little dirt road that went into a field. I was slinging her and screaming at her. Screaming as loud as I could. I finally told her to stop the car, and when she did, I took off her clothes and stabbed her."

"Do you remember the weather that day?" Smith asked.

"Cold. It was really cold."

Soon, though, Wardrip's memory became selective. He was able to describe the white Camaro Toni Gibbs had been driving and what she was wearing, even the color of the jacket she'd worn, but he said he had absolutely no recollection of having a weapon with him or what might have happened to it after he committed the crime. "Probably," he finally said, "it stayed right there."

He said he began removing her clothing while they were still in the car. "I think she got away from me," he told Smith. "She got out the door and started to run. I think that's how we got out in the field."

Smith's impatience began to show. "Did you have sex with Toni Gibbs?"

"I don't really remember. I just remember screaming at her, screaming that I hated her. I don't remember if I had sex. I just remember screaming and screaming and screaming how much I hated her, how much I hated everybody."

"You said that you knew Toni and she asked if you wanted a ride," Smith said. "How did Toni know you?"

"From the hospital," Wardrip replied. "I met her when I worked there. But she never had anything to do with me. I just knew her from there. It could have been anybody. She just happened to be in the wrong place at the wrong time. I never set my sights on anybody.

"I would just get mad and get out and walk. I'd be in such a rage. I would just scream at the sky, scream at the trees, scream at God. Then, afterwards, I would just lay down for a while and sleep. Then I'd see it on the news, realize that something bad must have happened, and I'd trick myself into believing it wasn't me..."

* * *

Wardrip looked at Little, who decided it was again his turn. "I'd like to talk to you about another case I'm investigating," he said. "About the disappearance and murder of Ellen Blau in September of 1985. Do you know anything about that?"

Little waited, trying not to show his anxiousness, as Wardrip paused for several seconds. Then, he almost whispered his reply:

"Yeah," he said. "Same thing. I was out walking. Just walking."

He described walking by a nearby airbase when he saw a car parked in a convenience store parking lot. He asked the driver what she was doing, and she told him she was looking for someone. "There wasn't nobody around, so I just grabbed her and slung her up against the side of the car and pushed her in. I told her we were going to take a ride."

He described how he forced Blau to drive down a road on the outskirts of town, screaming at her, telling her how much he hated her. They turned down a dirt road. "I drug her out of the car, took her in a field, and stripped her clothes off. I don't believe I raped her. And I don't remember how she died. She probably broke her neck because I sure was slinging her. I was just so mad, so angry."

It was, he insisted, never the victim he was seeing, but instead the face of his first wife. Each time, it was his wife's face he looked into as he committed the crimes.

Little leaned back in his chair and glanced over at Smith to see whether he had additional questions. Smith wearily closed his eyes and shook his head.

"Faryion," Little said, "did you kill Ellen Blau?"

"Yeah, I don't remember how…"

"Did you kill Toni Gibbs?"

"Yeah."

"Did you kill Terry Sims?"

"Yes."

And so, in less than an hour, Faryion Wardrip resolved questions that had, for 14 years, hung over the city of Wichita Falls. Finally, it was over.

Or so Little and Smith thought as they made ready to return the prisoner to the jailer's custody.

"There's one more," Wardrip said.

With that, he began yet another horror story of the murder of a 26-year-old mother of two named Debra Taylor; the two investigators sat in stunned silence. "It ain't here," he said. "This one's in Fort Worth. I'd left Wichita Falls and gone there, hoping I could find a job. I was staying at this Travel Lodge that was full of people selling drugs. So I just stayed there, shooting drugs. One night, I went to this bar. There was this girl there, and we got friendly and started dancing. She was coming on to me, and after a while we decided to leave.

"We went out into the parking lot around back and I made my advance toward her. She said no and slapped my face. When she done that, I just snapped. I slung her around, and I killed her."

For several minutes Little questioned Wardrip in an attempt to pinpoint the date of the Fort Worth homicide. Wardrip said he could remember only that, after he murdered Ellen Blau, he hitchhiked to Fort Worth and committed the crime while there. (In fact, investigators later found that Wardrip killed Taylor before murdering Blau.)

Smith and Little looked at each other, neither saying a word. Hoping to clear three homicides, they now had confessions to four.

"Will you be willing to cooperate with authorities in Fort Worth to help them with that case?" Little asked.

Wardrip shrugged then nodded his head. "Yeah. It's all over with now. I've done what God said I should do. I've confessed to my sins."

"Were you promised anything in return for giving me this statement?" Investigator Little tied up the loose ends of the interview.

"Eternal life with God is what I was promised," Wardrip answered. "I was promised that I won't burn in hell. What I've told you is the truth. It's all over. I give up. I can't go on no more. You can kill me now; I don't care. I'm tired of living on this earth, tired of the pain and suffering that Satan brings to people." And then, for the first time during the interview, he broke down, slowly rubbing his clenched first against his temples, moaning.

"Oh my God, what have I done?"

* * *

In November, 1999, in a Denton courtroom where Wardrip's capital murder trial had been moved on a change of venue, the defendant surprised those awaiting the first day's testimony by ignoring the advice of his public defender, John Curry, and entering a guilty plea to the murder of Terry Sims. In doing so, he hopscotched the proceedings directly to the sentencing phase. With stern-faced families of Wardrip's victims seated in the gallery, Barry Macha methodically presented the gruesome evidence of each of the long-ago crimes, determined that the trial would not be just about Sims but rather all five of the women whose lives had been so brutally shortened by Wardrip.

Judy Floyd, the forensic lab supervisor at GeneScreen, testified that the blood samples taken from Wardrip and the saliva from his discarded coffee cup matched the semen samples taken from the bodies of Terry Sims and Toni Gibbs. Leaving heads shaking in the courtroom, Floyd said the frequency of such a match was an arithmetic fantasy; only one in 3.23 quadrillion—the equal of more than 500 million Earth populations—could have left the DNA found on the victims.

After hearing just five days of testimony, the jury returned with answers to three questions that ensured a death sentence for Wardrip: Yes, they believed he acted deliberately in causing the death of Terry Sims; yes, they believed he represented a continuing threat to society; and no, they did not believe there were any mitigating factors that warranted him spending his life in prison rather than being put to death.

In the days that followed, Wardrip was shuttled to courtrooms in Archer County (where he pled guilty to the murder of Toni Gibbs in exchange for a life sentence), Tarrant County (where he admitted his guilt in the murder of Debra Taylor, receiving another life sentence), and, finally, back to Wichita Falls, where he received a third life sentence for the murder of Ellen Blau.

By stacking the sentences—having them run consecutively—prosecutors ensured that, even should the 39-year-old murderer not be executed, he would serve a minimum of sixty years behind bars before becoming eligible for parole.

On New Year's Eve afternoon, 1999, District Attorney Barry Macha sat in his office, pondering the framed photographs of Wardrip's victims hanging on a nearby wall. "It's hard to believe," he mused, "that when this year began we still didn't even know who killed Terry Sims or Toni Gibbs or Ellen Blau. We'd never even heard of Debra Taylor. Yet within a year's time, we've gone from an arrest to four convictions."

He breathed an audible sigh and slowly shook his head. "It's amazing," he said. "Absolutely amazing."

"Without DNA," John Little says, "there would never have been a case."

Catie Reid, Terry Sims' youngest sister, disagrees. "Without John Little, there would have been no case," she insists.

A few weeks after the Denton, trial Reid visited the investigator in his office, bringing along a fitting token of her family's appreciation. On an ordinary red brick, a reminder of another time in his life, were inscribed the words, "Our Hero, John Little."

◆ *Dallas Observer*, July 2000

POSTSCRIPT:

For this article, I drew on material gathered while researching a book on the case, *Scream at the Sky*, published in 2003. Just weeks following the book's publication, Terry Sims' sister, Catie Reid, who first alerted me to the case, died in an automobile accident.

While Wardrip remains on death row, appealing his sentence, John Little was honored by the state's district attorney's as the Investigator of the Year.

Chasing a Ghost

Much of what's known about the life of Loel Patrick Guinness is fact. He is the handsome and personable heir to the vast Guinness brewing and banking fortune, horse breeder, free-spending polo enthusiast, and jet-setting international playboy. Then there are the dark shadows of myth and accusation that constantly follow him on his secret travels throughout Europe and the United States. A wanted man who is the only one with answers to questions that trail him wherever he goes. Guinness, nephew of the Aga Khan, has, in the minds of many, become an evil ghost, a man with a deadly mission and a slippery disappearing act that some say he's elevated to an art form.

Depending on who one talks with, the 41-year-old one-time patron of the celebrated Stingray polo team, winner of Deauville's 1993 Gold Cup, is seriously ill, sequestered, and well-guarded at his sprawling horse farm estate in France. Or perhaps he's living a reclusive life in his homeland Switzerland. Others claim to have seen him and a female companion walking the streets of Manhattan or strolling the beaches of Texas' picturesque Padre Island. He's supposedly been seen at homes he owns in Britian and a leased residence on East Mountain Drive in the posh Southern California community of Montecito. From the social grapevine came recent word he was seen just last summer—or was it summer-before-last?—at a royal wedding in Spain. Some say he regularly jets into Mexico for medical treatment. Still others are certain he's been a recent patient in the American Hospital in Paris.

He is everywhere and nowhere.

Today, Loel Guinness is invisible to his mother, Delores, and sisters, Victoria and Alexandria, who insist they have not seen or heard from him in more than two years, a high profile private investigator who has tracked him across two continents, and a frustrated Palm Beach attorney determined to lure him into a Florida courtroom to answer civil lawsuit charges that he "maliciously, willfully, and wantonly, in complete disregard for the health and safety" of his client "engaged in sexual relations with her without advising her of his condition."

The client is 39-year-old Palm Beach socialite Maria "Mimi" Lambert, Guinness' onetime girlfriend who charges he was HIV positive during the two years they lived together in the early '90s yet never told her of his condition. Today, Lambert, stepdaughter of the late Vincent de Paul Draddy, who made his fortune from the LaCoste-Izod clothing empire, is being treated for the deadly disease, now suffering from many of the symptoms of full-blown AIDS. She says she's spoken with others—a German fashion model, another Palm Beach socialite, a young woman in New York, a girl whom Guinness met while playing polo in Argentina, and two others in France—also infected by Guinness and now seriously ill.

A disturbing story continues to circulate that a visitor to Guinness' French estate just outside Normandy was shocked to find photographs of each of the women he's been involved with displayed throughout the house. Like trophies, Lambert suggests.

Meanwhile, Guinness' Miami-based attorney, Calvin David, continues to insist, "[T]here is nothing to this...Loel Guinness," David told the media, "says he is not HIV positive."

If that is so, argues famed lawyer Bob Montgomery, who represents Lambert, why has Guinness gone into hiding, refusing the simple exercise of a blood test to quickly prove his attorney's claim? If falsely accused, why has he not lashed out at the British and American tabloid media which has feasted on the story, portraying him as a psychopathic, spoiled-rich playboy with no concern for the well-being of others?

It is, in fact, a story filled with a tragic litany of unanswered questions.

* * *

It began, however, as something more akin to a romantic fairy tale: handsome heir and beautiful heiress; love and passion played out in the mega-rich social stratosphere with not the slightest hint it would one day turn into a gothic horror story. Both could boast lineages of great privilege, profile, and accomplishment. In addition to remarkable success in banking and brewing, Guinness' father and grandfather rubbed elbows with Princess Margaret, Lord Snowdon, and the American Who's Who. Generous with their money, they were quick to finance the expeditions of underwater explorer Jacques Cousteau and eager to lend financial backing to help NASA claim victory in the space race. In addition to the fortune Draddy earned in the clothing business, Lambert's stepfather, a gifted athlete in his undergraduate days at Manhattan College, established and chaired the National Football Foundation's College Hall of Fame and once lost a bid to purchase the New York Yankees by the slimmest of financial margins. His wide circle of friends ranged from British royalty to American celebrities like golf legend Ben Hogan and entertainer Bing Crosby.

Swiss-born Loel and Cuba-born Mimi first met in 1980 at a New York celebration to mark the birth of a son to Guinness' sister, Victoria, one of Lambert's closest friends. It was not love at first sight, however.

"I met Loel at a party," she recalls, "but wasn't particularly interested in spending much time with him. He was drinking too much back then, and I was aware of his reputation for doing a lot of drugs." She'd also heard whispers about Guinness' past—how, as a teenager, he'd been shipped by his grandfather to a private school in the United States after getting a girl pregnant; how, during his collegiate days at Columbia, he'd been fascinated by theology while at the same time insisting he was an atheist.

Additionally, both were dating others at the time. Lambert was seeing Victoria's brother-in-law, Greek shipping tycoon Spiro Niarchos; playboy Loel's romantic interest was spread among a number of European fashion models.

Twelve years passed before they saw each other again. Late in '91, Victoria telephoned Lambert to say her brother, depressed over his breakup with the latest in a lengthy succession of girlfriends, was planning to visit Palm Beach and asked if Mimi would introduce him to people in her circle of Florida friends. "Victoria made it clear that she didn't like the woman to whom her brother had been engaged and wanted to be sure that he didn't get back together with her," Lambert says.

Immediately, Guinness was attracted to the vivacious Lambert, the dark-haired young woman with a soft, gravely voice who spoke French and Spanish fluently, had friends with names like Kennedy, Mellon, and Hitchcock, and nurtured interests ranging from horseback riding to antique toy collecting. A whirlwind courtship began almost immediately after they were reacquainted.

"He was charming, a perfect gentleman," Mimi recalls. "He called constantly, took me to dinner, bought me little gifts. I found him to be very intelligent and sweet. Very protective. And he had impeccable social graces." The Loel Guinness she soon began to fall in love with was far removed from the man about whom she once heard gossip and rumors. He now drank only moderately. Older and wiser, he insisted to her he hadn't done drugs in years.

If he did have an addiction, he warned, it was to the game of polo. Though still generally viewed by those in the sport as a novice, he took lessons, invested in the best ponies money could buy, and served as patron of a team judged highly competitive by fellow members of the polo community. Already he had played a season each in France and Spain and was looking forward to the upcoming winter matches in Palm Beach.

Many are less gracious about Guinness' talent. Reflects one player who competed against him in France and the U.S., "He became obsessed with the game—was very enthusiastic about it—but he was never the most coordinated player. He hired a full-time coach and practiced daily but never advanced beyond the rating of a one-goal player.

"Quite honestly, he was one of those people who literally bought his way into the sport."

None of which concerned Lambert. Though supportive of his athletic endeavors, regularly attending matches, she had avocations of her own which she attended with the same enthusiasm that Loel gave to polo. An environmental activist, she regularly stepped from her role as a high society figure to passionately lobby the town council for more aggressive anti-litter laws on nearby beaches and better protection of nesting sea turtles. She was also active on the board of directors of Ballet Florida.

To those who knew them, the couple seemed ideally matched. While Guinness improved his polo skills, Lambert pursued her own interests. "They were very attentive and supportive of each other," says a friend, "but they didn't seem to have a smothering relationship. It was very adult, very mature. There seemed to be a mutual respect between them." When Guinness found it necessary to jet back to France to tend business interests or check on the progress of polo fields being built on his farm, Lambert would take a scuba diving trip to the Florida Keys. "There was no evidence that one was jealous of the other's interests," the friend observes.

In the months following their reunion, Lambert and Guinness saw each other regularly. He was a house guest of Mimi and her mother, Maria, during the '92 Christmas holidays. If mutual friends had doubts about the growing seriousness of the couple's relationship, they were set aside when Mimi took her new boyfriend home to meet her mom.

During that visit, Mimi recalls, she and Guinness had sexual intercourse for the first time.

Sitting in the den of her mother's home, just a hallway removed from where the intimacy took place, Mimi reflects on the tragic irony of that carefree Christmas past. "The gift he gave me," she says, "was AIDS. It's a horrible thing to say, but it is true."

It would be some time, however, before the grim truth emerged.

Early in '92 they co-signed a lease on a Palm Beach house next door to one where Lambert grew up and began living together. "The following year," she says, "Loel found a house in Lantana next to his grandfather's home near the beach that he liked, and we moved there."

Throughout the two-year relationship, they shied from the public spotlight. "We went to very few social functions," Lambert says. "Loel is a very private person and was quite reclusive except for his polo, so we stayed home much of the time, occasionally having friends over for dinner."

None who knew the couple had any hint when problems began to develop. That Loel was spending increasing amounts of time away, on trips to New York and France, went unnoticed by most. Mimi, however, began to suspect he was seeing other women, perhaps secretly returning to drug use. His demeanor grew increasingly sullen and dark. It finally ended, Mimi says, when Guinness began to talk openly about "shooting up." "I'd been around a lot of drugs when I was younger," Lambert admits, "and didn't want any part of it. I told him I was too old for that sort of thing. He kept telling me of fantasies he was having, of us getting high together, things like that." Talk of separation soon replaced their once intimate conversations.

Finally, after returning from a few days in the Keys, the decision Lambert had struggled with was made easy for her. Guinness informed her he'd invited a German model he met on a trip to Europe to be his house guest. The signal was clear. Lambert left immediately, asking the housekeeper to pack her things and have them sent to her. Mimi recalls: "I told him, 'Fine. You go your way, I'll go mine.'"

Antique jewelry Guinness purchased as a birthday gift for Lambert instead was given to his new girlfriend.

Thus ended the fairy tale. The nightmare began 17 months later.

* * *

"The German woman who had come to visit him after I moved out phoned me," says Mimi, "and urged me to be tested for the HIV virus. She was obviously upset and told me she had tested positive. She said she was sure that it was Loel who had infected her." Stunned, Lambert immediately contacted Guinness' sister. "I asked Victoria if Loel had AIDS, if everything was okay with him. I explained to her that I wanted to one day have children and had to know. She assured me I had nothing to worry about. It had to be nothing more than a rumor, a lie."

In truth, tragedy all too often dotted the history of the wealthy Guinness clan. Plagued for generations by Kennedy-like misfortune, the accusations against Loel Guinness represented just another in a lengthy list of family crises. Loel's father, Patrick, died in an automobile accident in 1965. His uncle Sheridan died ten years earlier of the same disease Loel was now suspected of transmitting. More distant relatives committed suicide, died of cocaine and heroin overdoses, and were involved in a series of fatal car crashes.

Lambert quickly decided to schedule a test. "A few days before I was to see my doctor," she says, "I received another call from a man who refused to give me his name. All he would say was that he knew Loel and that I needed to see a doctor as soon as possible because I could be seriously ill. He said, 'Trust me, get tested. You have been exposed to the HIV virus.'"

Two weeks later—on October 19, 1995, just two days before Loel Guinness' birthday—Lambert's test results confirmed the words of the anonymous caller. Frightened and angry, she phoned a lawyer.

An attorney with no less than 56 multi-million dollar judgments to his credit (including the staggering $11.3 billion awarded the State of Florida in its 1997 suit against the American Tobacco Company), Montgomery cautioned his client that making such accusations against a person of Guinness' position was a sensitive proposition. "Still, I was impressed with what she had to say," he recalls. "I suggested we keep the matter low-key until we could fully determine the merits of her claim."

Montgomery quietly filed a suit on Lambert's behalf and contacted Guinness' lawyer. "I explained to him that I recognized the sensitivity of the situation and suggested that the best thing to do would be to have Mr. Guinness and Mimi submit to blood tests. We could then have a DNA sequencing done that would determine if, in fact, he was the responsible party."

David agreed to the testing and promised to contact his client. In good faith, Montgomery withdrew the civil suit pending the results.

Soon, however, Montgomery learned from a source close to Guiness that he had been secretly visiting a clinic in Lausanne, Switzerland where a revolutionary method of blood transfusion had been developed and would, in effect, mask the presence of the HIV virus for short periods of time. "I again contacted Guinness' lawyer," Montgomery says, "and told him that I had learned from a very good source that Guinness was going to this clinic and that it was there he planned to provide the blood sample we were requesting.

"I explained that we expected everything to be on the up-and-up and told him what we wanted was for Guinness to be quarantined in an agreed-upon hospital for 48 hours prior to the taking of the blood sample. We also wanted it understood that the sample would be drawn by an independent physician so that we could be assured of having a true replica [sic] of Loel Guinness' blood."

Guinness refused, Montgomery re-filed the lawsuit, and the chase began.

* * *

Chicago native Pat McKenna escaped the bitter winters he'd dreaded since childhood by moving to Palm Beach to work as a parole officer in the late '70s. By 1981, he'd moved into the public defender's office where he ran the alternative sentencing program for recovering drug addicts. So detailed and colorful were the pre-sentencing reports he wrote that a number of local lawyers began asking him to do investigative work for them. By 1984, he'd opened his own private investigations office.

Among those who liked his work was high profile Palm Beach lawyer F. Lee Bailey. In short order, McKenna was spared the drudgery of window-peeking jobs assigned most P.I.s and instead found himself doing federal criminal defense work and consulting with lawyer Roy Black, who was defending William Kennedy Smith in a much publicized rape case. Still, not until he was summoned to California to become an investigator for the "Dream Team" defending murder suspect O.J. Simpson did McKenna became nationally recognized.

Hired by Montgomery, McKenna set out to find Guinness and see that he was served the subpoena demanding his appearance in court. It took almost a month for the search to finally bear fruit.

"In early April of '96, we finally located him at a residence he had leased in Monticeto, California," McKenna recalls. "I got in touch with a process server in Los Angeles and carefully went over the details of how best to approach Guinness." The server, he says, "was supposed to phone me from his car once he was outside the residence. Then I would phone the house to make sure Guinness was there."

Things didn't go as planned. The process server, excited by the fact Guinness' car was in the driveway, bypassed the prearranged phone call and went directly to the door. The man who answered insisted he was not Loel Guinness but, rather, a student and house guest named Eric. When the server asked his last name, the man replied, "Just Eric."

The server handed him the subpoena and left. Guinness' lawyer insisted his client assured him he received no papers from a California process server. By then, Loel Guinness had returned to Europe.

"Eric," says McKenna, "was quite likely Loel Guinness, but we blew it. We had to start all over." Compounding his frustration was the fact that under law, a subpoena in a civil case must be served within 120 days of filing the suit.

Working against the legal deadline and with a growing network of informants, McKenna next received information Guinness and a female companion were registered in a Manhattan hotel under assumed names. This time, armed with a photograph of Guinness for identification purposes, the assigned process server confronted him on the sidewalk in front of the Carlisle Hotel.

Pleased that the mission had finally been accomplished, McKenna sent flowers to Lambert and forwarded an affidavit detailing the serving of the papers to her attorney. Montgomery, in turn, sent a copy to Guinness' lawyer—only to learn Guinness, no longer in the United States, again denied he was ever served.

"Because he was traveling so frequently, sometimes in his private jet, sometimes on commercial airlines," McKenna says, "it became increasingly difficult to keep up with his movements. It was soon apparent to us that he wasn't staying anywhere for any length of time." Loel Guinness possessed English, French, and Swiss passports. In every sense of the phrase, he was a moving target.

When it was learned in early July of '97 that Guinness and his girlfriend were staying on South Padre Island in Texas, McKenna's agents hurried to the resort area, staking out the hotel. When his car left the parking lot early one morning, the process servers followed—only to find Guinness' companion behind the wheel. She told them Guinness left days earlier for New York then France.

Challenged by the increasing difficulty of cornering his prey, McKenna began a full-time coordination of efforts in Europe and the U.S. to once again locate the elusive millionaire. The next time, he said, a photographer would accompany the process server to document the moment when papers were, in fact, handed to Guinness.

That opportunity finally presented itself when McKenna learned the elusive playboy planned to visit a Dallas doctor. "I had learned that he had an appointment for some kind of treatment at the University of Texas Medical Center. I found out the name of the doctor he was seeing, where the doctor's office was located, and that Guinness' appointment was for three in the afternoon. I decided that we would wait until he came out of the hospital before serving the papers. That way, I figured, there might be some chance that medical records could be subpoenaed to determine if the treatment he'd received was AIDS-related," McKenna explains.

The sequence of events that followed served as proof positive that even the best laid plans can go awry. "The papers," McKenna remembers, "were in New York, in anticipation of Guinness' return there, so I called and told them to FedEx them to Dallas immediately so they would be there well before his 3 p.m. appointment. I then called Dallas, and we went through the plan carefully."

Finally, the investigator was confident, the months-long chase was nearing an end.

"That afternoon I waited by the phone. I was a nervous wreck, anxious to hear how things had gone. The later in the day it became, the more nuts I got. Finally, I called them."

What he learned defied belief. The papers never arrived. After a series of angry calls to Federal Express officials, McKenna learned the plane carrying the crucial document to Dallas caught fire on a New Jersey runway and never left the ground.

Once again, Guinness slipped away. And he remains in hiding.

* * *

Seated at a favored table in Testra's, a trendy Palm Beach restaurant, Mimi Lambert picks at a salad as she reflects on the course her life has taken. There is no self-pity and, surprsingly, very little anger in her voice as she recites the medical problems she's encountered in recent years. "I've been on medications that were like taking cobalt and chemotherapy treatments at the same time. It was painful. I was disabled for two years." She suffered blindness in one eye, her brain swelled, and she had what doctors diagnosed as a mini-stroke that caused nerve damage to her left side. For the first time in her life, she battled with pneumonia.

Now with limited strength, she no longer enjoys the horseback rides, scuba diving, and jogging which had been so much a part of her previous life. As she speaks, she rubs her left hand, which gives her constant pain.

"Finally, last March," she says, "a doctor gave me the best advice I'd heard in a long time. He told me to get off the medication and enjoy what's remaining of my life." And while her T-cell count is now dangerously low, indicating full-blown AIDS isn't far off, Mimi Lambert looks remarkably healthy.

Still, she bears wounds unseen, invisible pain beyond the physical. "Many of my friends are now afraid of me," she whispers, sadness creeping into her voice. "I'm not allowed to hold their babies for fear I might infect them. Not long ago, I was visiting a good friend's home and was playing with her dog. The dog licked me on the mouth and she went into a rage. She said I had contaminated her entire family and asked how I could be so irresponsible. I cried over that for a week. .

"I understand the concerns, but I'm so resentful over the fact I've been put into such a position."

Guinness' mother and sisters, initially offering Lambert their support and encouragement after learning of her illness, no longer call.

"I'm a born-again Christian," Mimi says, "and as such, I have tried to forgive Loel for what he did. I had to put the anger and hatred behind me for my own peace of mind. Still, I want him to be held responsible for what he did to me and the others. I think he's really a coward for refusing to acknowledge the horrible things he's done. Would I like to see him in jail for the rest of his life? Nothing would give me more satisfaction."

Montgomery and McKenna share her feelings. "We'll get him one day," Montgomery insists. "Even if he dies before we find him, I'll file suit against his estate. He will not escape responsibility." Adds a frustrated McKenna, "This guy is filthy rich and dirty as hell. The next time we track him down, I'm going to pay my own way to wherever he is so I can serve him myself."

At the lush Palm Beach Polo Club where Loel Guinness once struggled for acceptance, his name now rarely comes up in conversation. When news of Lambert's claims first surfaced, a number of players, mindful of the blood that aggressive players sometimes exchange during the course of a match, quietly reported to their doctors to be tested for the HIV virus as a precautionary measure. All tested negative.

Preparing for a recent practice session, a player who asked that his name not be disclosed struggled to remember specifics about the days when he was often in Guinness' company. "He was quite odd, really. I don't know if I could even describe him as a real person. Though he worked hard at polo, he was just a playboy at heart. He had too many other things going on in his life to leave time for really close friends.

"He'd set a goal for himself to become a world-class player in five years. After a few years, I think, he realized that it wasn't going to happen and became very disillusioned. Looking back, I think it was probably that realization that caused his life to go off track."

He pauses and shakes his head. "You know, I can't even remember when I last saw Loel Guinness. I hadn't thought about him in some time.

"Is he still alive?"

◆*Polo*, 1999

The Resurrection
of Charles Ray Giddens

The cells on Death Row at McAlester's Oklahoma State Penitentiary are five feet wide and eight feet deep. Covered in coat after coat of clabber gray paint, each has a bunk, a toilet, and a wash basin. At night, an inmate can lie in bed and touch both walls of his miniature world. There are no light fixtures, no mirrors, no electronic outlets—nothing that might serve as an improvised tool for self-destruction. The architects of the maximum security prison were careful to do everything possible to make sure its condemned residents don't find some way to escape the court's promise of death.

When 18-year-old Charles Ray Giddens stood in front of Cell 49 on the morning of March 27, 1978, waiting for the guard to remove his handcuffs and leg chains, there were eight men on the Row, all marking the slow crawl of time either until appeals restored their hopes of life or their executions were finally carried out. Unfortunately, Giddens carried an extra burden: he was innocent.

A few cells down was a man who committed one of the most heinous mass murders in Oklahoma history. He had forced six people into the meat locker of a well known Tulsa steak house, made them lie face down on the cold floor, then fired a single bullet into the back of each one's head. Another inmate had abducted a family and burned them to death in their own truck. And there was the kidnapper who had held a young woman for ransom but later, when caught, admitted he'd killed his hostage even before beginning negotiations with her family. In another cell was an inmate who told of finding his wife and another man in bed upon his return from work one evening. Without a word, he returned to his car, got a pistol from the glove compartment, went back in, and shot them both. There was a 17-year-old who, after being stopped for speeding by a highway patrolman, calmly stepped from his car and blew the officer's face away with a .12-guage shotgun.

And there was a fat, ugly man in his late 20s who had sexually molested and murdered a 13-year-old boy. In a grinding case of irony, only the air-tight security of Death Row was keeping him alive. Even before he had arrived at McAlester, word spread through the prison population that he was coming, and a bounty had been placed on his life. In prison, there is no inmate more despised than a "baby killer."

"After I'd been there a while," Giddens says, "the thing that really stuck in my mind was the fact that most of the guys on Death Row didn't look like they were capable of the things they were there for. I guess we've all got this picture in our minds of what a murderer is supposed to look like. I just couldn't figure it. A lot of those guys were well educated and had good jobs on the outside. In the back of my mind, I knew what they had done and why they were there, but, quite honestly, most of them were pretty likable people."

In time, Giddens came to consider most of those with whom he was incarcerated as family.

"You help each other as much as you can in a place like that," he says. "Guys share with each other, they talk to each other, and they listen to each other. The bottom line is, you're all each other has. When someone's birthday was coming up, we'd all pass a card around and sign it. Stuff like that. I remember this one dude we sent a card to. It said, 'Happy 21st Birthday. Too bad you won't be around to see your 22nd.'"

Black humor, Giddens says, is very much a mainstay behind bars.

Most of the men on Death Row talked from time to time about the crimes they had committed, some simply bragging, others in a never-ending attempt to unburden themselves. Within the confines of the state prison, only a few continued to insist on their innocence.

But from the day Charles Giddens arrived, convicted of the brutal murder of a country grocery store cashier, he insisted he was not guilty of the crime. He did so when he was arrested and taken to jail in the small town of Idabel, Oklahoma. The young black man repeatedly swore his innocence from the witness stand at his capital murder trial, which, incredibly, lasted only three days before an all-white jury found him guilty and a judge sentenced him to die.

The jurors deliberated for just 15 minutes before finding Giddens guilty, giving little consideration to the evidence presented. Giddens' lawyer had discovered a number of glaring discrepancies in the testimony of prosecution witnesses. Giddens' uncle swore Charles was at his house when the crime occurred. The most damaging testimony implicating Giddens came from a young man named Johnny Gray, a friend who said he'd accompanied Giddens to the store where Faye Tapley was killed. Oddly, Gray was never indicted for the crime, despite his admission. And the jury chose to ignore an important point of Oklahoma law requiring corroboration of accomplice testimony by additional outside evidence.

"Everything that happened," Giddens remembers, "seemed crazy to me. Unbelievable. On the night I was arrested, I knew it had to be a mistake and that I would be out on the street the next morning. Then, when I went to trial, I was certain there was no way the jury could find me guilty because there was no evidence that I had been involved in what happened. Even when I got to prison, to Death Row, I couldn't believe it was happening to me."

For the next three years and six months, he joined fellow inmates in the agonizing wait for death. He was no longer Charles Ray Giddens, the high school dropout, the soft-spoken kid who idled away the hours riding around in a one-horse town, drinking beer, smoking a little pot, and shooting craps in the back room of a nightclub on the black side of the railroad tracks. The other prisoners on Death Row, always quick to give nicknames to newcomers, called him Charlie Brown. The state of Oklahoma labeled him inmate No. 96903.

* * *

On the morning of September 14, 1977, Johnny Gray pulled his late model Impala onto the main drag, driving slowly through the downtown section of Idabel as he accepted a beer offered him by his friend and passenger, Charles Giddens.

Both dropouts, they were two young men going nowhere, spinning their wheels, killing another day.

Charles had quit school for good at the end of his ninth grade year, despite the frustrated protests of his traveling salesman father and the aunt and uncle with whom he lived. Determined not to go back, Giddens got a part-time job loading trucks and cleaning up in the warehouse of a local furniture store. When the minimum wage he earned didn't stretch far enough, he sold a little marijuana to friends for pocket money.

Mostly, though, he cruised the streets of Idabel with friends, drinking and talking, hustling girls and listening to music. It was a treadmill kind of existence and, by his own reflective admission, a dead end course toward trouble.

Around 11 a.m. that day, he and Johnny Gray ran into another Idabel man named Robert Brown in front of Butler's Grocery, a place that served up the finest hot links in McCurtain County. Brown, a year younger than the other two, joined Gray and Giddens, shared their beer, and later invited them to stop by his house. There, he offered them beers from his own refrigerator as they sat in the kitchen.

"We'd been there thirty minutes or so," remembers Giddens, "when Robert got up, went into the bedroom, and came back with a pistol, a .25

automatic with a pearl handle. It was a nice looking gun, and he was really proud of it. Johnny and I both looked at it. I even asked Robert if he wanted to sell it, but he wasn't interested."

The last time Charles Giddens saw the gun that was ultimately linked to the crime of which he was convicted, it was back in the possession of Robert Brown.

Following their visit with Brown, Gray and Giddens rode around town for another hour or so, stopping by the high school football field to talk with a couple of female students. Later, again cruising through the downtown area, they picked up Gray's cousin, Robert Braxton, whom they'd seen walking in the direction of the Dairy Queen.

Which is all to say, it was a pretty ordinary day in the increasingly boring life of young Giddens.

"Earlier that morning," he recalls, "I had talked with Johnny about giving me a ride to Clarksville [Texas] later that afternoon. My car wasn't running, and I wanted to go down there to see my girlfriend. I told him I'd pay for the gas and the motel room if he would take me."

Gray, with nothing better to do, agreed to the trip, and as he dropped Giddens off at his aunt and uncle's house around 2:30 that afternoon, he indicated he was going home to see about borrowing some money from his mother. He said he'd be back later in the day to pick Charles up for the short trip down Highway 37 to Clarksville.

Around 4 p.m., Charles' uncle, David Giddens, called into his bedroom and said Johnny Gray was outside waiting for him. Not expecting his friend so soon, Charles asked his uncle to invite Johnny in while he turned off the television and packed a change of clothes for the trip.

Gray had already gassed the car and seemed anxious to get on the road.

Charles tossed his bag into the backseat of the Impala and noticed eight-packs of beer—Michelob and Miller—in the seat. "These cold?" he asked.

Leaning over to get a beer, he saw a woman's purse in the floorboard. "Hay, man," he said, "your mama left her purse in the car. Maybe we better run it by to her before we get out of town."

Gray shrugged and grinned slightly. "It ain't her purse," he replied.

Nothing more was said about it as they drove southward toward the Red River and the Oklahoma-Texas border.

* * *

The following day, they returned to Idabel shortly before noon. The visit to Clarksville had been pleasant; Charles' girlfriend had accompanied the two young men to a club that evening, where they danced and listened to music until closing time.

Because the motel at which they stayed had just one room available—which Giddens and Gray were forced to share—Charles and his girlfriend cancelled their more intimate plans.

Back in Idabel, they again stopped by Robert Brown's house and found him in the front yard helping his brother work on his car. They talked for an hour or so before leaving so Gray could drop Giddens off at home.

Later that afternoon, Giddens picked up the Idabel Gazette and read a front page story about a robbery-murder that had taken place at the Tapley Grocery Store, seven miles east of Idabel. The story told how Beulah Faye Tapley, the owner's wife, had been shot and killed by the robber.

Giddens scanned the report with interest. He'd seen Mrs. Tapley on numerous occasions when visiting the small roadside store during summers spent with his grandparents, whose farm was just four miles away.

It was the first time, he thought, anyone he knew personally had been the victim of a violent death.

* * *

Two weeks later, Charles was again in the company of Johnny Gray. They had been at a craps game for several hours, lost all their money, and had driven to the parking lot of a nearby apartment complex. Gray wanted to visit a girl there, but he expressed concern that her boyfriend might see his car and cause trouble. He suggested Charles take the car home with him that evening and pick him up the following morning.

"He was pretty nervous about what might happen if the girl's boyfriend found him or his car at her place," Charles recalls, "and talked about taking a .30-.30 rifle in with him. I told him that was crazy. If the guy did come and tried to start something, there was a good chance somebody might really get hurt if there was a gun around."

During that early evening discussion, three Idabel police cars suddenly appeared in the parking lot. Gray and Giddens both ran.

"I ran for a couple of minutes," Charles says, "then stopped and sat down on the steps of one of the apartments. What was I running for? I hadn't done anything. So I just sat there and waited for one of the officers to come to me."

Giddens was handcuffed, read his rights, and told he was being taken to jail on suspicion of attempted burglary of an automobile.

As he was being led to one of the patrol cars, an off-duty policeman who lived in the apartments appeared and pointed at him. "That's one of them," the officer said.

Puzzled and angry but still not really frightened, Giddens had no idea what the policeman was talking about.

The following day, he learned he was in far more trouble than he thought. Late in the afternoon, his aunt and uncle appeared at the city jail accompanied by the McCurtain County sheriff. "I remember my aunt asking why they weren't going to let her make bond and hearing the sheriff tell her that he had pretty strong evidence that I had been involved in a robbery and murder.

"I was sitting on a bunk at the time and jumped up and began screaming. I wanted to know who I was supposed to have robbed, who I was supposed to have murdered. Suddenly, everything went crazy, made no sense. I couldn't believe it."

The following day, the Gazette ran a story reporting 18-year-old Charles Ray Giddens was the prime suspect in the murder of Beulah Faye Tapley.

* * *

In the last week of January 1978, the fifty-seat State District courtroom was packed as the jury heard testimony in the case.

A bizarre sequence of events had already transpired even before the trial began. An attorney whom Giddens' father had hired, agreeing to pay an up-front fee of $10,000 for his son's defense, died in a house fire shortly after taking the case. And word reached Giddens in jail that his friend Johnny Gray had agreed to be a witness for the state and would implicate him in the crime.

During the course of the trial, Gray was, in fact, the state's star witness, telling the following story:

He and Charles drove out to Tapley's Store on the afternoon of the robbery-murder, and he (Gray) went inside to purchase beer. While inside, he dropped a bottle and broke it, apologizing to Mrs. Tapley and telling her he had to go back out to the car to get money to pay for the beer. At the car, he told Giddens he needed to get his money, but Charles said he would go inside and pay. Gray testified that he remained outside and was standing by his car when he heard two shots. Seconds later, he saw Giddens run from the store, carrying the two eight-packs and a woman's purse. They drove away and split the approximately $140 in small bills that was in the purse. Gray said they threw the purse from the car about a mile from the store.

Robert Brown then testified he'd given his .25 automatic to "either Giddens or Gray" on the day of the shooting. He also testified he received the gun back the following day but could not remember whether it was Gray or Giddens who returned the weapon to him.

Giddens' court-appointed attorney, Gail Graytor, argued the witnesses' stories were replete with contradictions to earlier sworn testimony. He called Charles' uncle to the stand and had him tell the jury his nephew was, in fact, at home between 3 and 4 p.m., the time the crime occurred. The attorney called a witness who found the purse several days after the murder, not a mile from the store, but several miles away in a direction opposite that Johnny Gray testified they had gone.

Finally, Charles Giddens took the stand and told his story, describing his activities on the day of the murder. He freely admitted having seen the gun at Brown's home earlier that day. He'd even held it while sitting at the kitchen table. But he had no knowledge of Brown giving the gun to anyone. And he had no knowledge of the murder aside from the facts he had read in the newspaper the day after his return from Clarksville.

"After the jury returned with its decision," Giddens remembers, "they took me back to jail. When I walked in, all the other inmates started cheering and clapping. They were sure I'd been found not guilty." .

Giddens went into his cell and, for the first time since his arrest, expressed his anger. Picking up a small radio the jailer had allowed him to keep, he threw it against the wall.

"Hey, man, you're putting us on," one of the inmates yelled. "Don't shit us. We know they didn't find you guilty."

Giddens glared at him. "If they had found me innocent," he spat, "would I be back in here?"

He knew when the jury came back with a guilty verdict that the death penalty would soon follow. Many in the courtroom that day verbally expressed their shock that he'd been convicted and would likely be sentenced to die on such flimsy evidence.

His attorney, stunned and too embarrassed to even look him in the eye when the jury announced its verdict, filed a motion for a new trial, pointing out the multitude of discrepancies in the testimony of prosecution witnesses and reminding the judge Oklahoma law required corroboration of accomplice testimony.

While Johnny Gray freely admitted he was, in fact, an accomplice in the commission of the crime, he was never indicted.

* * *

A month later, still in the McCurtain County jail awaiting transfer to the state penitentiary, Charles Giddens escaped.

The girlfriend of the man who occupied a cell next to his had smuggled two hacksaw blades into the jail in a family-size bag of potato chips. For three nights, six inmates sawed at the bars. They planned to crawl through the air conditioning vent to the top of the jail, steal cars at a nearby used car lot, and make their getaway.

"They kept telling me they were going to take me with them," Giddens says, "but I really didn't want to go. First of all, I figured we'd all get caught sooner or later. Second, I was still—for whatever reason—convinced that somehow all the mess I was in would get cleared up."

When he refused to saw the bars of his cell, others did it for him. Seven inmates escaped that night, five white men and two black men.

"We went to the roof, climbed down, and ran over to the car lot," Giddens remembers. "We broke in and grabbed a bunch of keys and began trying to find cars they would fit. Finally, we located two cars and a pickup. The other black guy and I got in one of the cars, and we all started toward Hugo, where one of the guys had a sister he thought he could borrow some money from.

"The car I was in ran out of gas just outside of town, so everybody stopped and they gave us the pickup. In Hugo, this guy got twenty dollars, and we decided to split it up and go in different directions. We took our ten and headed for Texas."

Arriving at an uncle's house in Waco in the early morning hours, Giddens told his story over breakfast then went to the back bedroom to sleep. His uncle telephoned Charles' father to advise him where his son was. Martin Giddens left Idabel for Waco immediately.

"When he got there," Charles says, "we talked for several hours. He knew I hadn't killed that lady but was afraid if I kept running they would find me and shoot me. My uncle had already told me he would help me get to this Indian reservation out in Arizona where nobody would know me. I could just sort of disappear there. It sounded pretty good to me because I wasn't real sure I was ever going to get a chance at another trial.

"Finally, though, my father persuaded me to go back with him. He told me, 'Son, just come on back to Idabel, and I promise I'll get you the best lawyer I can find and we'll have you out in two years. I know that sounds like a long time, but it beats running from this all your life.'

"I finally agreed to let him call the sheriff and tell him he was bringing me back in."

Less than 24 hours after his escape, Charles Giddens turned himself back over to the custody of the McCurtain County Sheriff's Department.

His next stop would be the Oklahoma State Penitentiary.

* * *

"I didn't see any way I was going to make it in the prison system," he says. "I'd heard horror stories about how inmates hassle the young guys.

189

What kept going through my mind was that the first time somebody tried to mess with me, I would go crazy and really kill somebody—or get killed myself."

In time, though, Giddens learned the rules of prison survival. "One of the things about Death Row," he says, "is that there is so much security that it's hard for anyone to get to you. Even the guards wouldn't come into the cell block very often. They'd just open the main door, take off your handcuffs, and leave you on the runway. Death Row is kind of a no man's land."

For the next year he was allowed out of his cell for only three minutes twice a week to shower. Otherwise, his world measured 5x8 feet, and his days became nights, his nights became days. "Everyone on Death Row sleeps during the day and stays up at night," he explains. "If you're awake during the day, you can hear the rest of the prison population doing things; out in the yard playing ball or working at their jobs. If you listen to that, you just get more depressed. So you sleep, trying to put the outside world out of your mind."

At night, he recalls, there were no lights on Death Row, so he, like his fellow inmates, sat in the small square of moonlight filtering through the bars, reading, drawing, and writing letters.

After the first month, the cotton in his four-inch thick mattress packed down to a rock hard inch and a half. He came to expect the food and morning coffee delivered to the Row to be cold. He tried to exercise for the first few months but found there wasn't really enough room and quit.

His first execution date was set for July 5, 1978. "A lot of guys had told me not to get too worked up about that first date," he remembers. "They said nobody goes on the first date because the appeal process hadn't run its course. It's the second one they get you on. Still, it wasn't easy to sit there and read a piece of paper that says on such-and-such date they're going to kill you. This may sound kind of strange, but the first thing I thought of when I saw that date was that my birthday would be six days later. It really made me angry that they weren't even going to let me live to see my nineteenth birthday."

After that, the first real fear of dying invaded his thoughts. "Once that first date has passed, you know that any time they can set the next one. It's just a matter of waiting it out. That's when you really get scared."

As the days passed, Giddens continued to learn the ways of life behind bars. Rule One was self-protection. Everyone on the Row, he quickly discovered, carried some kind of weapon. A friend who worked in the kitchen smuggled him a knife fashioned from the twisted wire end of a mop.

"What you do," he says, "is make up your mind to accept the fact you're there and try to figure out what you can do to make yourself as comfortable and safe as possible. And you've got to let everyone know you aren't weak. See, it's the weak guys who have the most trouble. If someone starts trying to give you a hard time, you've got to give it right back to him."

Confined to his cell for that first year, there were few instances wherein he felt threatened. Only after the state passed legislation permitting Death Row inmates occasional *en masse* trips to the prison yard for exercise and fresh air did he actually come into physical contact with his fellow prisoners.

In the next two years, he saw three people killed—one of them his best friend in prison—and watched one inmate, who had spent months collecting medication from others on the Row, attempt suicide. Two white inmates from the general population, having murdered their cell mate, were moved to Death Row and immediately began to pit whites against blacks. For weeks, everyone carried their makeshift knives into the yard.

"Finally, one day this guard came to the Row and talked to everybody. He had heard what was going on and wanted to stop it before somebody got hurt. He was one of the few people at the prison who seemed to really care about people, a guy who would take the time to talk to you. He was sitting in my cell one evening and said, 'Okay, Charles, I know you've got a weapon. I guess everybody here does. I don't want to see it. I just want you to get rid of the damn thing. They're coming in tomorrow morning to shake down everybody's cell. I'm just warning you."

Giddens hid his knife well. Two days later, however, a second surprise search took place. A guard found the weapon taped inside a radio and immediately sent Giddens to solitary. He stayed there for the next 47 days in a room with only a concrete slab for a bed.

It was the closest he would ever came to insanity.

* * *

Marvin Giddens, keeping his promise to his son, hired an Oklahoma City attorney named Ralph Samara, who, after reviewing the files and transcript of the Idabel trial, was incensed Charles' case had even gone to trial on the weak evidence gathered by the prosecution.

The conviction and death sentence, the attorney said, were the gravest miscarriage of justice he'd seen in his lengthy career. There was, he railed, hardly enough evidence to even get a grand jury to indict, much less to conduct a legitimate trial.

In December of 1979, he filed a scathing brief with the Oklahoma Court of Criminal Appeals. In his conclusion, he urged the case against his client be reversed and remanded with instructions to dismiss. Unless the prosecution could provide additional evidence not heard at the first trial, Samara wrote, he could not even see grounds for the state to retry his client.

* * *

The guard who worked the day shift in the prison's solitary confinement wing felt some sympathy for those hidden away in the darkened corner of the Oklahoma State Penitentiary. When no other guards were around, he turned the radio on his desk up to a volume that allowed the isolated inmates down the hall to hear it.

Giddens had been in solitary for three weeks when one morning, as he sat on his concrete bed eating breakfast, only half-listening to the radio newscast, he heard his name.

Suddenly, voices from other cells called out: "Hey, Charlie Brown, they said your name on the radio!"

Later, when the noon news came on, he strained to hear if he was mentioned again. His wait was short. His case was the lead item on the broadcast: "The conviction of Charles Ray Giddens, sentenced to death for the 1977 murder of an Idabel, Oklahoma, grocery store clerk, has been reversed and remanded to the courts..."

"Man, I jumped up and down, waving my arms, crying and clapping my hands," Giddens remembers. "I kept saying, 'I told you so...I told you so.' All along, I'd told everybody that I hadn't killed anybody and that one day I'd be getting out. But when I finally realized that it was going to happen, I was in a state of shock."

With the help of the prison chaplain, Martin Giddens was granted a special visit with his son despite the fact Charles was still restricted to solitary confinement. "Son," he said, "it took longer than we expected, but you're coming home."

"When?" Charles wanted to know.

"Just as soon as the judge down in Idabel decides what he wants to do. He can either ask for a new trial, or he can just dismiss the case. The attorney says he can't see any way they'll bother with another trial."

* * *

Freedom wasn't as quick in coming as Charles Giddens hoped. Not only was he forced to serve out the remainder of his time in solitary, but he also spent another eight months in prison while the wheels of justice sat motionless. In Idabel, obviously, there was little interest in granting him his release.

In time, the Oklahoma Attorney General's office, prodded by Ralph Samara, sent a letter to the district judge, informing him he would be allowed just ten more days to reach a decision on the matter. If, after that time, he hadn't responded, the A.G.'s office would assume responsibility for drawing up the release papers.

The judge never responded.

"The people in Idabel just didn't want to admit they had made a mistake," Giddens says. "They didn't want me back there, reminding them they had convicted the wrong man."

On the evening of July 3, 1982, a guard, clearly angered, walked onto Death Row, unlocked Charles Giddens' cell door, and said, "Get your shit together. You're going home."

"Don't kid me," Giddens replied.

"Get your stuff," the guard said. "Your papers have been sitting up there in the office since early this morning. I found them when I came on duty. They should have already cut you loose. You got somebody you can call to come get you?"

Later that night, the horror story begun almost five years earlier was finally over. Issued a pair of slacks, a sport shirt, and the standard $50 in cash, Charles Ray Giddens walked out the front door of the Oklahoma State Penitentiary a free man.

He was also more frightened than he had been in years.

* * *

Return to the free world, he knew, would not be an easy task. In prison, he'd learned how to take care of himself. If it meant fighting, he fought. He knew the same rules wouldn't apply beyond the McAlester walls. In truth, he was no longer certain what the rules of real life were.

"I knew I had to deal with people in a completely different manner," he says. "I knew if I walked in some place and some guy started giving me a hard time, I'd have to just walk away, leave it alone. It was just the opposite from the way I'd dealt with things in the pen just to make it from one day to the next.

"In prison, they knock you down to a level where you think only of taking care of yourself, regardless of the price. I knew I couldn't carry that same kind of attitude with me into the outside world.

"My dad and I talked about it a lot. He knew it wasn't going to be easy for me.

"There was this big family reunion in Idabel the day after I was released. Dad suggested that I come home, see all my relatives, and then start thinking about going somewhere else, getting far away from Idabel."

Martin Giddens, like most black men in that small southeastern Oklahoma town, knew the racial climate of the region many still refer to as Little Dixie. As late as 1979, the nation's attention had briefly focused on race riots erupting in Idabel after a young black was found hanged on a barbed wire fence behind a nightclub in a white section of town. Before calm was restored, two other people were killed.

Idabel was at peace that summer when Charles Giddens returned. But the railroad tracks which ran through the heart of town still marked the dividing line between the black and white populations of the community.

"But, dammit, I wanted to go back," Charles says. "I had the right. It was my home. My friends were there. And I wanted people to know I was free, that the courts had finally acknowledged the fact that I was innocent of the crime they sent me to prison for. So, I decided to stay in Idabel."

For most of a year, he remained there, unsuccessful in finding anything more than part time work. And he heard the constant flow of rumors that certain members of the white community didn't like the idea of a convicted murderer walking their streets. The intimation was subtle but clear: Charles Giddens had better watch his step. In the closed minds of many, he was still a killer. He'd just somehow managed to beat the system.

When more and more whites were seen slowly driving through the black section of town, sometimes stopping to ask youngsters playing in their yards or on the playground if they had seen Charles Giddens around, he got the message.

"I knew if I was going to be able to start a new life for myself, it would have to be somewhere else," he says.

In a manner of speaking, Idabel tried him a second time, again found him guilty, and sent him away.

For a while, he lived and worked in Waco then moved to Dallas, leaving his past behind. He made new friends but told them nothing of Idabel or McAlester.

And now, every day creates greater distance from those troubled times.

"I was bitter for a while," he admits. "There were a lot of days while I was sitting on Death Row when all I thought about was getting back at the people who put me there. I wanted to find Johnny Gray and ask him why he did what he did to me. I wanted to look up the sheriff and the judge and the district attorney and all those people on the jury. I was also angry with everyone who had refused to help me. I wrote to the NAACP while I was in the pen, begging for them to look into my situation, and never even got a reply. I thought if I ever got out I would spend a lot of time looking up people and letting them know how I felt. But I never did. Now, I don't even want to.

"That's all passed. It's history. And that's where I'm going to leave it. I don't think about it any more."

Finally, Charles Giddens has a future. And he doesn't want the ghosts of the past getting in his way.

◆*D Magazine*, 1986

POSTSCRIPT:

For a time after the story was published, Charles stayed in touch. He seemed happy, had a good job, and spoke less frequently of the nightmare of his teen years. Then he moved from Dallas and we lost touch. In Idabel, no one was ever tried for the murder of Faye Tapley.

The Newton Gang

If we went into a town, looking to rob the bank and saw police in the vicinity, we just kept driving. It was better to say, "There he goes" than "Here he lies."
■ Willie Newton to author Claude Stanush

Many youngsters of my generation looked upon the outlaw exploits of such legendary figures as Pretty Boy Floyd, Bonnie and Clyde, and Ma Barker and her boys with a skewed sort of awe. Not that we wanted to grow up to be notorious bank robbers or chased by the law, mind you. But in that pre-tabloid time, they were the titillating stuff of romantic legend; their lives and criminal deeds chronicled on the front pages of our daily papers and in occasional B-movies. We followed their trails with the same enthusiasm we attached to collecting baseball cards.

But in the hardscrabble West Texas of my youth, I listened as my elders talked of a family of brothers whose exploits put all others to shame. They were the homegrown Newton Boys. If the stories I heard were true, they robbed half the banks in the country, made off with gigantic sums of money, and, the gentlemen that they were, never once killed anyone. They drove fast cars, carried out their crimes with great planning and nerve, and deserved to be listed among the most notorious outlaws of their time.

Yet the Newton Boys never received their just place in the annals of criminal history. Those of us with the provincial mind-set that demanded our bank robbers be duly recognized grumbled over the short shrift given the local boys.

Only now, decades after their glory days, has the world come to know Willis, Dock, Jess, and Joe Newton. They finally came to the attention of retired San Antonio-based *Life* magazine writer Claude Stanush and gifted Austin movie-maker Richard Linklater. Through their efforts, the Newtons have now been portrayed on the big screen in *The Newton Boys*, starring a who's who of young Hollywood stars. Based on the State House Press oral history of the brothers' Texas-to-Canada crime spree, *The Newton Boys: Portrait of an Outlaw Gang*, which Stanush coauthored after lengthy confessionals from Willis and Joe Newton, it stars Texan Matthew

McConaughey as Willis, Ethan Hawke as Jess, Vincent D'Onofrio as Dock, and Skeet Ulrich as Joe.

Finally, the story that fascinated me for a lifetime emerged from history's footnotes.

* * *

It was a time when the Republican Party enthusiastically endorsed a Calvin Coolidge platform and a wavy-haired youngster named Gene Tunney was being groomed as the next heavyweight champion of the world. The Great Depression was something that could never happen in a place like America, and the Jazz Age had spilled merrily into the Roaring '20s.

And, on the evening of June 13, 1924, Engine No. 57 of the Chicago, Milwaukee & St. Paul Express left Union Station with nine mail and two express shipment cars in tow. In less than two hours, it found its place in history and in the folklore of my hometown storytellers.

As it slowed for the hamlet of Rondout, Illinois, just outside Chicago, the Newtons prepared to stage the richest train robbery in American history. In a matter of minutes, the holdup men, accompanied by an Oklahoma cowboy named Brent Glasscock (portrayed in the movie by country singer/actor Dwight Yoakam) and Chicago postal inspector Bill Fahay, gathered $3 million in cash, stocks, bonds, and uncut diamonds.

Months of preparation had gone into the robbery. Willis and Jess Newton and Glasscock boarded the train in Chicago, posing as railroad employees. As the train moved along, they climbed toward the engine to order the engineer to stop the train at a pre-determined spot known as Buckley Road. The plan called for Dock Newton to take his position just outside the lead mail car while the others entered and located the pouches containing money and jewels.

There was, however, a hitch in the plan. The train crept another hundred yards down the track before the engineer could bring it to a complete stop. Dock ran alongside the mail car so that he might be at his appointed position. Irritated by the departure from the plan, he shouted toward a figure stepping from the rear of the train: "Hey, what the hell's going on?"

He was answered by five gunshots which hit him in the jaw, arms, hands and side. Before he could aim the shotgun he carried, Dock fell to the cinders, unconscious.

Only after the outlaws completed the robbery and were preparing to make their getaway did they notice Dock was missing. They located his crumpled body quickly. Not even bothering to pick up his hat, which lay nearby, his brothers lifted him into the backseat of one of the two cars waiting to speed them from the scene of the historic crime.

It had been Glasscock, startled by Dock and more than slightly unnerved by the situation, who fired the shots.

Close to death as he rode in the back seat of a car for two days and nights, Dock's condition ultimately caused the gang's downfall. Gangrene set into his jaw, and it was obvious that, without the attention of a doctor, he would never live to spend any of the newly accumulated fortune. Thus his brothers took him to the Chicago address of an underworld doctor, who removed part of Dock's infected jawbone and mended his other wounds.

Other underworld figures were questioned repeatedly by Chicago authorities and soon became irritated with the accusations that they were involved in the train robbery. They began suggesting, "[T]hat shot-up guy over on North Washtenaw Avenue might be able to tell you what happened."

As a result, the gang was apprehended. In exchange for lenient sentences, they returned the stolen money and fruit jars filled with diamonds. Fahay, the postal inspector who was the robbery's architect and inside man, received a 25-year sentence. Willis and Dock Newton were sentenced to 12 years in Leavenworth, as was Glasscock. Joe received a three-year term.

Jess, the youngest of the brothers, ultimately spent a short time behind bars, but only after leading law enforcement officers on a merry, winding chase.

Says Stanush: "Jess was the only one not arrested, and he took off to Texas with some of the money they'd taken from the train. He apparently hid out in San Antonio for a time and one evening, after getting quite drunk in a bar, hired a cab driver to take him somewhere out in the country where he supposedly buried something like $35,000."

According to the stories his brothers told me, Jess woke up the next day and, applying more sober reasoning, decided to retrieve the money and take it into Mexico with him. Trouble was, he couldn't remember where he buried it. And when he finally located the Mexican cab driver, that guy couldn't remember either. "I was very drunk, too," the driver explained.

The buried money was never found.

Eventually, authorities tracked Jess to Piedras Negras, a city in northeastern Mexico near the Texas border, where he spent most of his time drinking tequila and entertaining locals with stories of his talents as a bronc rider. Since no extradition agreement existed between the U.S. and Mexican authorities, the federal agent who located Jess had to resort to a devious plan to lure him back into the United States.

After several nights of drinking with the unsuspecting Newton, the agent noted an upcoming rodeo just across the border in Del Rio. It would feature a horse that no man had successfully ridden.

"I damn sure can," Jess announced.

The agent offered a wager of $500, which the brash young Newton quickly accepted.

The following day, as he entered the rodeo grounds to get a look at the renegade horse, the agent placed him in handcuffs. Jess served a year and a day in prison for his part in the Illinois train robbery.

"The reason he got such a light sentence," says Stanush, "was the fact he'd never been in any trouble before and because of the sympathetic testimony of the train's engineer at his trial. He recalled that when Jess had approached him with the demand to stop the train, he'd smiled, shook his head, and said, 'Ain't this a helluva way to make a living?'"

Back in Texas, bankers breathed a sigh of relief at news that the Newton gang was finally behind bars. Their reputation became so widespread that they were routinely credited with robbing banks they'd never even heard of. On more than one occasion, they were reported in two places at one time—a surefire sign of notoriety.

* * *

Such were the stories I pursued once I became a journalist, digging through time weathered courthouse records and old news clips and listening to tales spun by those who'd known and chased after the Newtons.

It was left for author Stanush to provide details of the Newtons' upbringing, to offer some hint of why they turned to their lives of crime. Born near the Callahan County farming community of Cottonwood, their father was a sharecrop farmer who constantly moved from one dusty patch of land to the next.

"People say my daddy [Jim Newton] was a good man," Willis told Stanush. "They just never said what he was good for. He was what folks called a cyclone farmer, blowing all over the country, always looking for something better than what he had."

His mother, Janetta Pecos Newton, worked miracles to keep food on the table and outfit her eleven children in homemade clothing. When the seat of fourth grader Willis' pants finally frayed beyond the ability of his mother to repair, he avoided further embarrassment by simply dropping out of school. His brothers soon followed suit.

While the other children learned their multiplication tables and verb conjugation, the Newton boys grew up working in the cotton fields with their father. To escape the tedious work and dreary farm life, they occasionally hid out in boxcars and rode trains to such exotic places as

Cross Plains, Big Spring, and Abilene for a sample of big city life. The Newton boys were touched by wanderlust and an affection for bright lights early on.

Though official records reveal amazingly few depositions against them, they were generally credited by newspapers and historians with bank robberies in such Texas outposts as Winters, Coleman, Waxahachie, San Marcus, Boerne, and New Braunfels, as well as throughout the Midwest and into Canada. Stanush credits the gang with 60 bank robberies; Willis claimed an additional 20. They hit six trains in all, practicing for the multimillion dollar Illinois robbery by holding up mail trains near Denison, Bells, and Texarkana.

As colorful as they were daring, the Newtons thrived in the public imagination, bridging the Old West outlaw and the gangsters of the Al Capone era. The Newtons rode horses and drove Cadillacs. They wore cowboy boots and diamond stickpins.

What movie-maker Linklater fashioned was a similar hybrid: a Western gangster movie, the character study of a family of young men who robbed banks as an alternative to long, brain-baking days in the Texas cotton fields.

"The reason people haven't heard much about the Newton gang," actor Hawke suggested to a gathering of press while the movie was being shot, "is because they never killed anybody. They weren't a bunch of thugs. Robbing banks and trains was just their business, and they seemed to have fun doing it."

In time, apprehension of the gang became an obsession with Texas law enforcement officials. The public, on the other hand, wagered they would never be caught. The Newton boys, popular theory had it, were too cunning, their cars too fast. They spent weeks, sometimes months, planning each robbery, were careful to cut telephone and telegraph wires, and used nitroglycerine to blow safes—all methods that kept the law off-balance and unprepared. The reward money for their capture reportedly totaled $100,000.

There was often a dark comedy attached to their activities. One time they used a bit too much nitro and not only ripped the door off the vault, but also blew the entire front wall of the bank into the street.

Following the robbery of the Winters National Bank, word quickly reached nearby Ballinger that one of the Newtons had been killed in a shootout during their getaway. A sheriff's deputy chased a member of the gang as far as the community of Buffalo Gap and shot him in a downtown gun battle. He quickly sent word back to the Runnels County seat that he'd killed Jess Newton and was returning the body for all to see.

Later that day, the body was placed on a slab on the courthouse lawn so the townspeople might be afforded a view of one of the region's most notorious robbers.

J.P. Clifton, a Ballinger resident who had grown up with the Newtons near Cross Plains, was summoned to identify the body.

Clifton, the son of a former Texas Ranger, was residing in a rest home back in the late '70s when I visited him to hear his recollection: "They came and got me and said they'd shot Jess and wanted me to come officially identify him. We went down to the courthouse, where people were milling around everywhere. The fella they had shot was heavyset and bald. I told them right quick that it wasn't Jess Newton.

"Sometime before dark, Willis Newton came driving into town, big as life [there was no proof that he had been involved in the robbery, thus he was safe from arrest], and went over and looked at the body. He told the sheriff that he thought the guy's name was Ingram but that he wasn't sure what his first name was.

"The sheriff asked Willis what he should do with the body and ol' Willis just looked down at it for a few seconds, then said, 'You can throw the SOB into the Colorado River for all I care.' And with that he left town."

Jess Newton, the man who had caused such a furor on that day in 1917, died of cancer in 1960.

Clifton was not among those who remembered the Newton boys kindly. They grew up together in West Texas, and he'd had more than his share of run-ins with the brothers. "They were meaner than hell," he recalled.

"We were at a dance one night, and I'd just bought some new clothes at a store over in Cross Plains—a couple of pairs of pants and a new shirt. They were still bundled up and in the back of my buggy. The Newtons came to the dance and later in the night stole my clothes and hid out in the brush with them until the next morning when we got our guns and tracked them down."

Willis, who had already done prison time after he and Dock were convicted of stealing cotton from a local gin, was arrested and sentenced to two years for the theft of Clifton's new clothes.

In time, however, Willis and Dock matured to far more serious criminal behavior, luring their brothers along.

During January of 1921, they robbed the Hondo State Bank and the Hondo First National on the same Saturday night, making off with $150,000. They hit the Citizen's Bank of Houston two days later in broad daylight, taking away $80,000.

In February—they routinely picked cold weather for their work since townspeople and authorities were less inclined to brave the elements—they took $150,000 from the First State Bank in Boerne and robbed the New Braunfels State Bank of $115,000. The last Texas bank robbery credited to the brothers occurred in 1924, when they took $24,000 from the San Marcos Bank and Trust.

The Newtons got around. They robbed a bank in Spencer, Indiana; one in Deer Trail, Colorado; another in Moosomin, Saskatchewan; hijacked a mail truck in a Chicago suburb; and robbed a bank clearing house in Toronto.

Writes Stanush, "By their own accounting, they made off with more loot in a four year period than Jesse and Frank James, the Dalton brothers, Butch Cassidy, and all those other famous outlaw gangs put together."

* * *

After serving their respective sentences in Leavenworth, Kansas, for the Illinois train robbery, the Newtons dropped from the criminal limelight, settling on small farms in Texas and Oklahoma. Dock married, but soon his wife and land were both gone. He moved to Uvalde to exercise the boilermaker trade he learned in prison.

Willis stole back for another fling with the law in 1962—52 years after stealing the bales of cotton that sent him to prison for the first time. At age 74, he was sentenced to a year in the Oklahoma state pen for kidnapping a man who worked for him on his ranch near Tulsa. The hired hand, according to Willis' testimony, had stolen some jewelry from him, and all Willis was doing was attempting to scare him into telling where he hid it. The jury determined chaining the man and forcing him to ride halfway across Oklahoma in the trunk of a car was a bit too severe.

By then, Dock was collecting Social Security back home in Uvalde, suffering from arthritis brought on by the numerous bullet wounds he suffered during the infamous 1924 train robbery. His heart was failing.

Joe, having divorced himself from his early ways, became a well-respected rancher near Uvalde.

There is, however, a nostalgic footnote to the Newton gang's career:

On the evening of March 5, 1968, 78-year-old Dock Newton found himself back in the country he'd known as a boy, taking his last look at the far-reaching West Texas plains, the scrubby mesquites, the windmills, and the cotton fields he'd so long despised.

Late that night, in the tiny community of Rowena, hometown of the legendary Bonnie Parker, Dock and his Uvalde friend Robert Talley entered the First National Bank, carrying with them two .38-caliber handguns and a .30-.30 rifle.

Across the street, Butch Lisso, a boyhood friend of famed Texas Ranger Frank Hammer—the man who finally tracked down Bonnie and Clyde—was startled from his sleep by the bank's alarm, which was located in the rear of his liquor store.

Lisso quickly summoned the sheriff from nearby Ballinger. After a brief gun battle shattered the silence of the sleeping hamlet, Dock Newton was back in custody, along with his partner. A third party, whom Lisso thought he'd seen enter the front door of the bank, escaped.

Forty-four years after receiving his sentence for the legendary Illinois train robbery, brought into the courtroom on a stretcher, Dock pled no contest to the Rowena charges in an out-of-the-way courtroom in Fort Stockton, Texas. He was sentenced to two years in prison.

I watched that day as a sad-faced, gray-haired man squinted into the sunlight as he was taken from the courtroom and walked toward a car waiting to return him to his jail cell. He moved in the shuffling gait of a tired old man.

There was time for only one question as he passed by. Why, I wanted to know, had he done it?

He smiled faintly as he pondered my question, then shrugged. "Who knows why anyone does anything," he replied.

After spending eight months in a prison hospital, Dock was released and settled in a nursing home in Uvalde. He died in 1974 at age 83.

* * *

On a visit to Claude Stanush in San Antonio, I made no attempt to hide the envy I felt for his having had the opportunity to hear first-hand accounts of the Newtons' exploits from Willis and Joe before their deaths. The 79-year-old author explained they came to him in 1973, looking for someone who might help them tell their story.

"I'm not sure what I expected," Stanush says, "but neither of them looked like hardened criminals. Willis was dressed like an elderly businessman, wearing a suit and tie; Joe was dressed like the cowboy he'd always really been.

"What they wanted to do was set the record straight. While they acknowledged robbing a lot of banks in their day, they were also credited with a lot of crimes they hadn't committed. And according to Willis, the reported amounts of money they'd taken was often inflated by bank owners who, he felt, were just as criminal-minded as he was.

"And while I found the stories of their bank robbing days interesting, that wasn't really what attracted me. They seemed to have such a wonderful recall of history, of the climate of the times in which they had grown up.

They were intelligent men who were fascinated by nature and the outdoors."

In time, he says, they became more than the subjects of a book. They became his friends. They visited his home; he visited theirs. Stanush was at 90-year-old Willis' bedside when he died in 1979.

"The thing I remember about that night," he says, "was this fella who was a patient in a nearby bed telling me, 'You know, I really liked that old man. '"

So, obviously, did Stanush.

In 1989, the last of the Newtons, Joe, died at age 88.

But before they were gone, Stanush taped hours of their reminiscences for the book he would write. He also teamed with Trinity University professor David Middleton to produce a film documentary of the life and times of the Newton gang. Shown at film festivals and on college campuses, it earned numerous awards.

And, he says, Willis and Joe seemed to enjoy the spotlight shown on them during their final years.

On one occasion, when the San Marcos State Bank was in the midst of an anniversary celebration, it had as its featured guests the two surviving members of the Newton gang, which had robbed it back in 1924. "They answered questions and were treated like celebrities," Stanush remembers. "They thoroughly enjoyed themselves."

I wondered how they would have greeted the feature film that chronicled their life. And what became of all the money they stole?

"They spent it," Stanush says. "You've got to remember, they were just young kids back when they were riding high. They all liked to have a good time, dress well, and drive new cars."

They put nothing back for a rainy day?

"Oh, maybe a little," the author acknowledges. And with that he was off on another story:

"Once, when I was in Uvalde," he says, "I was introduced to [former Texas governor] Dolph Briscoe, who now owns the local bank. The meeting gave rise to another question I needed to ask Willis and Joe. I wanted to know why they had never robbed the bank in their hometown.

"It was Willis who answered what he clearly felt was a rather dumb question. 'Hell,' he said, 'we had to have some bank where we could keep the money we were robbing from the others. '"

♦ *Texas, Houston Chronicle, 1997*

Likely Suspect

There are some who see the glass as half empty, others who see it as half full. And there are those who will learn that we are the glass. This is evolution. This is power…

> ■ Gina Cotroneo

They were, to those who knew them, young and bright and quickly gaining ground in their race toward the American Dream. A rising star disc jockey for a Dallas radio station, Gary Faison had begun to taste the intoxicating fame to which he'd long aspired. Gina Cotroneo, meanwhile, was prospering as an art director for a local ad agency, involved in a relationship possibly headed toward marriage, and eagerly anticipating her debut speech to the Toastmasters organization she'd recently joined.

He was black, 31, charming, flashy and fun-loving, a celebrity whose stature had grown with every morning drive-time broadcast on KKDA and each nighttime appearance at trendy local nightclubs. She was white, 30, pretty and outgoing, so positive in attitude that simply finding a shiny new penny on her way to work would make her day.

And then, in the early morning of June 19, 1997, it all turned into a nightmare. In a brief, violent span of time in the pitch dark of 4 a.m., the lives of these two strangers collided and crumbled. He was arrested, tried, and convicted of crimes his friends and coworkers couldn't believe he would have committed. She lost her job, the marriage she'd looked forward to never took place, and even her strong faith in God was tested.

He went to prison, convicted of rape. She went into therapy.

Recently, both spoke about the life-altering chain of events that continue to link them. For Cotroneo, telling the story has been an ongoing therapeutic exercise. Unlike many survivors of rape, she has boldly stepped into the light, appearing on talk shows and telling her story to a national women's magazine. For Faison, the decision to speak out came after five years of silence.

* * *

205

The route taken to Dallas by Cotroneo, daughter of an electrical engineer father and bookkeeper mother, wound from her hometown of Rome, New York, to Tampa Bay, Atlanta, and Portland before her arrival in Texas in 1993. Along the way, she'd not only polished her artistic skills to a point that they landed her a well-paying job, but she'd also developed a fascination with quantum mechanics, all things spiritual, and the mysteries of the paranormal. Her mission in life, she says, became an ongoing search for knowledge and understanding. Gina welcomed the answers she found in the esoteric books she read constantly and thought-provoking, late-into-the-night discussions with friends.

In time, she even began to think her calling might not be in the advertising world but, instead, as a motivational speaker. It was for that reason she joined Toastmasters, a training organization for aspiring speech-makers. On that Wednesday evening in '97, she carefully organized her note cards, and her boyfriend listened as she practiced the talk she planned to give on modern day miracles. As soon as he left, Gina removed her contacts and prepared for bed. A good night's sleep, she felt, would improve her chances of success the following day.

Cotroneo never got to deliver her speech. Instead, she was providing law enforcement officials and hospital attendants with details of the most harrowing night of her life. Those attending her and taking her statement agreed she was lucky to be alive.

She told a dark, ugly story, one no woman dares allow herself to even imagine:

She'd been startled from sleep by the sound of her front door slamming. For a split second, she thought her boyfriend might have returned, but that notion vanished as a large, dark figure rushed into her bedroom and was quickly on top of her, placing a beefy hand over her mouth. "Do you want to die?" her attacker asked in a Jamaican accent. "I'll kill you if you scream." And then he raped her.

She struggled as he attempted to place a pillowcase over her head, then felt the searing pain of being raped vaginally and anally.

"Do you have any money? The intruder demanded. Cotroneo could not make out the man's face, only smell his foul breath and feel his large, fleshy hands pressing down against her. "In my purse," she replied.

"After the first 20 or 30 seconds," she remembers, "some of the terror eased, and I made myself think only about survival." She struggled to focus her thoughts on a favored photo of a guardian angel that hung above her bed, silently praying for its protection.

When the rapist ordered her to accompany him to the bathroom and shower, she managed to assert herself for the first time. "I turned on the water, and he started pushing me. I told him that I wouldn't get in until the spray had warmed. That seemed to shock him a little, but he let me wait. He just told me not to look at him and set down on the commode, waiting for me to get into the shower," she remembers.

As she did so, she got her best look at her attacker. Peeking from behind the curtain she "saw only the top of his head. Still, without her contacts her vision was seriously hampered. She did, however, get the impression he had "deep set eyes" and would later estimate the man at six feet tall and 250 pounds.

The humiliation wasn't over. Following her shower, the intruder forced her to perform oral sex on him and ejaculated into her mouth. He then shoved her into a closet, closed the door, and disappeared into the night.

What the attacker, exercising what he thought was extreme care to leave no physical evidence behind, hadn't anticipated was his victim's calm and resolve. Once certain he had left her apartment, Cotroneo exited the closet, hurried into her kitchen, and spat his semen into a plastic freezer bag. "All I could think," she says, "was that I wanted to be sure this guy was caught."

The evidence of her attack preserved, she telephoned her boyfriend, then the police. When they arrived at her apartment, they were amazed at her controlled demeanor. "People deal with trauma in different ways," she reflects. "At the time, I felt a lot of strong emotions—fear, violation—but not guilt. I knew I had done nothing wrong. What had happened was in no way my fault." Above all, Gina Cotroneo was angry.

That mindset got her through the days immediately following her assault. Instead of returning to her apartment, she moved into a spare room at her boyfriend's home for a while before going in search of a new place of her own. She missed only a single day of work and, in keeping with her lifetime quest for knowledge, began searching the internet for information on rape and its victims.

"After about three weeks," she says, "I felt I was ready to be on my own again, to get my life back to normal." Thus she attended a Toastmasters gathering, not anticipating that the first speaker's topic would deal with ways to prevent home break-ins. "I had to get up and leave," she says. "A lady in the group noticed me and came outside to ask if I was okay. When I explained why I'd left, she gave me the name of a counselor she recommended I contact.

"I felt I'd been handling things pretty well, but I also knew I didn't want to be one of those who suddenly suffers a breakdown in the middle of a shopping mall a year later. So I spent the next six months in therapy."

"She had an incredible determination to work through what had happened to her," says Patsy D. Phillips, a licensed professional counselor who specializes in trauma. "It was made easier by the fact she absolutely refused to see herself as a victim. Gina was a young woman with a strong spiritual foundation, and she used that to her advantage. She saw what had happened to her as something she needed to learn from. I admire her a great deal."

Cotroneo's progress, in fact, was well ahead of what law enforcement was making with its investigation. They found no data base match to the DNA sample, singled out no suspect.

And the rapes of Dallas women continued.

* * *

The man eventually arrested and charged with attacking Cotroneo and five others had come a long way since leaving Dallas' Hope Cottage when he was just eight days old, adopted by James and Vera Faison. He'd grown up in a home where his father, a Tom Thumb grocery store manager, demanded discipline and hard work. His mother made sure her new son regularly attended services at the neighborhood Baptist church.

"He was as good a little boy as you could hope to have," says his now widowed mother. "He'd even save part of his weekly allowance so when Christmas came he could buy gifts with his own money." She proudly remembers him singing in the church choir, always quick to lend a hand to others. Her's is the unwavering love of a mother for her child. "I pray for him every day," she says.

By the time he'd entered Garland High School, Gary had become a popular youngster who could bring home A and B report cards with very little study, was an outstanding linebacker on the football team, and, according to former teachers and fellow students alike, was the school's reigning class clown.

Only in the final days of his senior year did serious trouble visit.

It was, he reflects, the first time he'd "stepped out of bounds." He had begun dating a 16-year-old white girl despite her parents' displeasure. Still, he says, he was stunned when he learned the girl, accompanied to the police station by her mother and father, had filed rape charges against him. "She had told them that she was drunk and I sexually assaulted her," Faison recalls. The charges, he insists, were unfounded, triggered by an irate father angered over the fact his daughter was dating a black man.

Nevertheless, he was convicted in 1983 and sentenced to eight years in prison. The planned visits to the campuses of Rice, SMU, and Angelo State, where football coaches were promising scholarships, never occurred. Instead of a college campus, Gary Faison called the Texas Department of

Corrections' Ferguson and Beto units home for the next 32 months.

Once paroled, he found rebuilding his life difficult. He worked in a snack food warehouse, then a printing company, and, finally, in a grocery store deli. Briefly, he tried to revive his athletic career, joining a local semipro football team. Then, in the summer of 1988, he made a serendipitous phone call that led to a new lease on life.

"I was a big fan of the Tom Joyner Show [on KKDA]," he says, "and called in one day to answer a trivia question." Soon, he became acquainted with Joyner and other on-air personalities like Willis Johnson and Chris Arnold and reestablished ties with an old kindergarten classmate, Aaron Michaels, who was doing a late night show.

"One night," he says, "Willis invited me to go with him to Players, where he sometimes worked as a DJ." Soon, Faison, in his mid-twenties and up to 250 pounds, was serving as Johnson's assistant and bodyguard at clubs. One evening, a waitress questioned his age, pointing out that he looked too young for admittance. Surprised to learn Faison had just turned 25, she remarked that his baby face made him look much younger. Gary thus adopted a new moniker that remains to this day. Tinkering a bit with the King's English, he assigned himself the nickname "Babyfase." And he began visiting the Grand Prairie studios of KKDA, spending evenings watching as his old friend Michaels did his late night show. "He began to teach me," Faison says, "and would occasionally let me talk on the air."

In time, Faison was hired to work at the station, and he and Michaels became a team. When he wasn't bombarding his audience with an endless stream of jokes and music, he was out in the community doing street promotions, offering first callers and those who answered trivia questions correctly a free fill-up of gas, tickets to concerts, or copies of the latest releases of popular black artists.

Former class clown and ex-con, Gary "Babyfase" Faison had found his niche. By the late '90s, he was one of the metroplex's best known radio personalities, not only hosting a daily show with climbing ratings and earning top dollar as a club DJ, but so active in the black community that he began to win praise and plaques from the NAACP and other civic organizations. Word was that rival stations were trying to lure him away, promising bigger audiences and better pay. When TV talk show host Montel Williams shot the pilot for his successful syndicated show, Faison was among those asked to lend a hand.

He was, by his own admission, living the dream, having money in his pocket, driving a new Z-28 with personalized plates (Babyfase, naturally), rubbing elbows with celebrities, and being a constant target of women admirers who seemed not at all put off by the fact his weight had ballooned to 320 pounds. Though unmarried, he was the father of two daughters and a son and maintained a close relationship with them and their mothers.

Then, on a Saturday night in July of 1998, Faison's bright star suddenly went dark.

"I'd been invited to a party," he remembers, "and on the way home I had to take a leak. I'd recently had an appendectomy and had been drinking. I was in pain and needed to go pretty badly." Thus, he says, he pulled into an apartment parking lot and ran across the street to a row of unlighted bushes where he planned to relieve himself. Almost immediately, however, the beam of a security guard's flashlights was shining in his face and he was being ordered to lie on the ground. Two other guards soon arrived, one handcuffing him while the other placed a call to the Dallas police.

During a 45-minute wait, Faison learned from those detaining him that a woman living in a nearby apartment had been attacked just a week earlier by a man who had hit her with a bar stool from her dining room. There was also talk of the series of break-ins and rapes that had occurred in the general vicinity. "I finally snapped on the fact they were thinking I might be the guy doing all that," Faison says.

When the police arrived, however, they immediately ordered the handcuffs removed. "One of the officers seemed a little irritated at the security guards, looking at me and then handing one of them a flier and asking if he'd read it," he remembers. On it, the suspected rapist was described as weighing between 180 and 200 pounds, a weight range the 6-1 Faison hadn't enjoyed since his teenage years.

Thus he was released. Before returning to his car, he remembers, he shook hands with the security officers and the police. "I told them I understood they were just doing their jobs and that there were no hard feelings." Aside from receiving what he perceived as a few too many speeding tickets from them, Faison insists he had no negative feelings toward law enforcement in those days. In fact, he says, he'd been occasionally dating a woman lieutenant with the DPD tactical squad, even riding along with her on patrol now and then. In his billfold he carried an Honorary Deputy Constable card.

Early the following week, however, the KKDA station manager entered the control room where Faison was on the air, asking if there was someone who could sit in for him for the remainder of his show. The manager explained there were detectives in the lobby with a warrant for his arrest.

Soon after being escorted from the station, Faison was fingerprinted, a blood sample to be used in DNA testing was taken, and he was placed under $1 million bond.

In her Garland home, Vera Faison thought it strange that her son hadn't finished his show, which she listened to daily. She began dialing his cell phone number repeatedly but got no answer. In fact, she didn't learn until the following day that Gary had been arrested. She says she was dumbfounded when a Dallas Morning News reporter phoned to ask her response to the charges being filed against her son.

"What charges?" she asked. Rape, she was told.

Sitting at her dining room table, surrounded by family pictures and dozens of still shiny trophies that remind her of her son's athletic triumphs, she shakes her head as she remembers the day. "I was in shock," she says.

There were long, dark hours before Gary was finally allowed to telephone her. She began to weep at the first sound of his voice. "He told me, 'Mama, don't cry; don't believe this.'"

Now, five years and two trials later, she still doesn't.

* * *

During the mid-to-late '90's, an ominous cloud of fear settled over a northeast section of the city populated by singles apartments. Police were convinced that not one, but several serial rapists were terrorizing the neighborhood. Ultimately, a 43-year-old man named Ollie Ray Diles, who had been labeled "The Box-Cutter Rapist" after victims described the weapon he'd used to subdue them, was caught in 1997, convicted for three sexual attacks, and given three life sentences. Next to be apprehended was Sammie Luckus Cook, Jr., 31, who was linked by DNA evidence to as many as fifteen rapes dating back to 1995.

The litany of details provided by Cook's victims was numbing. Their assailant, each reported, had worn a bandanna over his face and either gloves or socks on his hands to prevent leaving any fingerprints. He used purse straps, belts, or electrical cords to bind their hands and feet and threatened them with a knife or scissors. In one case, a woman told of coming out of her bathroom to find a man holding a kitchen fork to the throat of her six-year-old daughter. The mother managed to grab the youngster away but was eventually raped as the terrified child looked on. Another had been eight months pregnant at the time of her attack.

Police, however, didn't believe Diles and Cook were the only rapists terrorizing northeast Dallas.

There had, for instance, been the young woman who, after returning from a week's vacation, was wakened at 2 a.m. by an intruder who entered her bedroom and placed a towel and a gloved hand over her face before raping her. During the attack, he threatened to cut out her eyes if she screamed or resisted. When he asked for money, the victim provided him with her ATM pin. Then, before leaving, he forced her to shower in an effort to do away with any physical evidence of the attack. She later told police she never saw the assailant's face.

There was, however, a photograph of a man using the ATM near the woman's apartment following the assault. Additionally, police lifted a palm print from a window screen that had apparently been removed from the victim's apartment and found nearby.

Then, two weeks before Christmas in 1995, a 26-year-old SMU graduate student was attacked in the early morning hours by a man who entered her apartment through a sliding glass door. The assailant covered her head with a pillowcase, bound her hands with a pair of pantyhose, and raped her. Throughout the attack, he warned he would cut her if she screamed. Following the rape, he also demanded she shower before he disappeared into the night.

The victim, who never saw her attacker's face, could only describe him as being 5-10 and weighing approximately 190 pounds. The only clues left behind were partial prints left by the intruder on the front door deadbolt and a strip of tape used to disable a locking bar. Unfortunately, as with the previous case, the police had no suspect with whom to compare the prints.

The following July, a young married woman whose husband was out of town on business was getting dressed for work when a man burst into her bedroom and threw a blanket over her head. He sexually assaulted her, then took $20 and a Discover card from her purse. Through the traumatic event, she later told investigators, she talked about being the mother of a young son and begged that her life be spared. She also asked her attacker to use a condom during the rape. All she could remember the man saying in response was for her to "settle down and shut up."

Though she was unable to provide police with a description of the man who attacked her, a neighbor later told authorities of seeing a black man looking into the woman's apartment window. Another resident said she'd been walking her dog two days earlier and saw an unfamiliar African American male near the rape victim's apartment.

While relatively certain the same person had committed all three rapes—and perhaps as many as a half dozen others—frustrated investigators had no real suspect. The man they had been desperately searching for was little more than a faceless ghost. Until Gary Faison was arrested.

* * *

A year had passed since her attack when Gina Cotroneo received a call from Dallas police detective James Skelly, informing her that a suspect was in custody. He asked if she would come down to the station and look at a photo lineup. Despite arguing that she hadn't gotten a look at the assailant's face, she carefully studied the pictures of six young black men placed on a table in front of her. None looked familiar.

"Still, I could tell that Det. Skelly was excited about the man they had in custody," she remembers. He explained, in fact, that Faison was a suspect in several assaults. A sample of his blood was being sent off to determine if his DNA matched the semen sample she had provided investigators. First, however, he would be tried for a rape where fingerprint evidence had been found.

By September of 1998, Faison had been indicted on three additional counts of sexual assault and one of aggravated assault with bodily injury. Det. Skelly told members of the media that there was the possibility that "three to five more cases" might be linked to Faison once DNA testing was completed.

At the end of the year, Faison had been convicted and sentenced to 90 years for the '95 rape of the SMU student. Though the victim could not identify him and there was no DNA evidence presented, a partial fingerprint lifted from the deadbolt latch of the young woman's door and a thumbprint from the strip of tape found at the scene matched Faison's. The jury deliberated only 90 minutes before finding him guilty ..

And even before Cotroneo's trial date was set, Faison's troubles continued to mount. A woman who had been attacked in the parking lot of her apartment in 1991 saw his photograph in the newspaper and told police he looked like the man who pulled her from her car, slammed her to the pavement, and attempted to rape her. The assault, she told authorities, had been interrupted by the arrival of another car, and the man attacking her had fled to a nearby Toyota.

However, the second trial convinced many of Faison's passionate defenders he was guilty; the prosecution offered DNA evidence that had only a one-in-300 million chance of being linked to anyone but the accused.

By the spring of '99, Gina Cotroneo had a new job and was regaining her positive outlook on life. Nothing, however, could remove the dread she felt as she prepared to take the stand and detail for a group of strangers the assault and degradation she'd been subjected to two years earlier. "On one hand," she recalled as she sipped at a cup of Starbucks coffee, "I felt a sense of relief that it was about to finally be over. By the same token, I really had to emotionally prepare myself for what I would have to do.

"I think a lot of my friends expected me to have some big emotional reaction to seeing the man who raped me sitting in the courtroom. Truth is, I didn't."

Not only did she tell her agonizing story in graphic detail, but others Faison was charged with raping took the stand to relive their nightmares.

Expert witnesses carefully explained the damning DNA evidence. Again he was convicted, this time to a life sentence.

The most dramatic moment in the proceedings came when Cotroneo was allowed to make a victim's statement at the end of the sentencing phase of the trial. Even now, she remembers it verbatim:

"When you raped me," she said as she faced Faison, "you took a piece of my soul with you, a piece that I've been grieving for and missing and wandering around without for two years. As I stand here, looking into your eyes, I take it back."

She recalls that he seemed to deflate in front of her. "I told him I could see him shrinking." By the time she thanked the members of the jury, the judge, and the prosecutor, there were few dry eyes in the courtroom.

As she reflects on the moment, she insists testifying against Faison was never a "personal" thing, rather just a means to ensure he was stripped of the power to ever again harm a woman. "I didn't know him; he didn't know me. Do I hate him? No, I don't have time for that."

Nor, she says, did her focus narrow only on the man seated at the defense table. "I was aware that his mother was in the courtroom," she says, "and I felt so badly for her. Seeing her there, imagining what she must have been feeling, was heartbreaking."

Some of those who crowded into District Judge Faith Johnson's courtroom in support of Faison or who testified as character witnesses remain convinced he didn't commit the crimes for which he was convicted. "I had visited him in jail shortly after he was arrested," recalls longtime community activist Chester Johnson, "and asked him point blank if he was guilty. He told me he wasn't. I've known Gary since we were kids, and that kind of crime is not like him in any way."

Rev. Doyce Wilson, Faison's minister at the Sweet Home Baptist Mission, agrees. "I never felt that his lawyer really put on a defense. Gary's told me many times that the Lord knows he's innocent."

Today, Johnson and Rev. Wilson are members of a Gary Faison support group that writes and visits him regularly.

* * *

Separated from his visitor by a glass partition at the Telford Unit near New Boston, Faison is finally speaking out about his arrest and convictions. Pleasant and personable, he talks in a rapid-fire manner, aware prison officials have allowed him only two hours to make a case for his innocence.

Even in his loose-fitting white jumpsuit, it's obvious he's far fitter than he was before incarceration. The 320 pounds have melted down to a trim and solid 210. "Today," he says, "I actually fit the description those women gave of the man who attacked them."

He talks only briefly of the grinding routine of prison life, of time spent reading and watching TV, writing letters, doing research in the law library, and looking forward to the weekend visits from family and friends. Mainly, though, he tells how he is an example of a black man who achieved a degree of success only to "get knocked down for it." Again, he points out, he had "stepped out of bounds." "I was an ex-con who had developed himself into something."

And then it was all taken away.

Someday, Faison insists, he hopes to get it back, to prove he wasn't a night-stalking rapist, but there is little real optimism in his voice. Still, he makes thought-provoking points about some of the evidence against him. None of those he was accused of attacking were able to identify him, most estimated his weight to be 100 or more pounds shy of what he actually weighed at the time. No hair or fibers linked to him were ever found inside any of the victims' apartments.

It's obvious he prepared himself for the first interview he's given since his arrest. "At my first trial," he remembers, "I was numb. [The victim] testified that her attacker was wearing gloves. Yet they found those partial prints on the door and lock that were supposed to match mine. That was the so-called evidence...and I got 90 years."

He shakes his head. "And she described the man who assaulted her as being six feet tall and weighing 180. The prosecution obviously couldn't find anyone who remembered me when I weighed less than 300. The whole thing made me wonder if common sense really applies in a court of law."

Flipping through the folder in front of him, he continues making his case: "That woman who was getting ready for work and was attacked and robbed? They had nothing that showed I'd ever been in that apartment. No hairs, no semen. All they had was a piece of broken glass—outside the apartment—that they said had my fingerprint on it." The recollection of the woman who said she was attacked in the parking lot before the assailant fled in a Toyota? "I've never driven a Toyota in my life," Faison argues.

What about the man in the ATM photograph, shown using a victim's card shortly after she was attacked? "The man," he says, "is wearing a hooded sweatshirt, and you can only see a small part of his face. But you can tell he's clean shaven. The only time I didn't have a beard back in 1997 was a four-day period after I'd lost a bet on the Tyson/Holyfield fight. I'd shaven it off but immediately began growing it back." And the DNA evidence? "All they said was that I could not be eliminated, never that there was a match." There was, he notes, a window screen, found 60 feet away from the victim's apartment that had a palm print the prosecution said matched his. "Even if it was my palm print—and I'm certainly not saying it was—that kind of evidence hardly placed me inside her home where the attack occurred."

Another woman, who lived less than a mile from Faison's residence at the time, said that the intruder who raped her entered her apartment through a small bedroom window she'd left open. Additionally, investigators found traces of semen on the living room floor where she'd been forced to perform oral sex. "I was finally eliminated from that one when there was no DNA match," he points out. Then, with the first trace of a smile, "Can you imagine someone 320 getting through a little apartment window?"

Noting that he never knew any of the women he was accused of attacking, Faison questions whether the police investigated the possibility that other apprehended rapists—particularly Cook—might actually have been responsible for the crimes.

Yet for all his denials, even his logical questions, there is one evidentiary snag that remains impossible to explain away. DNA matching, regarded as a foolproof crime solving technique, trumps all conjecture about partial or smudged fingerprints and conflicting descriptions. Five years ago, Gina Cotroneo spat into a baggie and handed it over to the police. The odds against her rapist being anyone other than Faison are off the mathematical chart. One in 300 million.

It is not a fact Faison is willing to concede. "When all that first came up," he says, "I knew it wasn't going to match. I was dumbfounded when they said it did."

Today, he remains so convinced that the physical evidence against him was somehow manipulated that he's asked DeSoto lawyer Fred McDaniel to file a motion requesting a new series of DNA tests. McDaniel, court appointed only for purposes of filing the motion, says they are rarely granted.

* * *

While Faison is doomed by the judicial system to endless days of dwelling on the past, Gina Cotroneo looks to her future. "He's on his own path," is all she wishes to say about the man convicted of raping her. "I'm on mine."

Today she insists that what occurred on that night five years ago didn't change her. "I changed me," she explains. Her friends have accepted what she went through and have put it aside. She insists she harbors no lingering suspicion of men and is again dating.

"In a way, what I went through convinced me that I now have the credentials to do what I want with my life." She looks forward to reaching out to others with a line of inspirational products she designed and plans to market. She's signed on with a lecture bureau, eager to pursue her goal of becoming a motivational speaker, and is working on a book.

Shortly after the Faison trial, Cotroneo took a trip to the jungles of Peru, visiting sacred Inca sites and participating in meditation ceremonies, returning to her quest for knowledge. "It was a profound experience," she says. "I came back feeling like the rising phoenix."

That, she says, is how she continues to view herself.

◆*Dallas Observer*, October 2002

Redemption

On those long dark nights when 45-year-old Donald Good lay in the bunk of his prison cell, silently pleading for the sleep that often refuses to come, he is haunted by the recollections of a flawed and failed life—the decision to leave education and the promise of athletic stardom behind in Lewisville, Texas, after the eighth grade; the addictive bouts with booze, pot, and crack cocaine; the menial jobs; the troubled marriage; and, finally, the endless string of break-and-enter burglaries meant to fund the drug habit that ultimately made it impossible to outrun the legal system.

Worst of all, however, are the constant thoughts about that which he did not do. For two decades, Good's tattered legacy has been indelibly underscored by his conviction for a brutal rape he didn't commit.

In June of 1983, he was charged with assaulting a 31-year-old Irving woman at knife point while her terrified eight-year-old daughter was forced to watch. Convicted, he was sentenced to a life term in the Texas prison system. For all his self-induced misery, it is that crime that became the nightmare benchmark of his life, landing him in a world where he's watched a fellow inmate be stabbed and killed after what began as a seemingly harmless argument over a Scrabble game, where he's spent 23 hours of each day in a five-by-nine cell, viewed brutal gang activity, and collected the spidery, tell-tale tattoos that now and forever brand him a convict.

By his own admission, Good's life prior to the rape conviction had been one train wreck after another. His tawdry criminal history, dating back to the mid-70s, included more thefts and burglaries than he can remember. His first visit to prison came in 1977.

It seemed impossible things could get worse.

He had been home on yet another parole in the summer of 1983 when the Irving police arrived at his parents' home, looking for his older brother Michael, who was a suspect in an aggravated robbery. Initially believing Donald was the man they were in search of, the police took him to the station for questioning. And while it was soon determined he was not, in fact, Michael Good, a computer check revealed Donald was the subject of an outstanding warrant for DWI. Back to jail he went.

Recently, as he sat in a cinder block interview room in the Dallas County jail, dressed in a baggy county-issue jumpsuit, he recalled the encounter which sent his life spiraling into a black hole. Irving detective Fred Curtis, he says, showed him a composite drawing of a suspect in a recent rape. "He told me that he thought I matched the drawing pretty well," Good says. "Then he walked me out into the hall, had me stand against a wall, and took some Polaroid pictures of me."

It was not Good's first run-in with the Irving officer. "There had been another time when he came to the house and took me down to the station to see if my shoes matched the prints that had been found at a burglary that had taken place near where I was living. When my shoes didn't match, he let me go but told me that he was 'going to get me,'" Good says.

Three days after his mother bonded him out of the Dallas County jail on the DWI charge, Irving police again visited Donald's home and again took him into custody. This time the warrant was for his arrest on suspicion of aggravated rape and burglary.

According to court records, the victim eventually viewed a montage of photographs and emphatically identified Good as her attacker. Pointing to his picture, she had said, "It's him, it's—my God—it's him," and then collapsed.

The school teacher's description of the attack was horrifying:

She had been in the backyard when she heard her daughter screaming inside the house. Looking into the den, she could see a dark-haired, dark-skinned man who had apparently entered through the garage. When the victim called out to her daughter to run, the nightmare began in earnest. The intruder put a knife to the child's throat and ordered the mother into the house. He used laces from her shoes to tie her and her daughter's hands and then ordered them into the bedroom. There, with a pillow case over her head, the woman was raped and sodomized as her terrified eight-year-old lay nearby on the floor, bound by shoestrings and her own hair ribbons. Finally, the assailant took money from the woman's purse and fled.

It took three trials to put Good behind bars for life.

The first ended in a mistrial when a lone juror steadfastly argued against conviction. During the three-day trial, the prosecution called the victim and her daughter to the stand to graphically describe the attack and identify Good as the same man they picked from a photo array.

"Someday," Good says, "I'd love to talk to that juror who held out." He'd like to ask why others didn't see the numerous flaws in the state's case.

Why, for instance, didn't they believe his younger sister who testified he'd been visiting her in her apartment at the time of the attack? "I was home from work with a kidney infection," Kathy Good remembers. "I could remember the exact day because I'd gotten a prescription filled and still had the dated pill bottle when he was arrested." Additionally, she testified her brother, who had come to help look after her infant daughter, had been on crutches at the time because of a knee injury.

Didn't anyone else have problems with the fact police reports identified the assailant as dark-haired and dark-skinned when Good is red-headed, fair, and freckled? Had it counted for naught that he'd voluntarily given investigators hair and saliva samples which matched none found at the crime scene? Why, when asked if her attacker had any noticeable marks on his body, had the victim not mentioned the ugly zigzag of scars on his arm, the result of being thrown through a plate glass window during a long ago bar fight? Hadn't it seemed strange that the mother told police a knife had been held to her daughter's neck while the daughter only remembered the assailant pulling her hair? And what of the unsuccessful search of his parents' home when law enforcement officials were so sure they'd find the victim's stolen panties? Later, they were discovered hidden beneath a mattress in the woman's bedroom.

Aside from the fact the victim and her daughter identified Good, no physical evidence linked him to the attack. With the science of DNA testing still far in the future, the prosecutor could only state that Good's blood type and matching biological evidence found at the crime scene could be narrowed to 30 percent of the nation's white male population.

After the mistrial, Dallas County assistant D.A. Winfield Scott immediately announced he and fellow prosecutor David Jarvis intended to retry the case. And they got their guilty verdict on the day following Good's 24th birthday, and he was shipped off to prison to begin serving his life sentence.

Two years later, however, the conviction was overturned because of what the Court of Criminals Appeals of Texas ruled prosecutorial misconduct. During closing argument at the second trial, the prosecution passionately argued to the jury that Good's "passive and unsympathetic" demeanor during the trial was in itself evidence of his guilt.

The appellate court ruled in 1986 that, in light of Good's alibi and insistence that he had not committed the crime, "it [was] not surprising that he would show no emotion or remorse throughout his trial."

Still, Good remained in prison while awaiting a third trial. During that time, he decided the counsel of fellow inmate Daniel Clark, a "jailhouse lawyer" serving a 99-year sentence who had aided him in successfully appealing his first conviction, was far better than his court-appointed attorney's. Thus, as the retrial neared, Good formally asked that Clark be present in the courtroom to serve as his advisor advocate. State District Judge Gary Stephens, who heard the case, denied the request and appointed Dallas attorney John Read to aid Good in his defense.

On Clark's advice, Good opted to serve as his own counsel and repeatedly insisted to the court that he wanted inmate Clark's assistance. "Your Honor," he said, "if it please the court, let the record reflect that I hereby respectfully request the presence of my advisor advocate, Daniel Clark, to assist me with my defense." The request became an ongoing litany interrupting the trial's normal flow.

Finally, Judge Stephens ordered the defendant handcuffed and gagged "to keep proper decorum in the courtroom." Three days later, the jury deliberated for only thirty minutes before voting to send Good back to prison for life.

With that 1987 verdict, Donald Good disappeared from public sight and mind, except for his parents, Mary and Delbert, who, as Good's mother now recalls, "wore out several cars making every-other-weekend visits" to see their imprisoned son.

* * *

Ten years after the rape for which he was convicted had occurred, Good was paroled and returned to Dallas where he was required to immediately register as a sex offender, was prohibited from associating with young children, even his own nephews and nieces, and ordered to attend costly and humiliating counseling sessions with others who had committed acts of sexual violence.

A neighbor, upon learning of Good's criminal history on the internet, posted signs throughout the neighborhood, warning residents, "a rapist is living in your midst."

One of his last memories of his father, who was ultimately a victim of Alzheimer's disease at age 76, is of him standing on the front porch of the family home, waving his cane at a television crew that had come to investigate the neighborhood uproar, yelling, "My son is innocent. He didn't rape nobody."

Good's mother, 74 and now moved from Dallas, also remembers the event—along with a late night gunshot that came through the front window of her home and another that pierced the fender of her car soon after her son's release.

For Donald, the court-ordered therapy sessions destroyed his hope of making a life for himself in the free world. When he refused to act out the crime he'd been convicted of or even admit his guilt during the meetings, his counselor reported to Good's parole officer that he was making no progress. "They kept saying that I was in denial," he recalls. If he didn't soon confess and play out the assault in front of fellow offenders, the counselor warned, he would recommend his parole be revoked and he be returned to prison to continue serving his life term.

"I finally had all of it I could deal with," he says. For nine years, he'd stayed clean and sober, dutifully reported to his parole officer and therapist, and earned a modest living remodeling apartments. However, when he was threatened with the revocation of his parole, he threw in the towel. Soon he was back on drugs, selling his car and furniture to pay for his reawakened habit. When he had no more personal possessions to pawn or sell, he went back to committing burglaries.

When he was arrested for stealing a set of tools from the garage of an Irving residence in May of 2002, Good agreed to plead guilty if authorities would give his wife, whom he'd married in 1993 and who had pawned the stolen items, a probated sentence. "I knew I was going to be convicted and had that life sentence hanging over me if I violated parole," he explains, "so I figured, what the hell, the best I could do was see if I could help out my wife."

For the burglary, he received five years, was found in violation of his parole, and returned to prison to continue serving his life sentence. Still, he had one last battle he was determined to wage against the legal system.

Lending a hand would be a man he's still never personally met, a man with a history of similar frailties and lapses in judgment, a once highly respected attorney whose career crashed into drug problems and prison time before he resurrected his life and career.

In a strange way, the lives of Donald Good and Mike Wilson merged.

* * *

In April of 2004, Mike Wilson, a case coordinator for the Dallas law firm of Modjarrad & Associates, listened patiently as Lillie Rollins, Donald Good's sister, recounted what she perceived as the years of injustice heaped on her brother. Wilson had heard similar rants during the course of his lengthy career and had rarely found cause to judge them valid.

Rollins had, she admitted, telephoned numerous other lawyers whose names she'd picked randomly from the phone book, but none had been interested in hearing her story. Neither had members of the local and national media she'd contacted. Even the famed Innocence Project, the national organization that investigates wrongful convictions, had been unsympathetic.

Perhaps, she now speculates, it was because of her own encounters with the legal system—the fact she, too, is a recovering drug addict and will be on probation for another seven years before she has fully paid her debt for burglaries in which she participated.

It was, in fact, not Rollins' angry tirade against an unfair judicial system that gained Wilson's attention. Rather, it was her mention that her brother had, in January of 2002, taken advantage of a new law that had gone into effect just eight months earlier and filed a *pro se* motion for post-conviction DNA testing—the scientific technique that hadn't yet been in use when he was tried and convicted—in a final effort to prove his innocence of the rape charge. In August of the following year, Good's motion was granted and the Texas Department of Public Safety lab in Garland performed the court-ordered test. It ultimately reported her brother's DNA did not match swab samples taken from the victim or collected at the crime scene in 1983.

"For whatever reason," she says, "Mike Wilson listened. And for that I will be eternally grateful."

Wilson promised her one of the firm's lawyers would soon be in touch with her. "She was a tough, determined lady," Wilson remembers, "and there was just something about her and her story that convinced me she was telling the truth." He telephoned several veteran criminal defense attorneys in Dallas to ask if they'd ever dealt with such a case. Several recalled clients who requested the post-conviction DNA test, only to have it reaffirm their guilt. None had ever had a client who was actually proven innocent.

"Well," Wilson told longtime friend and colleague Tom Mills, "I've got one who is."

The counselor, with his own dark history of hard-knock experience, was convinced Donald Good deserved another chance to rebuild his life.

Wilson, 59, had already received his.

Son of an East Texas oil wildcatter, star high school quarterback, and outstanding student, Wilson was on a fast track to success even before enrolling in the University of Texas at Austin, then SMU's law school. Fascinated by the intricacies of the legal process, particularly criminal law, he seized every opportunity to ride with the police on night patrols for a first-hand view of the dangers lurking in Dallas' back alleys. Soon after passing the bar, he'd been hired by the Dallas County D.A.'s office and quickly earned the reputation of an aggressive but fair prosecutor.

It was a time, however, when salaries were low and advancement slow for assistant district attorneys. Wilson moved into private practice and was soon driving a Porsche and living in a $300,000 lake-side home. Yet for all his success, he had his demons. By 1981, he'd acknowledged the fact he'd become a full-fledged alcoholic and sought treatment. Once sober, he helped initiate an Alcoholics Anonymous chapter whose membership was made up almost entirely of local lawyers.

Soon after he conquered his drinking problem, however, new addictions developed: cocaine and a beautiful and infamous Dallas socialite named Joy Davis Aylor.

By the time their paths crossed, she'd been indicted for orchestrating the highly publicized 1983 murder-for-hire of her husband's girlfriend. Wilson was soon neck deep in legal troubles as well, arrested for taking several kilos of cocaine as payment for legal representation of a drug-dealing client. While awaiting their respective trials, Wilson and Aylor fled the country together.

Soon disenchanted with life on the run and despondent over the collapse of his life, Wilson surrendered to authorities in Canada while Aylor continued to elude capture for over a year. Finally, she was tracked down and arrested in the south of France.

It was the kind of story that provided grist for a couple of true crime books and a network mini-series.

Aylor was eventually extradited, convicted, and sentenced to life in prison for the murder she commissioned. In federal court, Wilson received 15 years for his drug charges. In December of 1993, however, he was released after a successful appeal reduced his sentence to four years. On probation and stripped of his license to practice law, he energetically began working his way back as a highly over-qualified paralegal.

Though now eligible to seek full reinstatement to the bar, he continues to work behind the scenes at Modjarrad & Associates, coordinating cases, doing research, and preparing briefs. One day soon, he says, he'll retake the bar exam. For now, though he's happy at what he's doing. The pursuit of justice for Donald Good has become a mission.

* * *

As a bitter morning wind played outside last December, Modjarrad & Associates attorney James Krug reported to the Frank Crowley Courts Building, armed with research and paperwork prepared by coworker Wilson. Krug was there to hear the rape charge against Good dismissed and his life sentence vacated.

The hearing would be nothing more than a formality since the District Attorney's office, after reviewing the results of the DNA testing, had offered no objection. "If fact," says Wilson, "they bent over backwards to help us and to help Donald Good receive the justice he'd so long been denied. I'm firmly convinced they were as horrified by what had happened as we were."

Says District Attorney Bill Hill: "We have a specialized team of attorneys dedicated to evaluating DNA issues that arise during the appeals process. In this case, that group moved very quickly when the results came back exonerating Mr. Good. The DNA team then worked in coordination with other attorneys in our appellate section to rapidly inform the court that he should be entitled to relief."

For Good, however, it was but a first step toward freedom. Because of the five-year sentence for his 2002 burglary conviction (which had been ordered to run concurrently with his life sentence), he remains in prison awaiting a ruling by the parole board. Since he has now already served three years for the crime, quick parole seems likely.

Meanwhile, he waits in a cell in Huntsville, impatient to return to the free world. Once released, he says, he'll likely work with brother Carl, owner of a tire shop in a small Central Texas community. There, he plans to live with and care for his aging mother. And he'll follow sister Lillie's lead and enroll in alcohol and drug abuse programs. His first order of business, however, will be one last visit to Dallas and the Crown Hill Cemetery grave site of his father.

"I sincerely believe Donald's going to do well when he gets out," says his sister Kathy, 43, who unsuccessfully served as his alibi witness so long ago. "I've been impressed with his attitude. He sounds good when he calls, his letters are upbeat. He's no longer angry, just relieved that it is finally over."

With the help of Wilson and attorneys at Modjarrad & Associates, Good applied to the Texas Comptroller's Office for compensation set aside for the wrongfully convicted. According to law, Good, now exonerated, is eligible to receive $25,000 for every calendar year he served for the rape conviction.

"Since the day Mike [Wilson] first called my attention to it, this has been something more than just another case to our firm," says Sean Modjarrad, 33, who came to the United States from Iran with his parents in 1985. "There are two victims here: the woman who was raped...and Donald Good."

Good's family and attorneys aside, few involved in the decades-old case are now inclined to revisit it. Some, like the victim who was once so certain Good was her attacker, could not be reached. Others blamed poor memories and the passage of time.

"It was a lot of years ago," says former prosecutor Winfield Scott, now in private practice. When asked his thoughts on Good's conviction being vacated, he replied, "I can only refer you to the D.A.'s office." Detective Fred Curtis, still with the Irving Police Department, would not comment on the investigation of the 22-year-old crime. Douglas Parks, the court-appointed attorney whose repeated objections to the prosecution's references to Good's demeanor led to the first guilty verdict being overturned, says his recollection of those days in the courtroom are now fuzzy.

"But," he notes, "I do know I never thought he was guilty."

And what of the now nameless, faceless assailant who actually was? The statute of limitations on his crime ran out years ago.

◆*In Cold Blog*

Cisco:
The Texas Town Where Santa Claus Robbed and Murdered

For most who now call the quiet West Texas community of Cisco home, the changes occurred so gradually and so long ago that they've gone all but unnoticed. Many of the new generation know little of the hectic pre-1920 days when the roaring Oil Boom came, briefly increasing the population to ten times what it is today. Once known as Avenue D, the city's main street is now called Conrad Hilton Avenue, in honor of the famed mogul who launched his financial empire with the impulsive purchase of the local hotel.

And the old First National Bank long ago moved from its downtown location. For a time, the one-story red brick building, originally a retail store, became an auto parts shop, then was abandoned. Today it sits vacant, with only a Texas State Historical Commission plaque to proclaim it the site of the darkest, most violent day in the town's history.

The event that occurred there 87 years ago is now but a historical whisper, an ill-planned escapade that was daring, dim-witted and, unfortunately, deadly. It occurred just two days before Christmas in 1927, turning the town's holiday anticipation into a day of blind fear, reckless greed, and back alley bloodshed.

It was the day of a bank robbery during which four men, their leader dressed in a Santa Claus suit and beard in an effort to avoid being recognized, terrorized downtown Cisco and assured themselves an infamous place in Texas criminal history.

Over the years, local historians, one published book, and even Cisco Junior College playwright Billy Smith's regionally-produced musical, *The Great Santa Claus Bank Robbery*, have kept the strange and fascinating tale alive. And, as with all bigger-than-life legends, the passage of time has caused more than an occasional detour from fact. In time, the number of eyewitnesses to the famed robbery, the shoot-out, and the subsequent manhunt grew to include virtually all who called Cisco home at the time.

Everyone had a story to tell; everyone wanted to be remembered as a participant in the historic event that came to be known as "The Santa Claus Bank Robbery."

227

In all honesty, were it not for the tragic loss of lives and later mob violence that sullied the reputation of a nearby town, the story would read like a pulp novel, a dark comedy in which the bad guys simply aren't very good at their criminal craft.

* * *

Marshall Ratliff, a ne'er-do-well 24-year-old whose mother ran a small cafe in Cisco, was determined to excel at robbing banks. He and his brother Lee first tried it in the mid-'20s in the small Coleman County community of Valera, and, had it not been for their bragging while later hiding out in Abilene, they might never have been caught. However, when the local sheriff learned of the two young men who were living it up, spending freely, and drunkenly boasting of their recent crime, he sought them out and arrested them. Soon tried and convicted, the Ratliff brothers went to prison.

Paroled in just a year, they briefly wandered West Texas, unsuccessfully searching for oil field work before settling in a boarding house in Wichita Falls. By the fall of 1927, Marshall became convinced there were no legitimate career prospects for an ex-con and began planning another robbery.

This time, his target would be the oil money rich bank in his hometown of Cisco; the planning would be perfect, the get-away clean, and, most important, the lips zipped afterward.

Ratliff envisioned a four-man team executing the robbery in a matter of minutes: three men inside the bank to keep everyone under control while he gathered the money and a car and driver positioned in the alley, ready to spirit them away from the scene of the crime. Everyone would be heavily armed. He persuaded Henry Helms, 32, and Robert Hill, 21, two men he'd met while serving time in Huntsville, to join him and his brother for the robbery.

But even the best-laid plans are often doomed to fail.

The first problem occurred when Ratliff's less-than-brilliant brother committed a spur-of-the-moment burglary in Wichita Falls and was arrested and sent back to prison. At the last minute, Marshall Ratliff recruited a Helms' relative Louis Davis, a 22-year-old family man with no criminal background but an increasingly desperate need for money to take care of his wife and children.

Even the necessity of last minute recruiting failed to daunt Ratliff's confidence that his plan was foolproof. He'd even obtained a disguise he was sure would prevent anyone in his hometown from recognizing him.

Josephine Herron, his landlady, had sewn a Santa Claus suit for her husband to wear on Christmas Day, complete with a large white beard and a red stocking cap which her boarder asked to borrow, promising to have it back in time for her family's holiday celebration.

Rather than hiding his face with nothing more than a bandanna, Ratliff planned to walk into the First National Bank dressed as jolly ol' Saint Nick.

In the early evening of December 22, 1927, the four men set out for Cisco in a stolen Buick that, luckily, had a full tank of gas. Driving into the night, they drank bootleg whiskey and shared boisterous plans about what they would do with the stolen cash. It was well after midnight when they arrived at the oil field camp of Moran, home of Louis Davis' sister, Minnie Fox. When her husband refused to allow the drunken, late-night travelers into his house, they borrowed a tent and slept in the front yard.

* * *

Shortly before noon on an unseasonably warm Friday, the blue Buick arrived on the outskirts of Cisco, its occupants hung-over and weary from traveling 200 miles and getting only a couple hours of sleep. Ratliff, dressed in his Santa suit, stayed down in the floorboard until they were within a couple of blocks of their target. Then he quickly exited the car and walked along the main street sidewalk, waving at downtown shoppers and patting the heads of excited children delighted by his sudden appearance.

The disguise, he was certain, was the ideal diversion. As he played his holiday season role, the getaway car was driven to the planned spot in the alley near the bank's back door.

Across the street, six-year-old Frances Blasengame saw Santa entering the First National and urged her mother to take her to see him so that she might remind him of the gifts she hoped to soon receive.

As mother and daughter hurried across the street, Ratliff was already inside, responding to the friendly acknowledgments of the bank staff, customers, and two children, Emma May Robinson, 10, and Laverne Comer, 12.

Just moments after Mrs. Blasengame and her daughter entered, three men, pistols drawn, pushed past her into the lobby. The robbery was underway.

Louis Davis took his position guarding the door while Hill and Helms pointed guns at the employees and customers. Ratliff, the only robber whose face was hidden, ordered teller Jewel Poe to open the safe.

All was going as planned until the frightened Mrs. Blasengame suddenly hurried her daughter toward the back door before the robbers could block her path. Once in the alley, mother and daughter ran the half block to City Hall, calling out for police chief G .E. "Bit" Bedford. "The First

National Bank's being robbed!" Blasengame yelled.

The 6'4", 220-pound Bedford, a 25-year law enforcement veteran, grabbed riot guns from the rack behind his desk and tossed one to assistant chief George Carmichael and another to officer R.T. Redies. As they ran toward the bank, Bedford instructed his officers to take position in the alley while he covered the bank's front door.

Inside, Ratliff pulled a tow sack from beneath his Santa suit and filled it with $12,200 in cash and $150,000 in security bonds. Less than five minutes had passed since his arrival. The plan seemed to be working perfectly.

As Ratliff signalled the others he was done, Helms noticed a face suddenly pressed against the window of the bank's locked front door. Instinctively, he fired a warning shot in the direction of whoever was looking in. To his surprise, a sudden volley of crossfire from outside the bank answered his shot.

All hell broke loose.

Inside the small bank, the robbers wildly returned fire in the general direction of the doorways. It soon became obvious that shots were coming from others besides the three member Cisco police department.

* * *

Earlier in the year, the Texas Bankers Association, upset over the fact small banks were being robbed almost daily throughout the state, announced a $5,000 reward to any citizen who shot and killed a bank robber during the commission of his crime.

The possibility of earning such a reward was not lost on the people of Cisco.

As soon as the gunfire between the robbers and local police got underway, dozens of armed citizens, including two teenaged members of the high school football team, began arriving at the bank. At a nearby hardware store, the owner passed out shotguns, pistols, and ammunition to all comers.

Meanwhile, inside the bank, Ratliff frantically devised a plan to use the employees and customers as human shields while he and his accomplices attempted to make it to their waiting car.

As the volley of gunfire increased, several hostages were struck by bullets when they stepped into the alley, including bank president Alex Spears, who was shot in the jaw. Local grocer Oscar Clitt, who'd been in the bank to make a deposit, suffered a bullet wound to his foot, and Marion Olson, a Harvard student home for the holidays, was shot in the thigh.

Ratliff, though shielding himself with bank teller Freda Strobel, suffered wounds to his leg and jaw. Fellow robber Davis was even more seriously wounded, barely making it into the waiting sedan.

As the car sped down the alley, Officer Carmichael was shot in the head by the fleeing bandits; he slumped against the wall of the building, near death. Moments later, Chief Bedford, standing at the entrance to the alley, was also mortally wounded, his body riddled with five gunshots.

Taking the two young girls from the bank as hostages, the robbers sped away down the main street as Cisco citizens continued to shoot. One of an estimated 100 shots fired at the fleeing automobile punctured a back tire.

On the edge of town, briefly out of range of the pursuing townspeople, the bandits stopped to assess their quickly deteriorating situation. Two of them were bleeding badly, they had a flat tire and—if it's a bit of comic relief you're looking for at this point—the needle of the Buick's gas gauge was on E. For all their careful planning, no one had thought to gas the car following their lengthy trip from Wichita Falls.

It only got worse for the bumbling bandits.

As an Oldsmobile driven by 14-year-old Rising Star schoolboy Woodrow Harris approached, the robbers positioned themselves in the road, demanding that the driver stop. Ordering him, his parents, and his grandmother from the car and suggesting they run for their lives, the bandits prepared to take over a new getaway vehicle. They lifted the near unconscious Davis into the backseat. Ratliff pitched the tow sack of stolen money and bonds in behind him as Hill stood a few feet away, firing shots at the oncoming posse.

A rifle shot from one of the pursuers struck Hill in the arm, knocking him to the ground.

He got up and scrambled to the newly stolen car, only to learn that the quick-thinking teenage driver had taken the keys with him as he and his family fled to the safety of a nearby farmhouse. With no way to start the newly acquired getaway car, the pursing vigilantes and additional law enforcement personnel from nearby towns getting nearer, the robbers and their young hostages hurriedly returned to their limping Buick to continue their escape.

Left behind in the car they'd hoped to use was the badly wounded Louis Davis—and Ratliff's tow sack containing the robbery's spoils.

All that remained was the manhunt.

With the unconscious Davis left behind to be taken into custody and transported to a Fort Worth hospital, the remaining three men managed to get only a few miles down an Eastland County back road before having to abandon their car and continue their escape on foot. When authorities located the bullet-riddled Buick, the two young girls sat huddled in the backseat, crying and frightened but unharmed. Next to one of them lay a discarded Santa Claus suit.

However, the good news that Emma May Robinson and Laverne Comer were finally safe was soon muted by the fact that police chief Bedford, having never regained consciousness after being repeatedly shot during the bank standoff, died later that day

Even with the aid of law enforcement personnel from throughout West Texas, bloodhounds, and even a small airplane, a week passed before the remaining three robbers were finally apprehended. Alerted that they'd stolen another car and were hiding out in a wooded area just a few miles outside Cisco, a posse located the fugitives and engaged in yet another shootout. Helms and Hill managed to escape, but the badly wounded Ratliff surrendered. Before taking him into custody, an Eastland County deputy sheriff took six handguns, a double-barreled shotgun, a Bowie knife, and three belts of ammunition from the man who had disguised himself as Santa Claus.

Three days later, on December 30, 1927, Helms and Hill were captured near Graham and transported to the county jail in Eastland.

Davis died in the Fort Worth hospital.

* * *

Ratliff, still weak from six gunshot wounds he received during the bank shootout and his run from authorities, was the first to be tried in the Eastland County courthouse. Reporters from Fort Worth and Dallas were on hand to write of 10-year-old Emma Robinson and 12-year-old Laverne Comer bravely taking the stand to recall their horrifying time as captives of the robbers and identify the defendant as the man who had worn the Santa Claus suit and kidnapped them. Ratliff received a 99-year sentence for the robbery and abduction. It was the last trial held in the old courthouse, which was torn down soon after.

Later, in nearby Abilene, Ratliff stood trial for the murder of Chief Bedford and was sentenced to die in the electric chair.

Henry Helms, accompanied to court by his minister father, his wife, and his five children, was also given the death penalty. Robert Hill, who pled for the jury's mercy, recalling his life growing up in orphanages and reformatories, received a life sentence.

The story, however, seemed destined to never end.

Appealing his death sentence, Ratliff was returned to the Eastland jail in 1929 to await a hearing. While on Death Row, he had lapsed into what appeared to be an almost catatonic state, staring blankly into space for long periods of time, eating little, demonstrating no evidence that he even had use of his arms or legs. When he did speak, it was little more than babble.

Such was his apparent state one evening when Eastland jailers made their rounds to serve prisoners their evening meal. Leaving Ratliff's cell, they inadvertently left the door unlocked.

Moments later, the prisoner, suddenly both physically and mentally agile, slipped from his cell, hurried downstairs, and retrieved a .38 Colt pistol from one of the jailers' desks.

Deputy Tom Jones first confronted the convicted killer. Ratliff shot Jones five times before former sheriff and fellow jailer "Pack" Kilborn wrestled the gun away and returned Ratliff to his cell. Jones, suffering wounds in the abdomen, chest, and shoulder, was rushed to the hospital.

Outside, Eastland residents held a quiet vigil for the badly injured jailer. The following day, the crowd grew steadily, its concern turning to impatience. By 8 p.m., an estimated 2,000 people had gathered, anger spreading through the crowd.

Finally, two dozen men stormed the jail and knocked jailer Kilborn to the floor, pinning him there as they took his keys. The mob then raced upstairs to the cell where Ratliff lay nude on his bunk.

Taking the prisoner outside, stepping in time to the angry chant of the crowd, they moved the inmate near a telephone pole and placed a noose around his neck. They threw the rope over the guy wires and lifted Ratliff from the ground. When the first rope broke, the mob quickly found another and repeated the process.

Fifteen feet above the ground, Ratliff's dead body dangled at the end of the rope for twenty minutes before a county judge and justice of the peace arrived and ordered it taken down.

According to the granite monument that now stands on the corner of White and Mulberry Streets in Eastland, it was the last mob lynching ever carried out in Texas. Though a grand jury convened to look into the lynching, no legal action was ever brought against any of the participants.

In all, the casualty toll of the ill-planned bank robbery and its aftermath was staggering. Six citizens were wounded. The Palo Pinto County sheriff, having joined the manhunt, lost two fingers and was wounded in the leg when his pistol discharged by accident as he chased the fugitives.

Two Cisco police officers, Bedford and Carmichael, lost their lives in the initial gunfight. Eastland jailer Tom Jones died the day after Marshall Ratliff hanged.

Louis Davis died of the gunshot wounds he received during the attempted getaway. Henry Helms, sentenced to death for his crimes, went to the electric chair in Huntsville on September 6, 1929, two months before Ratliff faced mob justice in Eastland.

Robert Hill, who escaped prison twice before being caught and returned to Huntsville, was granted parole in the '40s and is said to have changed his name and moved back to West Texas—perhaps Midland or Odessa—where it is believed he lived out the remainder of his life as a law-abiding citizen.

For his presence of mind to take the keys while fleeing from the thieves who attempted to take his family's car during their getaway, Woody Harris was later presented an engraved gold watch by the bank's insurance company.

Laverne Comer, one of the young hostages taken by the robbers, was required to testify in so many trials that she failed seventh grade, and she had nightmares about the event throughout her life.

And there are those convinced one member of the gang that entered the First National Bank so long ago escaped.

The dying words of Cisco police chief Bit Bedford were, "It wasn't a man who shot me. It was a blond-headed woman. I was looking her straight in the eyes when she fired."

At the time, the veteran law enforcement officer's statement was viewed as nothing more than the incoherent blather of a dying man.

But the history of the robbery offers up questions. Some eyewitnesses vaguely recalled an unknown woman, dressed in a man's military uniform, in the bank at the time of the robbery. As the manhunt for Ratliff and his fellow gunmen began, a discarded woman's handbag, filled with antiseptic and bandages, was found in a wooded area into which the robbers had fled.

Minnie Fox, who had allowed the robbers to camp in her Moran front yard while en route to Cisco, later admitted to investigators that those involved in the crime had come to her home after the bungled robbery where she fed them and dressed their wounds. Law enforcement officials, however, were never able to directly link her to the crime.

◆*Abilene Reporter News*, July 2007

The Murder of Jennifer Servo

Dreams & Nightmares

Deep into the darkness peering, long I stood there wondering, fearing,
Doubting, dreaming dreams no mortal ever dared dream before.
  ▪ Edgar Allan Poe, "The Raven"

Sherry Abel remembers the dream as though it were yesterday, haunting and frightening, the kind that occasionally visits the dark, lonely nights of all loving parents. In it, she heard a knock at the door of her northwest Montana home and answered to find a state trooper standing there, hat in hand, with a somber look on his young face.

Without knowing why, she ushered him in, not through the front door, but instead through an adjacent laundry room, before he shared his horrifying news: Her youngest daughter, then a senior at the University of Montana, had died in an automobile accident.

Suddenly awake, Sherry sat up in bed, shaking and bathed in a cold sweat, hurriedly fumbling for a nearby phone in the 3 a.m. darkness. Only after her husband calmed her and discouraged a call at that time of night did the distraught mother agree to wait until morning to call Jennifer Servo's off-campus apartment in nearby Missoula.

When she did, she was relieved to finally hear a sleepy answer.

"Jen, are you okay?"

"I'm fine. Why?"

Sherry recounted the terrifying dream she'd had, and her daughter laughed.

"No, I'm okay. I'm fine. I'm alive."

In the three autumn months that followed, memories of the troubling night faded, replaced by better times. That spring, Sherry and Tom Abel proudly traveled to Missoula for Jennifer's graduation and listened as she talked of sending out audition tapes—filled with her on-camera reports of such events as an out-of-control forest fire in Whitefish, a Harley bikers' rally in Missoula, even a gruesome triple murder—to a number of televisions stations around the country. Having become fascinated with journalism while working part-time for a Missoula television station, KECI, and National Public Radio, she was eager to finally begin a career. Her sudden focus both amused and pleased her mother and stepfather. There had been a time when she was determined to become a high school Spanish teacher, then a band director; next she'd contemplated a career in the military, even persuading her mother to allow her to sign up for the Army Reserves at age 17. Now, however, she'd resolutely settled on a plan.

She hoped to get a job in Seattle, maybe even some small station in California, but, if that didn't work out, anywhere she could gain experience that would ultimately lead to her goal—one day anchoring a network newscast—would do.

A younger look-alike of Leslie Stahl of *60 Minutes*, the pretty blonde from Columbia Falls, Montana, ex-cheerleader, Lady Wildcats volleyball player, and flutist in the school band, dreamed big.

On her bulletin board at college she'd pinned the cover of a *TV Guide* featuring an article on network superstar Katie Couric as an everyday reminder of her aspiration. On a late-summer family trip to Oregon to attend the wedding of her stepfather's son, she'd elaborately described how things would one day be: At some point in the not-too-distant future, she'd be living in a penthouse apartment in Manhattan and send for her parents to visit. They'd be met by a limousine at the airport, and she'd wine and dine them in New York's finest restaurants.

Everyone had laughed. Jennifer said just wait and see.

Even when the only job offer the 22-year-old graduate received came from 1,600 miles away in a place she'd never heard of, Servo quickly accepted. Abilene's KRBC-TV and its paltry starting salary, she told her mother, was a start.

And, she confidently explained, she wouldn't be there more than a year before bigger and better things beckoned.

Sherry Abel tried to hide her concerns over her daughter moving so far away while Jennifer talked endlessly of the romantic Old West to which she was certain she was headed. The young woman who had grown up in a logging community of 3,600 that prided itself on being the "Gateway to Glacier National Park" spoke constantly of an imagined new world of cowboys, cattle, wide open spaces, and an audience of a couple of hundred thousand people to which she would soon be reporting.

* * *

On the afternoon of July 16, 2002, Sherry and Jennifer, pulling a U-Haul trailer packed with belongings, set out on a mother-daughter trip to Texas.

Jennifer had been pleased when her mom had agreed to accompany her and assist with all the details of getting settled. Neither did she mind that her mother planned to leave her Buick with her and return home by air.

As they pulled away from the Abel house just outside of Kalispell, Jennifer took one last sweeping look at the pine-covered mountain ranges and the picturesque Flathead Valley, as if to retain an image that might last her forever.

"I'm really going to miss this place," she said. "I'll probably never see it again."

"Oh, sure you will," Sherry replied.

* * *

The two-day trip ended at 4 a.m. when Jennifer shook her sleeping mother awake and excitedly announced, "Mom, we're here." Sherry Abel looked from the car window into the cheerless pre-dawn landscape, flat and barren, wind sweeping debris across the highway and peppering their windshield with dirt being blown from plowed fields. As they entered the city limits, the view got even more depressing as they passed a row of shadowed old buildings, deserted and badly in need of repair or demolition. In her tired and only half-awake state, Sherry thought to herself: "If this is Abilene, you're not staying." All she said aloud, however, was, "Let's see if we can find a motel."

Soon, the mother's perception of the West Texas city changed dramatically. Later in the day, following a few hours sleep, they set about searching for an apartment. While doing so, Sherry discovered a clean and busy downtown and quiet residential areas with well-kept yards and friendly people. Everyone they spoke with—in stores where they shopped for necessary household items, in a Mexican food restaurant where they had lunch, in the grocery store—was kind, warm, and welcoming.

By the end of the day, they put down a deposit with the manager of the Hunters Ridge Apartments and began moving in. The upstairs residence, No. 427, was small, just one tiny bedroom, a living room/kitchen combination, and a bath—but the monthly rent fit the tight budget Jennifer anticipated.

Having spent her college days living in a low-income apartment she'd leased for only $40 a month, Jennifer was delighted with her new home. Standing amid the unpacked boxes, she determined the bedroom would be used as a walk-in closet/storage area. The bed her mom had bought for her earlier in the day would go in the living room.

"That evening, while Jen was unpacking and arranging things, I cooked spaghetti," Sherry remembers. "I spread a tablecloth across a trunk we'd brought, unpacked some plates, glasses, and silverware, opened a bottle of wine, and we had the first dinner in her new place. Later we went downstairs for a swim. Since her bed hadn't yet been delivered, we slept on the floor."

By the time Jennifer dropped her off at the airport for her flight back to Montana, Sherry Abel had but one lingering concern over her daughter's venture into a new world.

* * *

Early in the summer of 2002, Jennifer met and started dating a University of Montana employee named Ralph Sepulveda. Ten years her senior, he had begun working in the university's Lab Animals Resources department following his discharge from the Army Rangers.

The relationship developed quickly and intensely, much to the concern of Jennifer's family, including her older half sister, Christa Slaten.

On the Fourth of July weekend that year, Jennifer invited Sepulveda to her parents' home in Kalispell and was met with a chorus of whispered, "What are you doing with this guy?" concerns from family members. The age difference and the tattoos covering his arms were, says Slaten, now a middle school teacher in Kalispell, "off-putting." So, too, was his reluctance to talk much about his past except to say he'd been raised in a large family that was split in half when his parents divorced. He and several of his siblings were raised by his mother, the others by his father.

By the time Jennifer was offered the KRBC position, she too had begun to question the relationship, thinking the long-distance move might offer an easy ending. She liked Sepulveda, she confided to friends, but he demanded her constant attention, to the point where she was beginning to feel suffocated.

Still, she didn't know how to say no when he announced he planned to quit his job in Missoula and move to Abilene. He'd done some online research, he explained, and felt sure he could find work at one of the three Abilene colleges or, perhaps, with the local police department.

When Jennifer tried to discourage him, he countered with a plan that had him taking up residence in an apartment far removed from hers. "I'll live on the opposite side of town," he promised her.

They could, he suggested, "start over" in Texas. He even bought her a book on Texas history and folklore, writing on its title page how he was "looking forward to Texas...we can visit Mexico...and learn to country dance."

And so, despite everyone's concern and Jennifer's own reservations,

Sepulveda arrived in Abilene on the same day Sherry Abel planned to return to Montana. Driving a rental truck containing little more than his clothes and a few personal items, he also brought along Jennifer's beloved cat, Mister Binx.

With no car and no job, he asked Jennifer if he could stay with her for a couple of weeks. Reluctantly, she agreed, convincing herself that, at least for a time, it might be nice to have someone she knew around as she adjusted to a strange place where she knew no one.

When Christa called to see how things were going, her sister assured her she'd given Sepulveda a short deadline for moving out.

Soon, she kept her promise. Expelled from Jennifer's apartment, Sepulveda found a place of his own just a few miles away at the Quail Run Apartments. And, while they corresponded occasionally by email, they no longer dated.

Jennifer, meanwhile, immersed herself in her new job, new friends, and new surroundings. On days off, she and coworkers at the station occasionally took short, spur-of-the-moment trips—to Buffalo Gap for shopping, to Arlington to watch a Texas Rangers baseball game, or out to Roswell, New Mexico, to visit the site of the alleged UFO crash in the 1940s—unfettered by the presence of her dismissed boyfriend. On Sundays, she attended various churches, looking for one in which she felt comfortable enough to seek membership.

Her regular calls home convinced her mother she was happy, doing well, and enjoying her new life.

And then, late on a Wednesday afternoon, September 18, 2002—just two months after Jennifer Servo's arrival in Abilene—an old, forgotten dream suddenly evolved into a dark and endless nightmare.

* * *

For several days, Sherry Abel had been calling her daughter's cell phone but had been unable to reach her. "For some reason I can't explain, I had this bad feeling that I just couldn't shake. I just wanted to make sure she was okay. When I couldn't reach her, I told myself that I was worrying too much, that she and some of her new friends might have taken one of their little trips, and tried to put it out of my mind."

Still, on that Wednesday afternoon as she returned home from shopping at a nearby Wal-Mart, she reminded herself to give her daughter another call after dinner.

The meal was never prepared.

At 5:30 p.m., she answered the front door to find a Flathead County Sheriff's deputy standing on the porch.

"Ma'am," he asked, "are you Sherry Abel?"

"Yes."

"Is your husband at home?"

Puzzled for a moment, she wondered what the deputy might want with her engineer husband who was due to return any minute from a business meeting.

"Would you mind if I came in and we called him? I'm afraid I have some bad news."

Sherry felt her legs weaken. Her heart instantly began to pound. Breathing was suddenly difficult and painful. Offering a mumbled apology for the fact the porch was under repair, she directed the officer to another entrance—through the laundry room.

Only minutes later, Tom Abel arrived to find his wife seated in the living room, pale and shaking. The deputy, clearly uncomfortable with his task, informed them that "earlier in the day Jennifer Servo was found dead in her Abilene apartment." An investigating officer with the Abilene police had called to ask that they be notified personally.

Sherry screamed and burst into tears as her husband attempted to comfort her. It was he who finally managed a question: "How did it happen?"

"Sir," the deputy replied, "my information is that it was a homicide."

A Portrait of Jennifer

We sent her to college and she came home. We sent her off to the Army and they sent her back to us. We sent her to Texas and she never returned...
- Pastor Dan Heskett at Servo's memorial service

Brian Travers, a meteorologist at Abilene's KRBC, was immediately attracted to the newly hired reporter from faraway Montana. Like Jennifer Servo, he too was a long way from home, having grown up in Williamsburg, Virginia, and was still trying to adapt to the dry-bed part of the world where his nightly weather reports were of vital interest to farmers who had spent their entire lives playing Russian roulette with the region's annual rainfall.

A year older than Servo, Travers was drawn to her energetic manner, her smile, and her eagerness to experience the new world she'd entered. It was no surprise to him when he learned that *Breakfast at Tiffany's* was her all-time favorite movie. Servo, he quickly decided, was the living reincarnation of the film's vivacious, fun-loving, and inquisitive lead character, Holly Golightly.

And on camera, she had what he and others in the industry call a "presence," a professional and appealing delivery to the stories she reported. Travers, like most of Servo's coworkers, was convinced she wouldn't be in Abilene long.

She was a young woman focused, determined, and more than a little headstrong. Such had been the case throughout most of her life.

At age 17, she announced she wanted to enlist in the Army Reserve, explaining to her mother it would not only help with college tuition but eventually provide her a means to see the world, perhaps even a lifetime career.

"I wasn't particularly keen on the idea," her mother recalls, "and, actually, could have nipped it in the bud since, being underage, she needed a parent's signature to enlist. But she was so determined, I finally agreed."

It proved to be a good decision. By the time Jennifer left for the University of Montana in 1998, just a year after she enlisted, she displayed a degree of maturity that far surpassed that of most of her friends and classmates. Too, her mother wasn't at all surprised when she learned Jennifer had quickly been assigned duty as a platoon leader. And she was proud when, in 2000, her daughter told her she was to be part of a task force deployed to spend two summer weeks in Chilangera, El Salvador, on a water purification mission following a devastating hurricane.

"Once she set her mind to something," Sherry Abel says, "it was almost impossible to persuade her differently."

Hidden beneath the ever-smiling, fun-loving exterior was a serious, thoughtful young woman. It seemed she'd always been so. Once, during a conversation with her mother, who had returned from the funeral of an uncle, Jennifer listened as Abel painfully described the difficulty she experienced when those in attendance were invited to parade past the casket and view the body. For a moment, Jennifer became quiet, pensive, then spoke: "When I die," she said with a conviction that belied her age, "I want to be cremated."

Her mother made some now-forgotten response, casually dismissing the remark by a girl far too young to contemplate such matters.

Then, on the day before the 9/11 tragedy, Jennifer made a dramatic alteration to her life. The 1996 divorce of her parents had been neither easy nor pleasant; her relationship with Norm Olson, her father, was severely strained even when her parents had still been together. Following the divorce, it deteriorated to a point where they rarely spoke or saw each other.

Jennifer Lynn Olson, at age 21, went to court and had her last name legally changed to her mother's maiden name. Thus, when she arrived in

Abilene, she was officially Jennifer Servo.

* * *

At KRBC, she immediately fit into the small, hard-working staff, making friends and eagerly attacking the long hours her new job demanded.

"She wasn't what I expected at all," remembers former weekend anchor Jennifer Shed. "We'd heard about her military involvement, for instance, and were probably expecting this very businesslike young woman. Then in walks this cute little blonde with a big smile. For the first week or so, she was even a little shy."

Soon, the two Jennifers were visiting each other's apartments, sunning by the pool on days off, becoming friends.

It wasn't long before fellow workers, aware of young Brian Travers' obvious fascination with the new employee, encouraged Jennifer Servo to accept the weatherman's invitation to a movie or an after-work pizza. Those who knew about her recently ended relationship insisted Travers was a gentle, caring kind of person—more her type.

"We began seeing each other," he remembers, "though it was clear to me that she was just looking for a friend, someone to hang out with after work or go with to a movie. I accepted that. She was just fun to be around."

And after a time, they became confidants. Travers felt comfortable asking if she was having any problems with her former boyfriend. No, she'd told him on a late-night drive back from a quick visit to Roswell in early September, but she did need to get in touch with Ralph Sepulveda soon and have him return the key to her apartment that he still had.

Shed had also asked about Sepulveda just a few days earlier.

"Jennifer said she hadn't heard from him but needed to email him," she recalls. She and Sepulveda, Servo explained, had agreed to share the expense of a rental mailbox shortly after his arrival in Abilene, and he hadn't picked up his mail in some time.

"Actually," says Shed, now an evening anchor with an out-of-state television station, "she didn't talk about him very much. I think early on, when they were still living together, she even went out of her way to keep us from meeting him. Honestly, I think she was a little embarrassed by him."

If so, that problem seemed to have been resolved. Sepulveda had moved into his own apartment, purchased himself a car, and found work in a nearby Winters, Texas, manufacturing plant.

* * *

On Sunday evening, September 15, 2002, Jennifer Servo and Travers worked until the 10 p.m. newscast ended then left in separate cars to stop by the apartment of a former KRBC employee and pick up a coffee table he'd promised her. After loading the table into her car, they drove to Wal-Mart where Travers needed to shop for groceries while Jennifer picked up cat food for Mister Binx.

Later, their shopping completed, they drove in tandem from the parking lot, and Brian had a fleeting impression that a dark, four-door car was following them. He quickly dismissed his concern, however, and thought no more about it until he pulled into his apartment complex. As he stepped from his car to await Jennifer's arrival, he thought he saw the same car drive past, slow briefly, then speed away.

Again he chose to forget about it.

"Jennifer helped me get my groceries in," Travers recalls, "and we talked for a while, making plans to see a movie the following night."

When she left, he insisted on walking her to her car.

"If something happened to you between here and your car," he said jokingly, "nobody would ever forgive me."

With that he kissed her and watched as she drove away.

It was the last time he ever saw her.

* * *

It was after midnight when Jennifer returned to her apartment at Hunters Ridge, yet she was probably not surprised when her cell phone rang. Since her arrival in Abilene, David Warren, a Missoula television reporter whom she'd dated while in college, regularly phoned to see how she was doing. And, though he didn't know Brian Travers, the two men had a good deal in common. Both were TV meteorologists, and both clearly had strong feelings for Jennifer Servo.

Warren later recalled that their hour-long conversation that night focused primarily on how their respective careers were progressing. Jennifer seemed happy, comfortable with her new surroundings, and perhaps a little homesick. If anything was worrying her, she made no mention of it.

Maybe, she'd finally told him before hanging up, they could get together when she returned to Montana for the upcoming Christmas holidays.

* * *

During mid-morning on the following day, Brian Travers dialed Jennifer's cell number but got no answer. Arriving at the station later, he confided to Shed that he felt Jennifer was trying to end their relationship.

"I've left messages," he said, "and she won't call me back."

Shed privately assumed the smitten Travers was, indeed, about to get the brushoff. "I didn't think any more about it," she says, "until I was told later that night that we were going to need someone to fill in on the Tuesday morning newscast. I tried to call her and see if she could do it but got no answer. That concerned me since Jennifer was always very conscientious about being available for work and returning calls."

On Wednesday, since both would be off work, Servo and Shed had made plans to meet for an afternoon lying by the Hunters Ridge pool. But, like Travers, Shed had been unsuccessful in reaching her friend to confirm the plan. Early in the afternoon, Shed phoned Travers and said she was coming to pick him up. She was getting worried. It was time, they agreed, to make a drive out to Servo's Texas Avenue address.

"As we parked, Brian looked over at Jennifer's car and saw that the coffee table he had helped her load was still there. I remember him saying, 'That's not good.'

"We knocked at her apartment several times but got no answer. Brian tried her cell phone number again. Then, I tried the door, thinking I'd just stick my head in and call her name, but it was locked."

Each remarked that they'd never before seen Jennifer's window blinds completely closed. It had been her habit to leave them slightly raised so Mister Binx could sit on the sill and look outside during the day.

Both recall an anxious feeling sweeping over them as they stood at the upstairs doorway. In a nearby tree, a shiny black grackle frantically flew from limb to limb, cawing angrily. Downstairs, an apartment maintenance man slowly walked along the sidewalk, repeatedly glancing over his shoulder in their direction.

"He gave me the creeps," Shed remembers.

Unsuccessful in their mission, Shed returned Travers to his apartment and drove back to KRBC. There, she told her boss, Toby Dagnhart, of her growing concern.

Dagnhart immediately telephoned the apartment manager, explained the situation, and asked her to check on the woman who, for the past two months, had been living in 427.

The answer Dagnhart and Shed waited for came not from the apartment manager, but from a police scanner in the station's newsroom. There was the electric crackle familiar to all reporters, then the announcement of a Texas Avenue address and apartment number.

"Possible DOA," a monotone voice reported. "Contact Major Crimes immediately..."

Jennifer Shed, already sobbing, ran from the building toward her car.

Horror at Hunters Ridge

There's the scarlet thread of murder running through the colorless skein of life, and our duty is to unravel it…
- Sir Arthur Conan Doyle, *A Study in Scarlet*

On the back side of the sprawling south Abilene apartment complex, the sudden flurry of activity was hidden from passersby on Texas Avenue.

By the time Jennifer Shed reached the Hunters Ridge Apartments, she already knew what she would find. Her friend, the young woman she was supposed to be spending time by the pool with at that very moment, was most likely dead, the DOA—"dead on arrival" in police-speak—earlier announced on the police scanner.

The scene Shed encountered immediately verified her worst fears. She arrived to see a grim-faced paramedic walking down the stairway that led from Jennifer Servo's apartment, slowly shaking his head. Nearby, a young woman—the apartment manager—stood alone, clearly in shock, wringing her hands. Parked next to a couple of police cars, an ambulance waited, its back doors swung open, yet there seemed no urgency to get a passenger to the hospital.

Shed tried unsuccessfully to muffle a scream with her hands, then walked hurriedly toward the ambulance driver. "What's happening?" she demanded. "Is she dead?"

He turned to her with what she remembers as an accusatory look. "How would you know that?" he responded. She began to cry.

It was then that the apartment manager approached and put her arms around Shed. "Yes, she's dead," the woman, who just minutes earlier had discovered the body, whispered. "I'm so sorry…"

Her hands shaking, Shed dialed Brian Travers' number and managed two words: "Jennifer's dead."

Minutes later he, too, arrived, his legs almost buckling as he hurried past police who were putting up the yellow crime scene tape. The KRBC weatherman saw the hurried and constant foot traffic of investigators up and down on the stairs leading to Servo's apartment.

For several seconds Travers stood silently, then yelled a curse and angrily hurled the bottle or orange juice he'd been carrying into a nearby brick wall. When he suddenly began running in the direction of the stairwell, determined to reach Jennifer's apartment, an officer grabbed him and firmly walked him back toward the parking lot.

The officer told Travers to remain there and that the police would want to talk with him later. Grief-stricken and puzzled, he asked why.

"Because, sir, we're conducting a murder investigation," the officer replied.

* * *

Inside the apartment, investigators went about determining what manner of horror had played out. A blood trail began in the living room and led to the small bathroom where Jennifer's body lay. The cloying smell permeating the apartment assured the investigators the victim had been dead for several days.

Still dressed in the shorts and T-shirt she generally wore to bed, Jennifer had suffered multiple blunt trauma wounds to the head. Bruising around her neck indicated she had also been strangled.

There was no sign of forced entry to the apartment or evidence the victim put up a struggle before the blows to her head had likely rendered her unconscious. Though personal items—her purse, car keys, and cell phone—were missing, nothing suggested robbery.

Investigators could find no obvious murder weapon.

Abilene Police detective Jeff Bell, who was assigned to the case despite having never been the lead investigator on a homicide, instinctively knew the case would hinge on DNA evidence. If, as suspected, the victim had been raped, hopefully the attacker had left behind hair or semen. Maybe lab experts would find the perpetrator's blood mixed with Jennifer's in the living room carpet or on the bathroom floor.

However, there were no obvious visible clues, with the possible exception of an empty Coke can found in the living room. Neither Jennifer Servo's refrigerator nor trash indicated she favored that brand of soda. Crime scene investigators hoped it had been left behind by her killer. If so, it might well provide fingerprints and DNA leading to a quick and definitive solution to the mystery Bell was charged with solving.

Meanwhile, there were numerous people eager to make Bell's job easier. Several of Servo's Abilene coworkers, as well as her parents in Montana, named the person they believed guilty of her murder: Jennifer's former boyfriend, Ralph Sepulveda.

* * *

Word of the Texas tragedy spread quickly. Soon after the sheriff's deputy appeared at the Montana home of Jennifer's mother to break the news, Sherry Abel began the weighty task of notifying family members.

Norm Olson recalls being surprised at first to hear his ex-wife's voice on the phone, then instinctively realizing that she wouldn't call unless something disastrous had occurred. "When she said that Jennifer had been murdered," he says, "I felt a physical pain like nothing I'd ever experienced."

Long after the call, he sat alone in the small living room of his Columbia Falls, Montana, home, his emotions ping-ponging between the darkest grief and most searing anger he'd ever experienced. He was relieved when he answered a knock at his door and found his next-door neighbor, an emergency room doctor, standing on the porch. He'd just heard on the evening news what had happened to Jennifer. Long into the night, the two men sat and talked of how to best deal with the dark visitors of grief and despair.

In Oregon, Jennifer's older half-sister Christa had initially been speechless upon hearing the news. She wanted to know when, how, why, but the words refused to come, as if blocked deep in her throat. Several minutes after she'd hung up, she regained some degree of composure and phoned her husband, Mark, at work to tell him they needed to make plans to drive to Montana as quickly as possible.

That night, Christa Slaten did not sleep. She paced for hours then sought out a box of her sister's letters and reread each of them, tearfully looking at the photographs Jennifer had regularly sent to her over the years.

Down the hall, Christa's infant daughter, Mallory, slept through the night for the first time. The fact that she'd never get to know her aunt only added to her mother's pain.

In Abilene, KRBC executive Toby Dagnhart placed a call to the Abel home and was in tears even before he heard Sherry's voice. "I feel responsible; I'm so sorry," he told her.

The pall that had settled over the station was palpable. On that Wednesday evening, there was no newscast with its usual happy banter and reports on school board meetings and area celebrations. Instead, there was only a brief report on Jennifer Servo's murder, a montage of reports she'd done during her brief stay, and a smiling portrait of her that remained on a silent screen for the remainder of the half hour.

* * *

In the days to come, Sherry and Tom Abel wrestled with one difficult decision after another. Tom spoke several times with Abilene detectives, learning little more than that the investigation was in its early stages. Told that Jennifer's body had been delivered to the Tarrant County Medical Examiner's office in Fort Worth for autopsy, they discussed an immediate trip to Texas. They finally decided there would be time enough for that later. Sherry could not bear the thought of seeing her daughter in death.

Instead, she requested Jennifer's cremation be done there while she began preparation for a memorial service.

On the morning of September 26, four KRBC employees—Dagnhart, sports reporter Tim Hill, Brian Travers, and Jennifer Shed—somberly boarded a chartered plane for a flight to Kalispell to attend the memorial service for Jennifer Servo.

On board with them was an unusual cargo: a box containing Jennifer's ashes was to be delivered to Sherry Abel, and Jennifer's cat, Mister Binx, was en route to his new home with Norm Olson.

The Investigation

Death cancels everything but truth…
- William Hazlitt, *The Spirit of the Age*

Just three days after Jennifer Servo would have celebrated her 23rd birthday, family, friends, and former coworkers gathered for her memorial at Northridge Lutheran Church in Kalispell. As the plaintive playing of Taps ended the September 26, 2002, service, whispers spread among those who had known her best.

Conspicuous by his absence was Ralph Sepulveda, the 34-year-old ex-Army Ranger who, just two months earlier, gave up everything to follow Jennifer from Montana to Texas. No only did he not attend the service, but he didn't even contact anyone in Servo's family to express concern or offer condolences.

In Abilene, meanwhile, the investigation into his former girlfriend's murder was on a fast track as a half-dozen members of the police department's Special Crimes Unit worked around the clock.

At a time of the year when the attention of the West Texas city was generally focused on the Friday night fate of the local high school football teams and the myriad activities of its dozens of churches, the high-profile murder was a constant topic in coffee shops and at office water coolers.

Abilene is a community in which many who call it home refuse to believe it could be visited by the degree of evil that had been played out at the Hunters Ridge apartments. Yet as word of the murder spread, people with no direct connection to the case, who had not even known the young victim, began calling the police department, seeking information on the progress of the investigation. If there was a killer afoot in their normally quiet midst, they wanted the culprit apprehended as swiftly as possible.

Such would not be the case.

* * *

Within hours after Servo's body was discovered, police were collecting evidence and conducting interviews, clearly acting on the time-honored premise that most homicides are solved within the first 48 hours.

Police soon reached the conclusion that, in all likelihood, the crime had taken place in the early morning hours of the previous Monday. The medical examiner's preliminary report placed the time of death at approximately two days before the body was discovered. And a neighbor in the apartment complex where Servo lived reported briefly hearing loud noises coming from her apartment sometime around 3 a.m. that morning.

Officers were also repeatedly hearing Ralph Sepulveda's name. During their initial contact with Jennifer's family, the first words her mother had spoken were, "Find Ralph." In questioning KRBC personnel, virtually everyone investigators spoke to named him as the most likely suspect.

After being taken to the police department on Wednesday evening, Sepulveda answered questions with only brief replies. Monday night, he said, he had been in his own apartment, sleeping. He insisted he hadn't seen or spoken with Jennifer Servo in several weeks. Already, detectives had checked databases and learned Sepulveda had no criminal history.

Throughout the interview, Sepulveda showed little emotion. At no point during the two hours of questioning did he ask what happened to Jennifer. He did, however, volunteer to provide a DNA sample.

Down a hallway, David Atkins interviewed Jennifer's badly shaken coworker and friend Brian Travers, the last known person to see her alive. At first, he was surprised at the tone of the detective's questions, but he quickly realized he was not being treated as a close friend of the victim anxious to help with the investigation, but, rather, as a suspect. Still, he readily volunteered fingerprints and a saliva sample for DNA comparison. Yes, he assured police, he would gladly accompany them to Jennifer's apartment to see if he might notice anything missing.

The hour-long interrogation had been disquieting. Returning to his apartment, Travers phoned his parents in Virginia to tell of the grisly drama playing out. His father recognized the seriousness of the matter and warned his son the police were probably considering him a suspect. The elder Travers promised to immediately contact a lawyer and that he and Brian's mother would be in Abilene as quickly as possible.

"It was all so unreal," Brian recalls. "I remember when my parents arrived my dad took me aside. The first question he asked me was, 'Son, did you do it?'"

Brian assured his father he had nothing to do with Servo's death and, in fact, planned to cooperate with the authorities in every way possible.

The following Friday, Travers, accompanied by his lawyer, joined investigators at Jennifer's apartment. Uncomfortable standing in the midst of a crime scene, the young meteorologist described the missing purse Jennifer usually placed on the kitchen table. During his last visit, he said, there had been several CDs stacked atop her television set. Finally, he pointed to an empty spot near the doorway, where he said a large ceramic frog had been the last time he was there.

* * *

The authorities soon realized the solution to the case would not be quick in coming. A canvas of the apartment complex yielded no eyewitnesses to anything out of the ordinary during the presumed time frame of the crime. When they attempted to interview one of Servo's neighbors, he informed them he'd already hired a lawyer and quickly shut his door. Questions raised more questions. The absence of evidence of forced entry into Apartment 427 strongly suggested Servo either knew her attacker or willingly opened her door to a stranger. The latter, friends and family assured police, was highly unlikely.

Nothing inside her cluttered home indicated a violent struggle had occurred before her death. Nothing suggested robbery as motive.

Detective Bell repeatedly told members of the media he and fellow investigators were talking with "persons of interest"—the modern, politically correct term for "suspects"—but privately he was convinced no confession would be forthcoming from anyone he'd interviewed.

The facts of the case were scarce, obvious within the first few minutes spent at the crime scene. It appeared Servo had been struck in the head by a blunt object—at least three times according to the autopsy—and strangled in the living room of her apartment. Then, inexplicably, her body had been dragged into the nearby bathroom.

The coroner found no skin under her fingernails, nothing to indicate she fought with her attacker. Neither could he suggest what kind of weapon caused the victim's head trauma.

Like most small law enforcement agencies, the Abilene Police Department lacks the sophisticated equipment needed to sort out the microscopic blood, hair, and fiber samples gathered at a crime scene. A mind-numbing waiting game followed their evidence gathering.

At the office of the Tarrant County Medical Examiner in Fort Worth, where the crime scene evidence was delivered, prioritizing testing is no easy matter. Local cases as well as others from cities and towns throughout the vast West Texas region simply had to wait their turn.

Meanwhile, outside the door of Servo's apartment, a memorial of flowers and candles grew daily.

* * *

For Sherry and Tom Abel, the days following Jennifer's death passed with agonizing slowness. The steady flow of calls and emails from their daughter's friends continued, and their mailbox filled with sympathy cards. They phoned Detective Bell regularly, only to learn he had no new developments to report. Finally, the parents agreed it was time to make the dreaded trip from Kalispell to Abilene and gather Jennifer's belongings.

Neither was prepared for what they saw in the small apartment. The bed Sherry had purchased for her daughter was bare, stripped of linens. A lengthy stretch of carpet leading toward the bathroom had been cut away and removed. Gray fingerprint powder was everywhere. Several boxes Jennifer had brought from Montana remained unpacked.

Tom hugged his wife as her shoulders slumped and she began to cry.

They completed their task late in the afternoon, and, realizing they hadn't eaten all day, Sherry directed her husband to the Mexican food restaurant she and Jennifer had visited just two months earlier. For almost an hour, the exhausted couple sat, idly picking at their food, saying little until Tom asked for their bill. Only then did their waitress acknowledge she knew who they were.

"I'm so sorry for your loss," the young woman said. "My manager said to tell you there is no charge for your meal."

Later at the police station, the Abels finally met the man in charge of their daughter's murder investigation.

Sherry recalls Detective Bell asking if they had found anything of Jennifer's missing.

"Her flute," Sherry remembers replying. "She played it in the junior high band and had brought it with her."

* * *

Soon came national media coverage. Forever fascinated by the dangers female television personalities face from admirers who form deranged attachments and often turn to stalking, they quickly recognized the murder of Jennifer Servo as a topic reaching far beyond the boundaries of Abilene, Texas. *Inside Edition* arrived to prepare a story. So did *America's Most Wanted*. Talk show hosts Montel Williams and Maury Povich phoned to ask Sherry to come to New York and talk about her daughter. *48 Hours* was interested in doing a segment on the case. A writer from *Cosmopolitan* magazine requested an interview.

Hesitant at first, Sherry Abel finally became convinced anything that kept her daughter's murder in the public eye might aid the investigation. In death, Jennifer Servo achieved the fame she'd aspired to in life.

Truth Seekers

Every murderer is probably someone's old friend...You cannot mix up sentiment and reason.
- Agatha Christie, *The Mysterious Affair at Styles*

Though it was his first assignment as a lead investigator on a homicide case, then 38-year-old Detective Jeff Bell knew well the responsibility it carried. He also knew the drill: Act as quickly as possible on any and all leads, cover all the bases, think of everything that needs to be done, and don't hesitate to reach out for help.

In the early stages of the investigation, two sergeants and eight investigators worked the Jennifer Servo murder case. They quickly located people to be interviewed. As procedure dictated, one officer accompanied the body of the local television reporter to Fort Worth to be present during the autopsy. They searched databases for information on the victim's friends and associates both in Abilene and back in Montana. They continued to gather, catalog, and deliver evidence to the Tarrant County Medical Examiner's office.

A native of nearby Clyde who had joined the Abilene police force in 1993 after serving seven years in the Army, Bell was admittedly nervous.

He soon compiled a list of no fewer than ten people—coworkers, apartment complex neighbors, people in Montana, and ex-boyfriend Ralph Sepulveda—whom he and fellow investigators believed might provide more information.

In the days after discovering the crime, the detective spoke with Sepulveda on four occasions. The story was always the same: Ralph had taken a job with a manufacturing plant in Winters and had little time to do anything but travel to and from work. On the night it was believed Servo died, Sepulveda said he'd been alone in his apartment, sleeping. He also insisted he'd returned the key to Jennifer's apartment weeks earlier and hadn't spoken with her in some time.

The parade of other people summoned to the Law Enforcement Center for interviews offered no real direction for the investigation.

Even the final report from the medical examiner lacked the definitive answers the detective hoped for. Servo, the M.E. said, had suffered blunt trauma wounds to the head, but bruising around the neck indicated strangulation as the actual cause of death. Whether she had been sexually assaulted was less certain. Though she'd been clothed when found, bruising evidence pointed to the possibility of rape.

As weeks passed, however, the frenzy of activity focused on the case gradually slowed. Other detectives turned their attention to new crimes while Bell proceeded alone, continually adding page after page to the growing case file stacked next to his desk. On his office wall, he placed a photo of Servo, a daily reminder of his commitment to the victim and her family.

In a 2003 interview with the *Abilene Reporter News*, Bell admitted the slow progress of the investigation had begun to "hurt."

"You get into this job to catch the bad guy," he said. "And to provide answers for those grieving over their loss. I talk with her mother every week, and even when she's in a good mood, you can still hear the pain in her voice. I would like to be able to tell her it's finished. I feel like I owe that to her family."

Tips, many of them bordering on the absurd, had initially flooded the department's hotline but soon slowed to a trickle. Regardless of their validity, each had to be checked out.

A woman phoned to say she bought a purse at a flea market she was certain had belonged to the victim. Other women told of boyfriends giving them gifts of jewelry that, for whatever reason, they strongly suspected had belonged to the dead woman. A resident at Hunter's Ridge, where Servo was found dead in her apartment, was convinced there was ongoing satanic activity in the complex, suggesting it might have something to do with the murder. An anonymous caller was convinced Servo's death was in response to a news report she'd done on the arrest of a group of drug dealers in an area community. Another pointed a finger at a member of the local Gold's Gym where Servo occasionally worked out. A father in the East Texas town of Jasper called to say he believed his son might have committed the crime. Only after a trip to the small town did police learn the father was simply angry with his son and had absolutely no evidence he'd been involved in the Abilene homicide. Another caller suggested the murder was the result of a late-night drug deal gone wrong. There were even those who expressed belief that it hadn't actually been Jennifer Servo who was found in the apartment, that she was still alive and on the run.

Briefly, there was even discussion that Servo's death might be connected to a series of murders in Baton Rouge, Louisiana. Police, however, were unable to place the prime suspect in the Louisiana killings in or around Abilene at the time of the Hunters Ridge homicide.

Impatiently, Bell waited for evidence of more substance.

When they learned Sepulveda left Abilene after only a couple of weeks with plans to reenlist in the Army, detectives Bell and David Atkins began tracking his movements—back to Missoula for a brief visit then to a sister's home in California. Learning he'd been assigned to San Antonio's Fort

Sam Houston for training, the investigators decided it was time to pay him another visit.

Bell, hesitant to divulge many specifics of his investigation, will only say that the interview with Sepulveda was "shorter than those that had been earlier conducted." Jennifer's mother, however, remembers the detective contacting her and describing the meeting in more detail. Sepulveda, he told her, had been quite agitated, particularly when the visiting officers confronted him with photographs taken at the crime scene. Sepulveda, she understood, had abruptly halted the interview and asked for an attorney.

Bell will only say, "He told us he was tired and wanted to end it."

* * *

A six-month wait for results of the forensic testing conducted in Tarrant County was equally frustrating. The testing of hair and fiber evidence had been particularly slow, complicated by the fact much of what had been collected was hair shed by Servo's cat. Blood sample tests matched only the victim.

"What we were hoping for," Bell says, "was DNA that didn't fit, that wasn't traceable to the people we already knew had spent time in Jennifer's apartment."

No such clue was found in the trace evidence expert's report. The investigation, once almost frantic, slowed to a frustrating standstill. Such would be the case as months turned into years with no resolution.

* * *

In Montana, Sherry Abel agonized over the lack of progress.

Pleased that the Abilene police initially stayed in touch, advising her of any new turn or advancement in the investigation, Abel eventually had to endure month-long stretches of time with no news. When she or her husband did call, the response was always the same: nothing to report.

Though she had been confident at first that the investigation was being conducted properly, certain that detectives Bell and Atkins, to whom she most often spoke or received emails from, remained determined to solve the case, the distraught mother found herself wondering if there was anything else that might be done.

Aware that the Texas Rangers are often called in to aid in difficult investigations, she searched the internet and discovered a Ranger stationed in Abilene. She phoned Calvin Cox and asked that he contact the Abilene Police Department to offer his assistance. In response, detective Bell asked the Ranger to review the case and see if he believed there was anything that might have been done differently.

A few weeks later, the Ranger called Sherry to tell her the police had, in his estimation, done a thorough job.

"He told me," she recalls, "that he'd looked over the case and wouldn't have done anything differently." It was, he told her, the same opinion he'd passed along to Bell.

Though reassuring, the Ranger's observation had a disturbing ring of finality to Sherry Abel.

* * *

In truth, Bell and his fellow investigators had reached out for help wherever possible as the case slowly drug into a second year.

"I felt we'd done a good job," Bell says, "but we just got to a point where we were running out of things to do."

He'd even presented the details of the crime and his subsequent investigation to a gathering of fellow law enforcement and judicial officials at a Texas Major Crime Review Board gathering in Austin in hopes of hearing new ideas, suggestions from those who might see the case from a more detached vantage point.

If there was anything of an encouraging nature that came from the gathering, it was the observation of a Harris County assistant district attorney who, after hearing the details of the circumstantial case presented, remarked, "I wish I had a case like this because I think I could take it to court."

Such isn't the mindset in Abilene.

That the Abilene Police have never even formally submitted the case to veteran Taylor County District Attorney James Eidson speaks to the fact there is virtually no physical evidence pointing in the direction of any viable suspect.

"I've followed the case from day one," Eidson says, "and have had numerous conversations with the investigators. I don't think they feel comfortable filing on anyone at this point."

Meanwhile, word soon spread through Abilene's Law Enforcement Center about a plan to establish a new investigative unit that would focus only on older, unsolved cases.

The Jennifer Servo homicide was fast reaching the age that would qualify it as a cold case.

Psychics & Select Societies

The mass of men lead lives of quiet desperation. What is called resignation is confirmed desperation.
- Henry David Thoreau, *Walden*

The numbing frustration felt inside the offices of the Abilene Police Department was shared in Montana. Though Sherry Abel stopped short of voicing public criticism of the investigation of her daughter's murder, she found herself wrestling with a growing concern that the case might never be solved, privately wondering if everything had been done properly and thoroughly.

She couldn't help but question: Had police searched dumpsters in the area of Jennifer's apartment immediately after finding her dead? Were small town Texas politics standing in the way of justice?

Well over a year had passed since the murder of Jennifer Servo and nothing, including the DNA evidence gathered from the crime scene, provided a break in the case. The mother's grief quickly evolved into an obsessive determination to find some new, unthought-of avenue that would lead to the answers she so desperately sought.

She regularly searched the internet for methods used to solve homicides and had begun watching hour after hour of cable TV true crime shows. One called *Psychic Detectives* caught her attention. One of its episodes profiled a Virginia woman named Noreen Renier. A self-described "psychic investigator," she'd earned a degree of credibility and celebrity during a two-decade career working on hundreds of unsolved crimes with law enforcement agencies in 38 states and six foreign countries. Among her most celebrated successes was a case in which she used her unique "gift" to help locate a downed plane containing the body of an FBI agent's relative.

Never promising miracles, Renier routinely insisted consultation with a psychic was to be considered only as a last resort after all other investigative efforts had been exhausted.

Soon, Sherry Abel contacted Renier. The psychic asked for no personal background on Jennifer or specific details of the crime, only that articles of clothing or jewelry belonging to the victim be sent to her as soon as possible.

Sherry quickly packaged up one of her daughter's shoes, her glasses, a ring, and a small swatch taken from the T-shirt Jennifer wore the night she died. Then she telephoned Abilene police detective Jeff Bell to tell him what she was planning and inform him Renier requested to speak directly with him after she completed what she called a "remote viewing."

Though skeptical, the detective agreed to hear what Renier had to say. When she phoned him in late May, he wasn't sure what to make of her "findings."

The weapon used by Jennifer Servo's assailant, she told him was "something that was very special, something loved, cherished, held in high esteem…The victim was at home when she was killed…she knew her killer was there but had been surprised by a sudden turn of events…Her killer lives close by…probably within walking distance…lives in multiple housing, maybe three or four stories…it's inexpensive, un-fancy…Most of the time he drives a light-colored pickup…I see a Mexican…tattoos…very jealous…He thought she was seeing someone else…She was strangled, then moved…but not very far…" Whatever items taken from her home, she offered, were personal things.

Bell asked if she had any thoughts on a weapon used during Servo's assault. "He's going to hide it… maybe at a relative's house…in a garage or building that's not attached to the house…He doesn't live there…"

Renier expressed a strong feeling that the assailant returned to Jennifer's apartment sometime after committing the crime. The murder, she said, had been carefully planned.

As the detective sat, reading the notes he'd hastily taken, he wondered what to make of the fact someone so far removed from the crime could claim intimate knowledge of what occurred.

Renier seemed convinced that the weapon used in the crime was a gun. At one point during their conversation she'd said it was hidden somewhere beneath a bridge, then in a garage or building adjacent to a relative's house.

"What she had to say was hard to make sense of," Bell says. "She jumped around so much. And there was nothing she said that indicated 'you need to go here.' But, when this case is said and done and we have someone in custody, there might be some similarities there."

Whatever degree of fact it offered, Bell determined there was nothing in Renier's "viewing" that advanced his knowledge of the case, nothing that provided a new path that might lead to an arrest.

* * *

In Columbia Falls, Montana, Norm Olson had also been searching for a way to advance the search for his daughter's killer. Online, he'd read about a unique crime solving organization calling itself the Vidocq Society.

Named for an 18th century French detective named Eugene Francois Vidocq, said to have been the inspiration for Detective Dupin in Edgar Allan Poe's "The Murders in the Rue Morgue," the Society had an invitation-only membership of 82—in honor of the years Vidocq lived—who arrive from throughout the United States to gather bimonthly in a walnut-paneled meeting room of Philadelphia's *Public Ledger* Building. There, the group, which boasts hundreds of collective years of crime-solving experience, review unsolved murders and disappearances that have come to their attention and vote on which to investigate.

Only if invited into a case does the Society, whose membership includes experts in forensic science, retired law enforcement officials, prosecutors, undercover specialists, judges, and lawyers, involve itself in an investigation.

By the time Olson learned of their existence, the 15-year-old Society had been involved in more than 100 cases, providing local investigators with new ideas and approaches, sometimes discovering the necessary scientific evidence for arrests and convictions.

In Lubbock, Texas, Olson had read, the father of a boy who had been missing and presumed dead since 1991 contacted the Vidocq Society after stymied local police proved unable to advance the case. There had been strong evidence that a violent crime had occurred—signs of a scuffle, a blood-soaked carpet, blood splatters matching the missing youngster's blood type—but no body. Society members quickly arranged for Lubbock detectives to consult with experts at London's famed Scotland Yard and several noted forensic pathologists. By July of 1997, the case had been solved and two men convicted of murdering the youngster.

Olson read of similar success stories in places like Philadelphia and Little Rock. Gathering all the information he had on the case, he wrote to the Vidocq Society, requesting that it consider involvement in the unsolved murder of his daughter. He then contacted Detective Bell to advise him of what he'd done.

Four months later, during yet another call to Bell, Olson was told a representative from the Vidocq Society had, in fact, called and left a message.

Bell said he hadn't had time to get back with them.

* * *

For Jennifer's family, hope was slipping away.

The DNA evidence gathered at the scene of the crime had yielded nothing. Hair and fiber evidence matched only those people who had spent considerable time in Servo's apartment during her two-month stay.

Blood samples matched only the victim. Forensically, nothing pointed to who committed the crime. The voluminous case files offered no new investigative direction. Locally, there was virtually no one left to question.

Most of Jennifer's coworkers departed KRBC for new jobs in distant states. Ex-boyfriend Ralph Sepulveda left Abilene and reenlisted in the Army.

The last hope, it appeared, might be a new investigative unit being planned by Police Chief Melvin Martin.

False Leads

Lying is done with words, and also with silence.
   • Adrienne Rich, *Women and Honor: Some Notes on Lying*

In late April of 2005, the Abilene police arrested a man named Juan Bravo in connection with the 1974 stabbing of 7-year-old Michael David Niles. Forensic evidence that had become available years after the brutal crime led to a reopening of the 30- year-old case and, ultimately, the long overdue resolution to the crime.

That success prompted a decision by Police Chief Melvin Martin to dramatically alter his department's Criminal Investigation Division. If a three-decade-old crime could be solved, perhaps there were others gathering dust that might merit another look. Throughout the nation, police departments were establishing cold case squads to take advantage of a quantum leap in forensic science and give new life to abandoned investigations.

The Abilene Police Department followed suit and established a two-man Cold Case Unit.

Assigned to it were Detective David Atkins, who worked closely with Jeff Bell in the early stages of the Jennifer Servo murder investigation, and veteran Sergeant Roger Berry, former head of CID and the most experienced member of the department. High on their list of unsolved crimes was the all-but-dormant September 2002 Servo case.

Atkins, an Abilene High graduate, enrolled in the police academy in 1985 and quickly rose through the ranks. By 1998, he'd earned his detective's shield.

Being named to the Cold Case Unit, he remembers, promised an exciting new chapter in his law enforcement career.

"The first thing we did," he recalls, "was go back to square one and go through everything we had on the case."

Atkins and Berry sat with Bell, listening as the former lead detective walked them through the myriad details of the lengthy investigation he had headed for more than two years. Berry read through the paperwork of the case, including the bulging folder filled with "tips," asking questions as he did so.

Bell, far from upset that the case had been reassigned, welcomed the renewed effort. "You always second-guess yourself," he says, "and wonder what you could have done differently, if there was something you had overlooked." He was pleased new eyes would be focusing on the case.

"All we were doing," Atkins says, "was making sure that nothing had been missed."

When they found no shortcomings in Bell's investigation, they determined the most logical approach was simply to start over.

For weeks, Atkins and Berry reviewed every piece of evidence collected at the crime scene two years earlier and poured over old lab reports. They visited the Hunters Ridge apartment where Servo had lived in an attempt to reconstruct the crime. Then began the process of re-interviewing everyone.

The only person they couldn't reach was Ralph Sepulveda, who, they learned, had recently departed the U.S. for a 12-month assignment in Kuwait.

And they also began to hear bizarre stories rivaling those reported earlier in the investigation: In the Tarrant County jail in Fort Worth, an inmate insisted a friend of his who had been dating Servo committed the murder. The inmate told of taking his "friend" to Servo's "house" on several occasions, even remembering dates of the visits.

"Five minutes into the interview," Atkins says, "it was apparent the guy knew nothing. He repeatedly spoke of Servo's 'house,' never mentioning that she actually lived in an apartment. Most important, the time frame he was giving us was well after the murder occurred.

"Finally, he admitted he'd recently seen something about the case on television and it had 'reminded' him of his friend's involvement."

In truth, it had been nothing more than an all-too-familiar shot-in-the-dark attempt by an inmate hoping to gain favor and perhaps a reduced sentence in exchange for information that might help solve a crime—another waste of investigators' time.

"We were inundated with rabbit trails like that," Atkins says, "particularly in the days immediately following any replay of one of the television shows [*Inside Edition, America's Most Wanted*] on the case."

After learning about the Servo case from television, a woman phoned from Minnesota to say she believed she was in possession of Jennifer's purse; so did a lady in North Carolina, who said she'd found it discarded on the side of a dirt road near her rural home.

Similar calls—none of any real substance—occasionally came in to the Taylor County District Attorney's office.

The investigation again became a house of mirrors: psychics and call-in kooks, false leads and one aggravating dead end after another.

As months passed, the Abilene Cold Case Unit got no closer to determining who killed Jennifer Servo than had Detective Bell during his time on the case. Berry and Atkins, like their predecessor, were fast running out of avenues to explore. They were grasping at straws.

"It was a stretch," Atkins remembers, "but we talked it over and decided to call out fifty officers to conduct a search for Servo's missing things in a wooded field between her apartment and the one where Ralph Sepulveda had been living."

On a day when the temperature neared 100 degrees, police officers methodically combed the field for several hours. The search yielded nothing. "We knew the odds were pretty small," Atkins remembers, "but we felt we needed to make the effort."

Such became the investigation's mantra.

* * *

In Montana, Sherry Abel had patiently waited through a long summer to hear from the men assigned to reinvestigate her daughter's murder.

Finally, in late August of 2006, she emailed Sergeant Berry to ask if there had been any progress. She wasn't prepared for the news she received. The Cold Case Unit, Berry responded, had been shut down for budgetary reasons.

For the first time since Jennifer Servo's death, her mother felt the police in Texas had given up hope of ever finding her daughter's killer.

Unfinished Requiem

Memory is a way of holding onto the things you lose, the things you are, the things you never want to lose.
  ▪ from the TV series *The Wonder Years*

As the cooling breezes of yet another fall swept over the northwest Montana landscape, four years had passed since the death of Jennifer Servo in Texas, four years without peace or resolution for her distraught family. And yet they wait, praying for patience while eternally hoping that one day there will be answers to their questions, justice for their daughter, their sister.

On the sidewalk that leads to the doorway of Norm Olson's modest Columbia Falls home, there is a faint but lasting reminder of better, more carefree times. Off to one side, scrawled in a 9-year-old's best printing is a single word written long ago: Jenn.

Inside, photographs of his daughter decorate Olson's living room. Here, alone with Mister Binx, once Jennifer's cat, for company, he tries to keep the memory of his daughter alive. His gentle, soft-spoken demeanor hides an ever-present anger and frustration to which he readily admits.

For twelve years, he worked at a local aluminum plant, but he's been on medical leave since January, battling with what doctors tell him are severe cases of stress and high blood pressure. The ailments, he knows, are the byproducts of his obsession with his daughter's death. He no longer plays golf or fly fishes in the Flathead River like he did in his younger days.

Downstairs, in a dimly lit basement, he sits for hours in front of his computer, counting the number of electronic visits paid to his "Justice for Jennifer" website. Some weeks, he says, there are as many as 280, often from people offering sympathy or sharing details of some cruelty that has visited their own lives.

"You find," he says, "that you bond with people and their tragedies." He now regularly corresponds via email with several parents whose children also met violent deaths. They have become Olson's faceless new friends.

If he feels disappointment over the years of disconnect with his daughter, he does not acknowledge it, instead pointing out that she drove to his home on the day before she left for Abilene to tell him goodbye. He regrets he was away from the house and missed her. It would have been the first time he'd heard from her since receiving a Father's Day card in June of the previous year.

Today, Olson's memories focus on a much younger Jennifer, the precocious little girl who put sentences together before any of her young peers, who wrote her own fairy tales, and who began reading the local newspaper by age 12.

More recently, he fondly recalls taking her to a 1997 Bonnie Raitt concert in Missoula.

And, yes, he admits Jennifer's decision to legally change her last name from his upset him greatly. So, too, did a quote from his ex-wife that appeared in a recent magazine article, referring to him as "not a good father."

Were he such an uncaring parent, would he have written the moving eulogy read by the pastor at Jennifer's memorial service?

As Olson talks, Mister Binx strolls slowly into the living room, gives me a cursory glance, then curls at his new keeper's feet. Olson reaches down and pets him. "I'm lucky to have him," he says, "lucky to have something that was Jen's."

The day the cat was delivered to him by the memorial service visitors from KRBC, he recalls, Mister Binx nervously walked about the house, inspecting each of its rooms. Finally, down a hallway, he entered the bedroom that was once Jennifer's.

He sleeps there now.

* * *

A half hour's drive away, the Abel home is busier, more upbeat. Tom and Sherry conduct his busy engineering business from an upstairs office. By mid-afternoon, however, Sherry is out of the house, en route to pick up her four-year-old granddaughter Mallory from preschool. That Jennifer's older sister, Christa, and her husband opted to return from Oregon to live in Kalispell reignited a flame in Sherry's daily life.

On weekends, the families often gather at Flathead Lake for an afternoon of sailing.

"I know that Jen would want me to move ahead, to seek out the joys of life," her mother says.

Still, a dark cloud lingers. It rolls in at the least expected times: when Sherry drives past Moose's, a pub and pizza place, which was a favorite of Jennifer's; when an email from one of her late daughter's friends appears on her computer screen, just to ask how she's doing; and late nights when, awakened for no reason, she quietly wanders the house filled with photos and memories of Jennifer.

The month of September, she admits, is the most difficult, the time when her daughter was born. And died.

Today, the Abels only hear from the Abilene police when they place the call. Routinely, any hope that the investigation might be progressing or that new leads have developed are dashed. No one can remember when the last call related to the case came in to the Crime Stoppers hotline. More recent crimes now demand attention. The rewards for information, established shortly after Jennifer's murder, remain unclaimed.

Investigators with whom the Abels now talk candidly admit they have nowhere to go, no new leads to follow.

Still, Sherry continues to feel strongly that the answers she so desperately seeks remain with her daughter's former boyfriend. Upon recently hearing that Ralph Sepulveda returned to Fort Drum, New York, following his stint in Kuwait, she contacted the Abilene police to ask if there were any plans to travel there and interview him again. She was informed they had neither finances nor manpower available for such a trip.

Later, she sent an email in which she and her husband offered to finance the trip from Abilene to upstate New York but has received no response.

Jennifer's father shares their frustration. Recently, Norm Olson posted

Sepulveda's whereabouts and photograph on his website with the following plea: "As Jennifer's father, I am asking and demanding that he [Sepulveda] consent to a polygraph exam."

To date, there is no indication that police, who insist they remain open-minded about who caused Servo's death, are planning any interviews in the immediate future. At the same time, the case hasn't been forgotten. The waiting game goes on.

At the Tarrant County Medical Examiner's office, Abilene investigators have been told, a new technology that can detect even smaller particles of DNA will be available in the not-too-distant future. Though he avoids specifics, Detective David Atkins indicates additional testing of evidence taken from Servo's apartment is planned.

* * *

On a warm, windy afternoon in late July of 2003, Sherry Abel made the difficult decision to disregard her angry vow not to dispose of Jennifer's ashes until her killer was apprehended.

With daughter Christa and son-in-law Mark in Kalispell for a summer vacation, the family sailed out to the picturesque Summer's Bay on Flathead Lake, a spot their daughter had called one of her favorites. There, two other sailboats, one carrying some of Jennifer's high school friends, another with her aunt and uncle as passengers, joined them, bobbing gently as Sherry whispered a final goodbye and Jennifer's uncle offered a prayer.

With that, Sherry Abel spread her daughter's ashes on the water.

◆*Abilene Reporter News*, October 2006

POSTSCRIPT:

The murder of Jennifer Servo remains unsolved but not forgotten. Abilene police investigators did finally travel to upstate New York in an attempt to re-interview Ralph Sepulveda, but he refused to speak with them. Detective Jeff Bell presented the details of the case to the Philadelphia-based Vidocq Society. After a thorough review, the membership agreed that local authorities had correctly done all that could be done. CBS's *48 Hours* and ABC's *Primetime* have recently done lengthy examinations of the case.

About the Author

Author-journalist Carlton Stowers has twice received the Mystery Writers of America's Edgar Allen Poe Award for the year's Best Fact Crime Book (*Careless Whispers* and *To The Last Breath*) and *Within These Walls*, which he coauthored with prison chaplain Rev. Carroll Pickett, won the Violet Crown Award for Texas' Best Book of Non-Fiction.